IMAGES
of America

MURRELLS INLET

I0806291

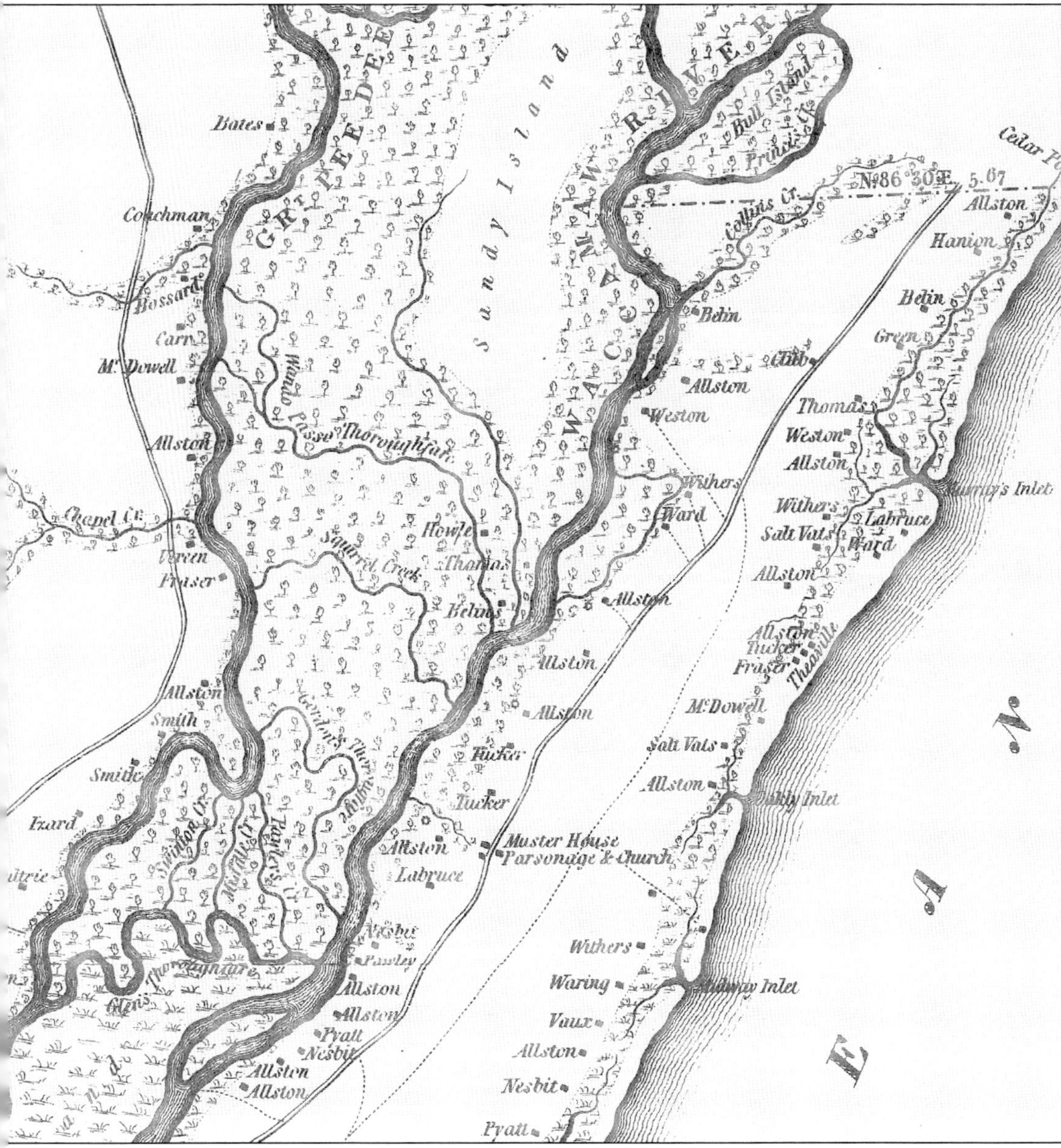

The 1825 Mills Atlas for the Georgetown District showed the entrance to Murrells Inlet as "Murray's Inlet", along with the names of the households there, including the Allstons, the Belins, the Westons, the Withers, and the Wards. This map shows the single "Kings Road" traveling north to south and the homes generally arranged along the river or the creek. (Courtesy of the author.)

On the Cover: The Army Air Force established a crash boat station in Murrells Inlet in 1941 to support the aircraft operations flown from the air base at Myrtle Beach. New pilots were trained to shoot at targets on the beach and target boats that were towed behind the crash boats during World War II. The typical P-134 crash boat shown here headed out from the Army dock towards the ocean in the main channel, passing the channel markers installed to help boats safely navigate the creek. Monte Watson was one of the crash boat captains in 1944 and took numerous photographs during his tour. (Courtesy of Gwen Watson and Murrells Inlet 2020)

IMAGES
of America

MURRELLS INLET

Steven G. Strickland

ARCADIA
PUBLISHING

ISBN 978-0-7385-9379-1

Published by Arcadia Publishing
Charleston, South Carolina

Printed in the United States of America

Library of Congress Control Number: 2011945927

For all general information, please contact Arcadia Publishing:
Telephone 843-853-2070
Fax 843-853-0044
E-mail sales@arcadiapublishing.com
For customer service and orders:
Toll-Free 1-888-313-2665

Visit us on the Internet at www.arcadiapublishing.com

This book is dedicated to my grandparents—Captain Charlie, Grace, B.C., and Lucille—who created our history and to my grandchildren (yet to come) who will benefit from it. A special thanks to Lucille Glenn Akers Fleming, who left me with a suitcase of old photographs that started this journey.

Contents

ACKNOWLEDGMENTS

This book represents the stories, pictures, and memories that were shared with me over many hours of interviews, lunches, and telephone calls. Many thanks go out to the numerous people who shared their experiences that continue to remind me why Murrells Inlet is home. So many people contributed their time (some more than they realize) to help document our history, including (in no particular order) the Eason family; Alzata Lee; the Chandler clan (Bill, Ann, Joe, Ann, June, Wayne, and Tookie); Don and Linda Lash; Susie Cooper Grega; Wayne, Wesley, Wes, and Joe Gordon; Taryn Gordon Wilson; the Morse girls (Judy, Gail, Pansy, and Ginger); Dick Vick, Johnny and Chester Lewis; Sandra Sing Bundy; Bill Moeller; Charlie, Glenn, and Colleen Welch; the Caughman family; Jerry Wells; Joyce Hughes Brett; Kelly Dorman; Mike, Johnny, Jean, and Wayne Strickland; Rae Wesley; Wendy Wesley Spring; Cecil and Beth Alston; Sissy Hughes; Robin Loud; Pearline Brown; Monica Eason Turner; Dean Hair; Nicki Lewis Queen; Mike Marchant; Jeff McKenzie; Nancy and Carolyn Altman; Gwen Watson; Tommy Gaede; Tom Swatzel; Guy Gentry; and the dozens of others whom I may have overlooked. This book is a memorial to the men and women who made Murrells Inlet what it was.

The people who knew the stories and their family history (part of the bigger picture) deserve special thanks—you know who you are and were willing to tell me more than once so I could remember how the pieces fit together. I am also indebted to the Murrells Inlet 2020 organization not only for the use of the photograph collection of Monte Watson but also and mostly for their love for Murrells Inlet and the will to protect and preserve our history. Special thanks go to Suzanne Cameron Linder and Martie Leslie Thacker for their work in *Historical Atlas of the Rice Plantations of Georgetown County*, from which the early Murrells Inlet history has been summarized. Big thanks go to David McMillan, Al Hitchcock, and Theodore Russell at Inlet Affairs and Drunken Jacks for being gracious hosts over the last three years—your support of the Murrells Inlet History Project is appreciated.

My gratitude goes out to Washington Lafayette Strickland (my great-grandfather) for taking the chance to come to Murrells Inlet, his son Charles Gennings Strickland for starting a maritime tradition of boat captains and fishermen, and my parents, Al and Glenda Strickland, for coming home and bringing us boys to paradise. And last but not least, a heartfelt appreciation of the patience my wife and children had cannot be overstated, for they helped support me during the past two years of this project.

INTRODUCTION

The land around Murrells Inlet has a record of settlement that goes back thousands of years, before written history, but evident in the shell mounds and archeological findings from the Atlantic Ocean to the Waccamaw River. The early inhabitants included the Waccamaw Indians, who took advantage of the natural resources provided by the creeks and rivers. *Wachesaw* is loosely translated as "place of great weeping," in reference to the burial grounds found along the high bluffs that contained European beads, urns, and other artifacts.

The recorded history of the area goes back to the land grants of the Lords Proprietors, when large portions of the Waccamaw Neck were divided into baronies that stretched from the Atlantic Ocean to the Waccamaw River. The baronies were typically tens of thousands of acres that were subdivided into long narrow plantations that ranged from 500 to 1,500 acres. The plantations of Murrells Inlet included the Oaks, Brookgreen, Springfield, Laurel Hill, Richmond Hill, and Wachesaw (from south to north). The first land grants were given in 1711 to Robert Daniell, who in turn sold to several other speculators, with the first planters arriving in the 1730s to begin building settlements. The most notable was Capt. John Murrell, who bought 2,340 acres that eventually became Wachesaw and Richmond Hill Plantations and built a house on the bluff there around 1733. He was a subsistence farmer and raised indigo as the primary cash crop. He passed away in 1771 and left his land to his son, Daniel, and his two daughters, Ann and Elizabeth, after which it became the two separate plantations. Wachesaw Plantation was eventually purchased by Allard Belin around 1800, and Richmond Hill passed through Murrell descendants until it was sold to an Allston some time in the early 1800s.

These plantations were owned by a host of famous planters and prospered during the establishment of the rice culture of the 1700s and 1800s. The Waccamaw Neck planters were represented in the state senate and house as well as in the governor and lieutenant governor's offices during the 1800s. The rice planters were also active in the establishment of social, educational, and religious organizations, including the Planters Club, the Winyah Indigo Society, the Hot and Hot Fish Club, the All Saints Academy, the Waccamaw Methodist Mission, and All Saints Waccamaw. The names of the families are shown on the various historic maps that date back as far as 1783—the listing of the Murrell family on the first maps is the most credible explanation of the origin of Murrells Inlet.

The rice plantation era came to an end after the Civil War with the emancipation of the slaves, resulting in the decline of the fields, dikes, and water-control structures required for rice cultivation, since planters had to rely on freedmen to work the fields. Several powerful hurricanes following the Civil War and up to the 1893 hurricane damaged the dikes in the rice fields and ultimately ended the production of rice on the Waccamaw Neck. The 1893 hurricane (when the Atlantic Ocean was reported to have met the Waccamaw River) became known as the Flagg Flood because the Flagg families who lived in houses on Magnolia Beach (Dr. Arthur; his wife, Georgeanne; his son Arthur Jr.; and Arthur Jr.'s wife and six children) were swept away in the storm surge.

After Dr. Allard Flagg's death in 1901, his daughter sold Wachesaw and the Hermitage to Samuel Sidney Fraser, a real estate speculator, who held onto the plantation briefly before selling to Robert Ernest Beaty in 1905. Clarke A. Willcox of Marion purchased Wachesaw and the Hermitage in 1910 for $10,000 to use as a summer retreat. The Willcox family retained the Hermitage but sold Wachesaw in 1930 to William A. Kimbel, who also bought Richmond Hill with the purpose of developing a large hunting estate. With his purchase of both properties, Kimbel had restored the boundaries of John Murrell's original plantation.

In 1920, Dr. Julius A. Mood of Sumter and a group of sportsmen bought Brookgreen, Springfield, Laurel Hill, and the Oaks to use as a hunting preserve. His daughter Julia Mood Peterkin made several visits to Brookgreen and used the area as the setting for some of her novels. She won the Pulitzer Prize for *Scarlet Sister Mary* in 1928. After numerous owners, railroad magnate Archer Milton Huntington purchased Brookgreen in 1930. At first, he and his wife, Anna Hyatt Huntington, intended Brookgreen as a winter resort. Eventually, they decided to use the plantation as an outdoor gallery for Anna's award-winning sculptures. The Huntingtons constructed Atalaya, a Spanish-style fort, on the beach to use for her studio and living quarters at what is now Huntington State Park. Brookgreen Gardens is open year-round and offers opportunities for investigating the old rice culture, modern art, and beautiful gardens for which Brookgreen is famous today.

Early shipping routes relied on the Waccamaw River to move materials and goods by schooners and steamships, stopping at Wachesaw Landing to deliver passengers and mail to Murrells Inlet. The Murrells Inlet creeks were also convenient places for blockade-runners and pirates to bring in loads of goods or ship cotton out when the entrances to Little River and Georgetown were blocked by Union ships. The shipping of goods into Murrells Inlet during the Civil War created many embarrassments for the Union navy from 1862 to 1864, until Confederate withdrawal of troops ultimately allowed the Federal forces to control the inlet.

The transportation corridors up to the 1900s were primarily the Waccamaw River and the Atlantic Ocean for boats and the Kings Road (used during George Washington's visit) and the River Road (along the Waccamaw River near the plantation houses) for horse and wagons. These dirt roads were crude, rough paths that bore no resemblance to today's modern highways. Highway 17 was paved around 1933 as part of a federal effort to provide paved roads across the United States. The original road through Murrells Inlet followed along the creek-front houses until the new highway was constructed.

The years from the Reconstruction until World War I saw an increase in the number of settlers who moved to Murrells Inlet to enjoy the natural resources provided. The families that moved into this area were from communities like Marion, Conway, Southport, and nearby counties.

Murrells Inlet received visitors from all over the United States because of the Army crash boat station established during World War II and the Myrtle Beach Air Force Base, which was reactivated in the 1950s; many of these military personnel ended up making Murrells Inlet their home. Some of these service members started families with the girls they met in Murrells Inlet, and others brought their family with them. The period after World War II up into the 1960s saw the growth of the fishing and seafood industries, and Murrells Inlet quickly gained the reputation of the "Seafood Capital of South Carolina." The charter fishing industry quickly gained fame after Alex Sing brought the fishing vessel *Captain Alex* to Murrells Inlet in 1967 and fishermen all over the Southeast read newspaper reports.

The growth of the population and the tourism industry during the 1970s and 1980s saw a transformation from a sleepy fishing village to the modern town of today. Hurricane Hugo hit Murrells Inlet in 1989, and the storm surge destroyed many of the last remnants of the past, including the Army docks. The closure of the Myrtle Beach Air Force Base in the early 1990s signaled a change in the local economy, and in 1997, there was a local push to improve Murrells Inlet, protecting and preserving the creeks and helping to improve the business climate. This resulted in Murrells Inlet 2007, which was the effort of numerous individuals and several small groups joining forces to speak with a united voice. This group (now Murrells Inlet 2020) has been successful in completing several projects to beautify and improve the community and plan for the future.

One

Boats

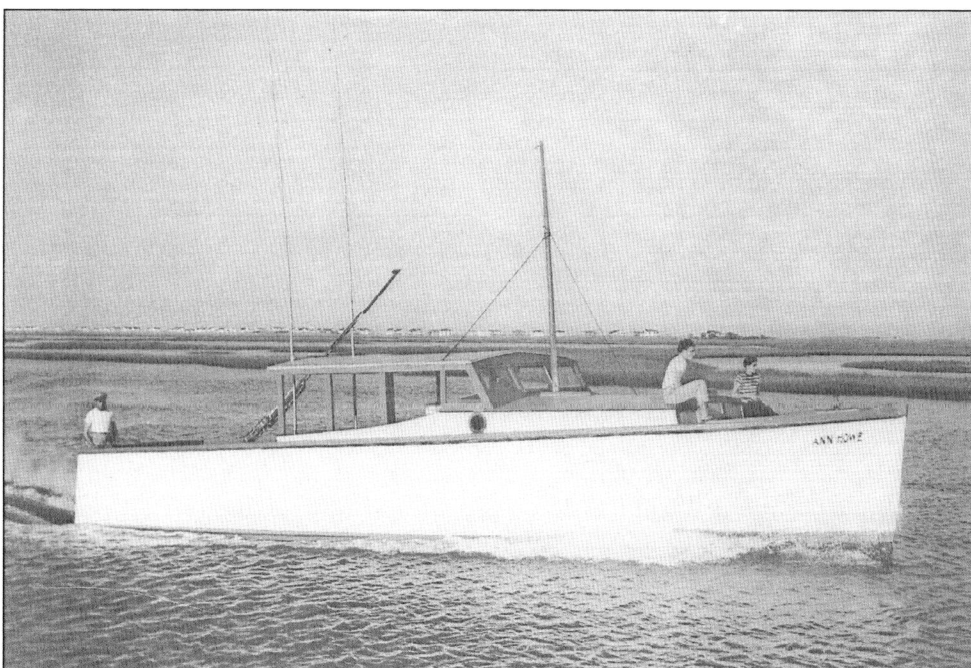

The *Ann Howe* was a wooden fishing boat constructed in the late 1930s by Luther Smith using the wood recovered from live oaks that were cut down during the construction of Highway 17 in the mid-1930s. This boat took many years to be completed (some called it Luther's folly), and when Luther was asked if he were finished with the boat, his reply was "and how," which was said to be the origin of the name. The *Ann Howe* ran from Smith's Landing during the 1940s, including a stint in the Army during World War II, and around 1951, it was sold to Capt. Mack Oliver, who moved it to Oliver's Lodge in 1953. Capt. Ira Vick also ran this boat for Luther Smith and Mack Oliver and rode out Hurricane Hazel on the *Ann Howe* tied to a channel marker. From left to right, Sam Barwick, Bill Chandler, and Buddy Martin are shown aboard around 1948. (Courtesy of the Smith family.)

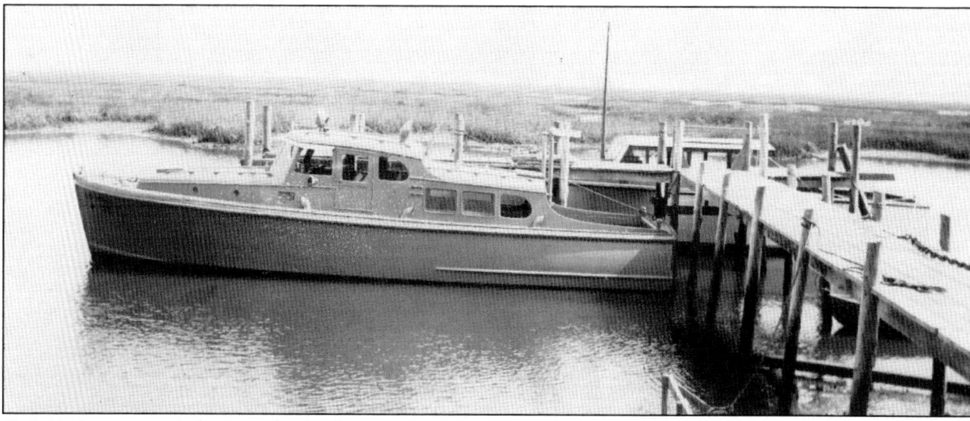

A P-32 Army crash boat is docked at Luther Smith's Landing near low tide in 1945. The Army Air Force operated crash boats out of Murrells Inlet during World War II to support flight-training operations at Myrtle Beach Army Air Force Base, using the crash boats to tow targets and pick up pilots who crashed in the water while practicing bombing and machine-gun training near the beaches of Garden City. The *Ann Howe* is also at the dock in this photograph. (Courtesy of Gwen Watson and Murrells Inlet 2020.)

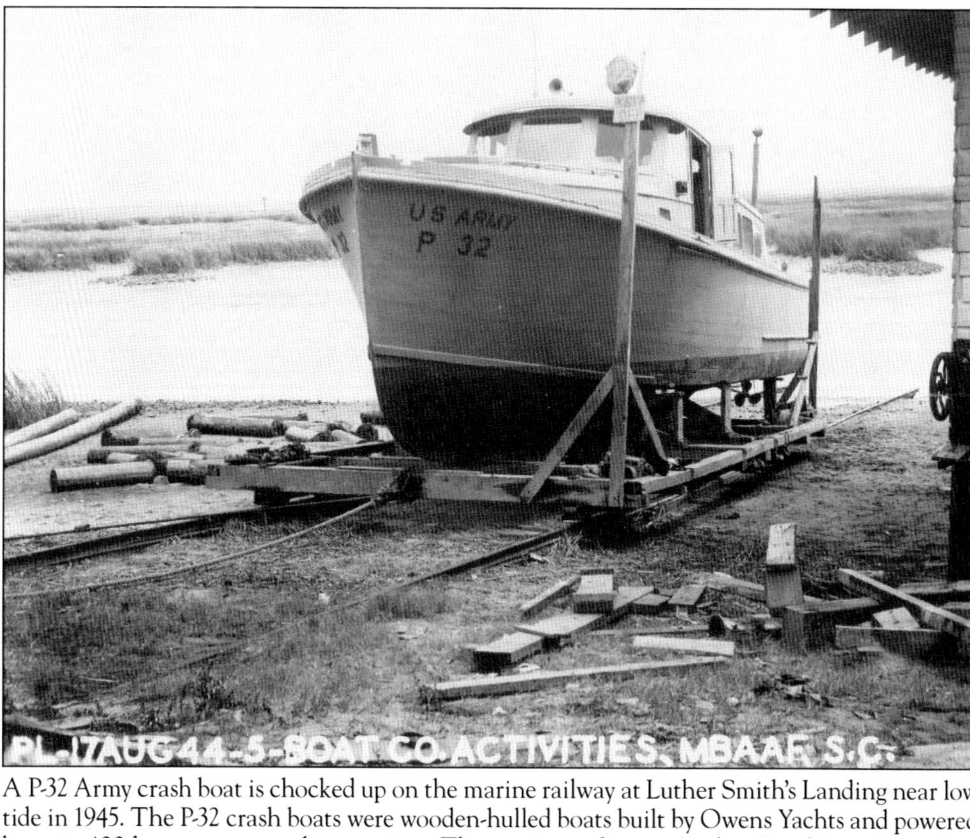

A P-32 Army crash boat is chocked up on the marine railway at Luther Smith's Landing near low tide in 1945. The P-32 crash boats were wooden-hulled boats built by Owens Yachts and powered by twin 400-horsepower gasoline engines. The marine railway at Luther Smith's used a timber cradle and steel wheels to support the boats, and the cradle was pulled out of the water using a large hand-operated winch that is still located at Flo's Restaurant nearby. (Courtesy of Gwen Watson and Murrells Inlet 2020.)

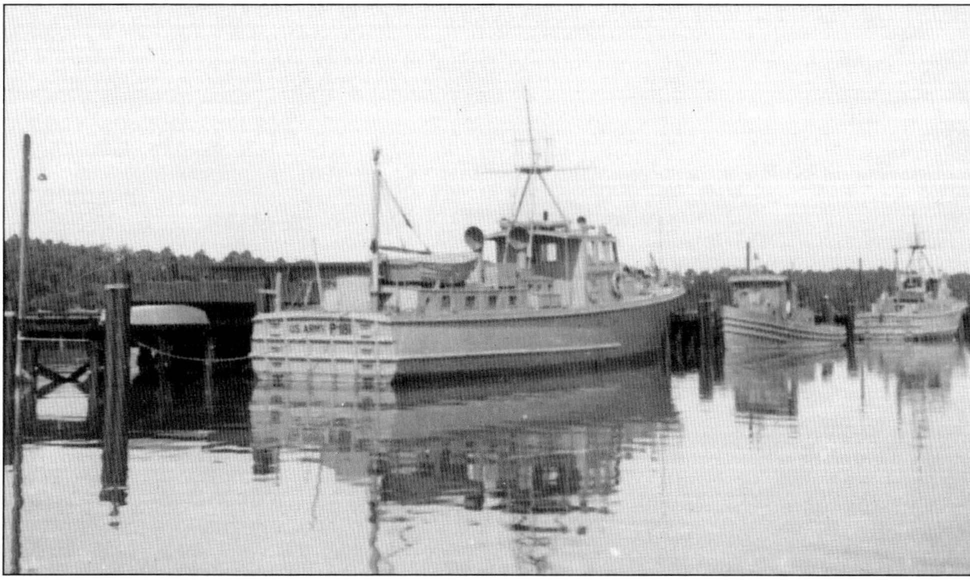

The Army dock was constructed in Murrells Inlet around 1941 to support flight-training operations at Myrtle Beach Army Air Force Base, starting at the Future Farmers of America (FFA) lodge that had been leased to provide crew quarters. Both military and civilian boat captains ran the crash boats that towed targets and picked up pilots who crashed in the water during training operations. A P-181 transport ship and two smaller boats are shown alongside the Army dock in the main creek at Murrells Inlet in 1945. (Courtesy of Gwen Watson and Murrells Inlet 2020.)

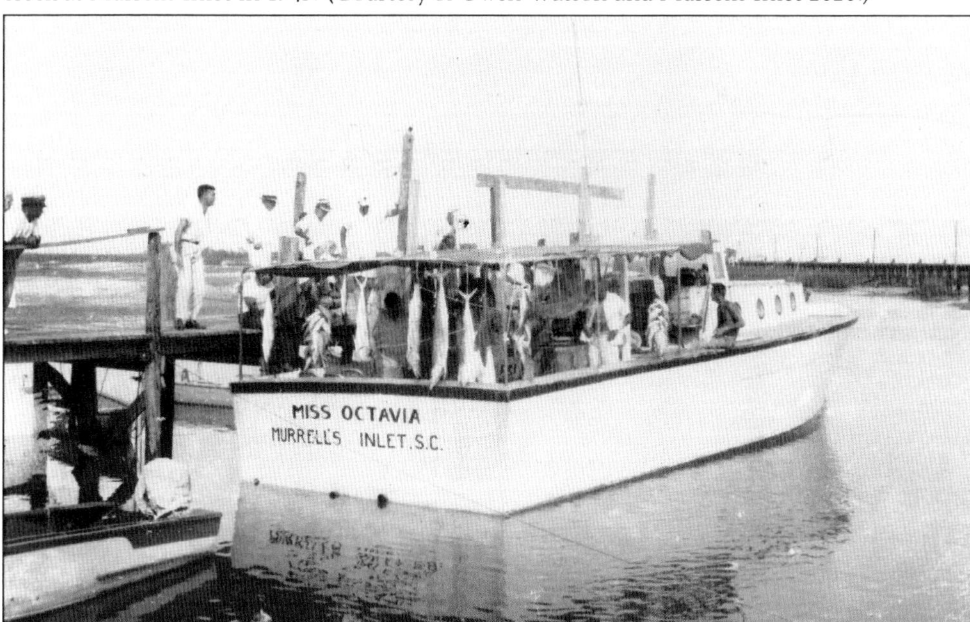

Capt. Sanford Wells built the *Miss Octavia* at his home on McDowell Shortcut and launched it at Smith's Landing around 1958. This wooden boat had a solid pine keel and fished the blackfish and snapper banks off Murrells Inlet, docking at Captain Alex's Marina. It is shown here after returning from a good fishing trip with king mackerel, mahi, and snapper hanging from strings around the rear deck; the Army dock is visible in the background. (Courtesy of the Caughman family.)

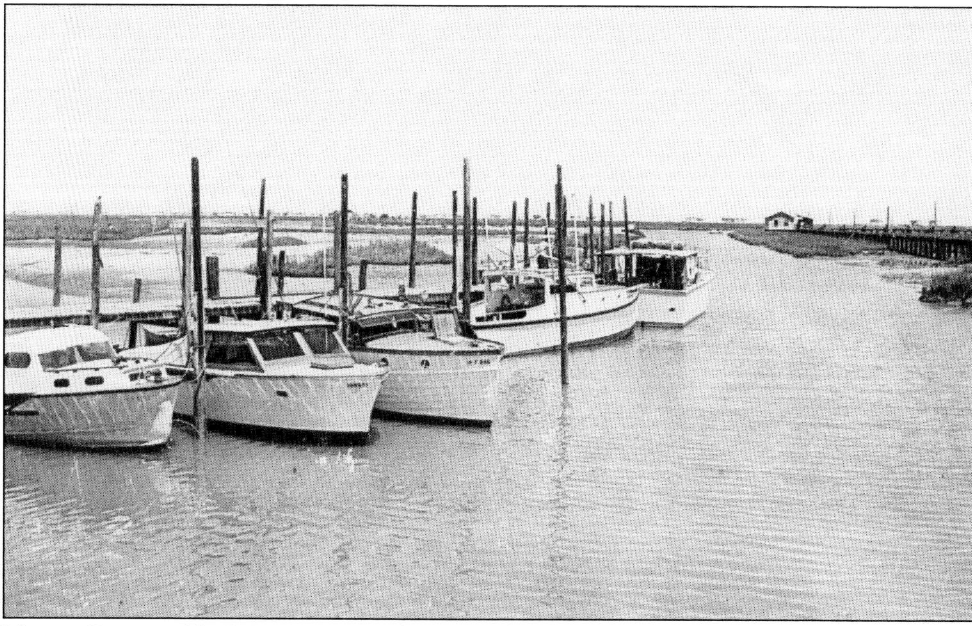

Here is Captain Alex's Marina around 1960 with the typical charter fishing boats, including, from right to left the *Miss Octavia* (Capt. Sanford Wells), the *Sea Queen* (Capt. Orsa Bashor), an unidentified boat, and the *Braxley Ann* (Capt. Sam Worrell). The marina basin and the channel out to the main creek beside the Army dock were dredged in the late 1950s. (Courtesy of the Sing family.)

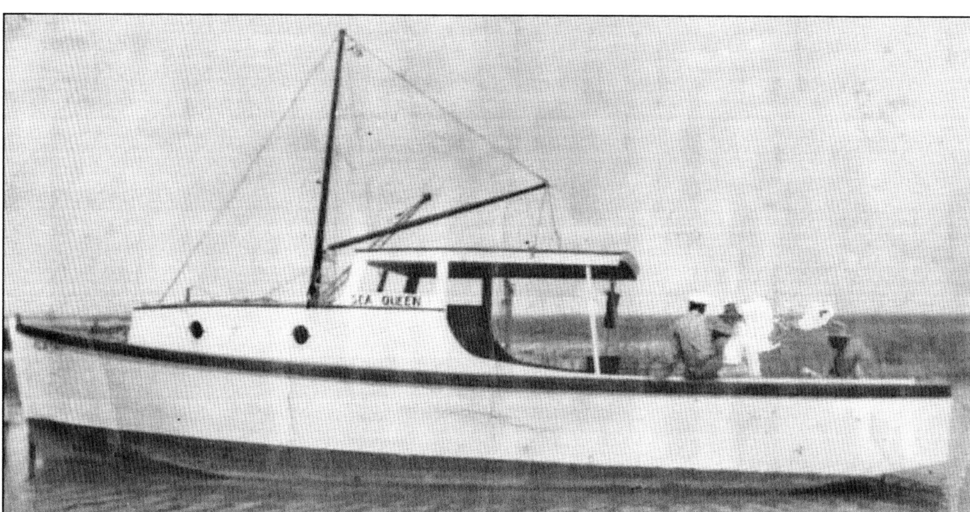

Capt. Orsa Bashor ran the *Sea Queen* out of Alex's Marina during the late 1950s and early 1960s for charter fishing trips both nearshore around Murrells Inlet and out to the blackfish banks. Orsa and his two sons built this 36-foot boat for Albert Jordan, who ran it as *The Joy* from Jordan's Landing. The Bashors were noted boat builders in this area, and their boats were sought out for both fishing and sailing vessels along the East Coast. (Courtesy of the Bashor family.)

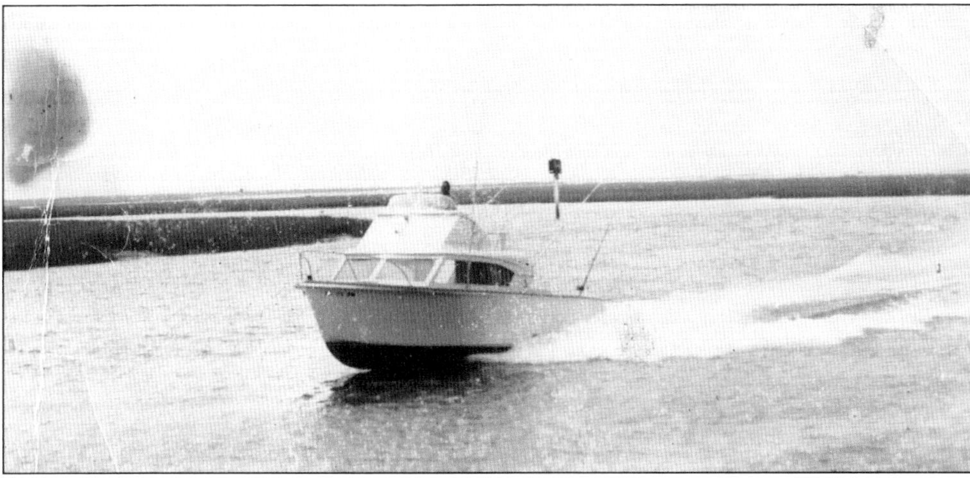

Capt. M.G. Caughman built the *Albacore* in 1962 behind the Garden City Grocery and launched it at Wachesaw Landing for the first sea trial, with Harold Harper riding on the flybridge and lifting powerlines over the boat while it rode on a lowboy trailer to be launched. The *Albacore* was a 28-foot fiberglass boat with twin Volvo engines capable of 35 knots. It was one of the first topwater trolling boats for big-game sportfishing to operate out of Murrells Inlet, fishing the offshore waters out to the Gulf Stream. (Courtesy of the Caughman family.)

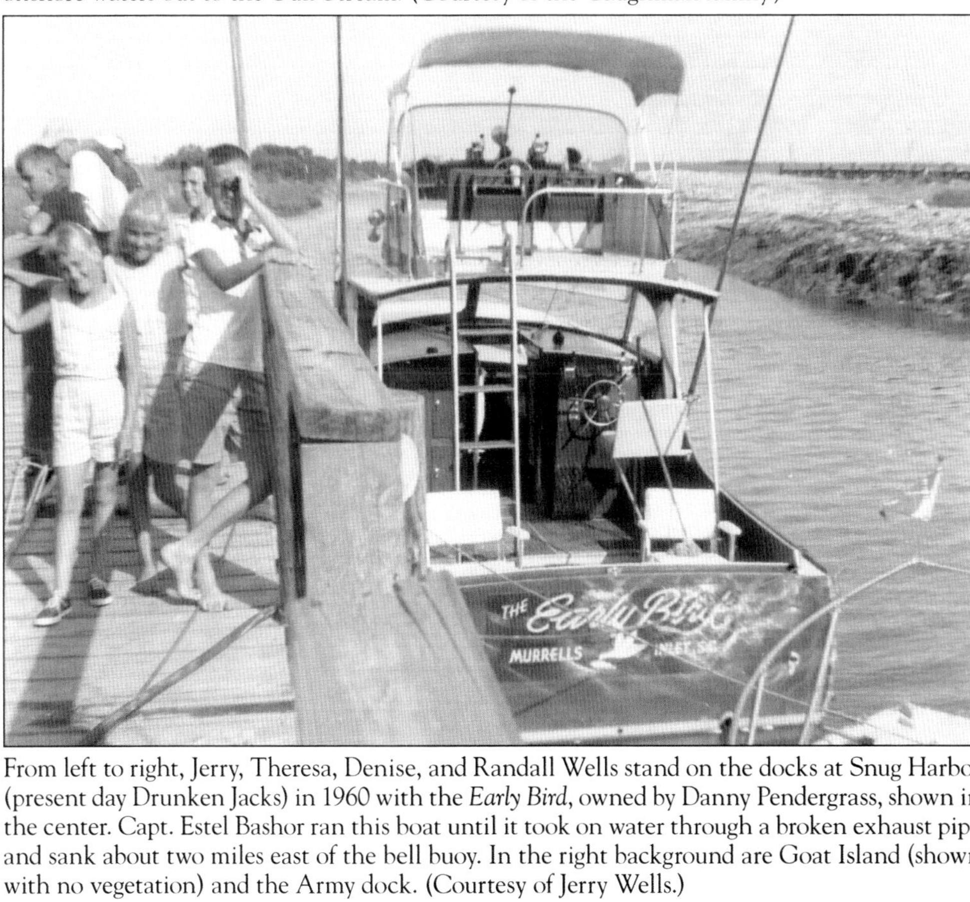

From left to right, Jerry, Theresa, Denise, and Randall Wells stand on the docks at Snug Harbor (present day Drunken Jacks) in 1960 with the *Early Bird*, owned by Danny Pendergrass, shown in the center. Capt. Estel Bashor ran this boat until it took on water through a broken exhaust pipe and sank about two miles east of the bell buoy. In the right background are Goat Island (shown with no vegetation) and the Army dock. (Courtesy of Jerry Wells.)

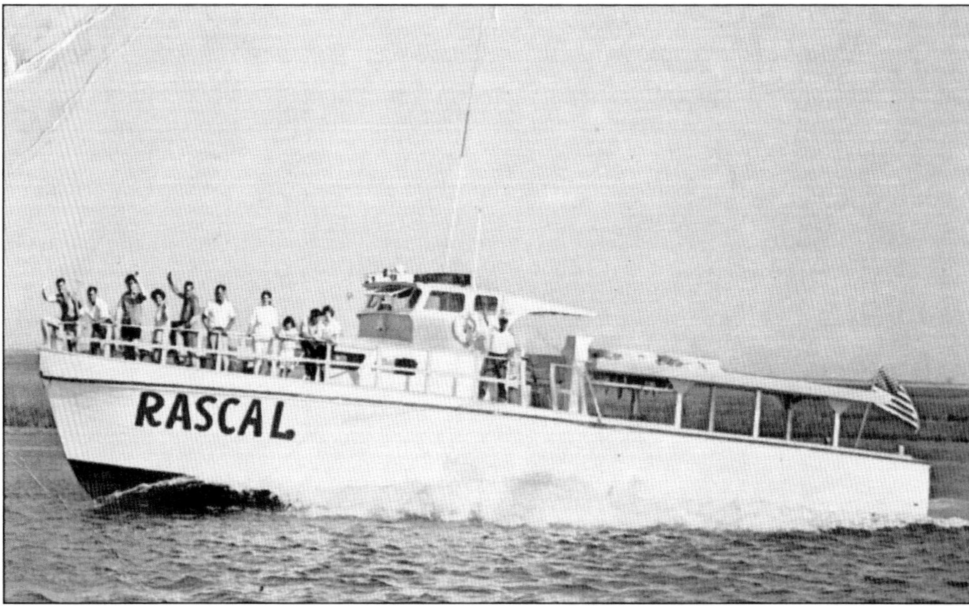

The *Rascal* was a converted World War II PT boat that fished the blackfish and snapper/grouper banks offshore, departing from Sam Barwick's dock from 1963 to 1965. This picture shows, from right to left, Capt. Lemuel Strickland, Peggy Turbeville, Wayne, Debbie, and Winnie Belle Strickland, Earl Reynolds, James Legette "Hoss" Johnson, and members of the Milligan family. (Courtesy of the Strickland family.)

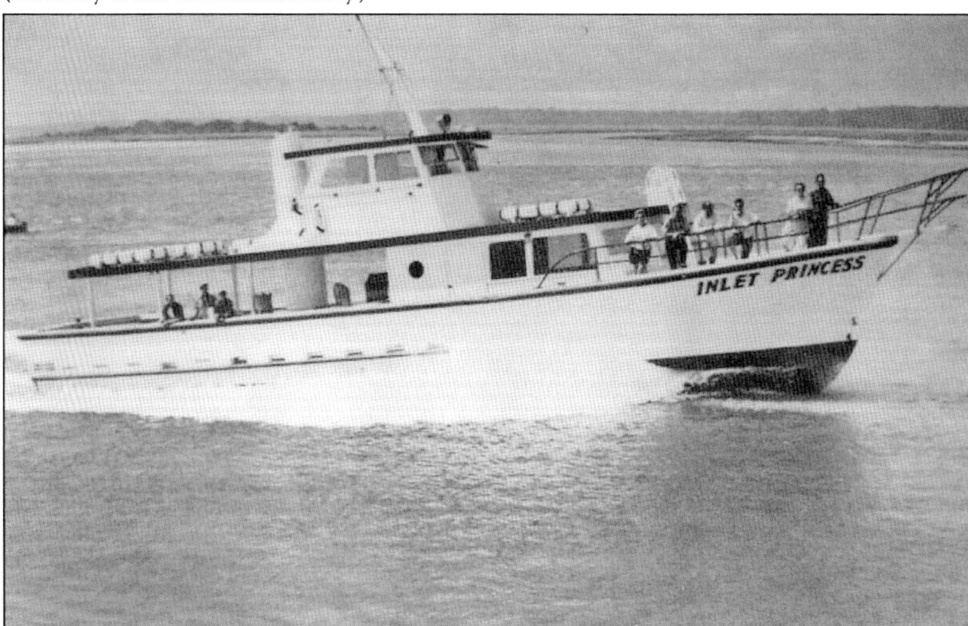

The *Inlet Princess* is shown during one of the initial sea trials after it was launched in 1963. The *Inlet Princess* was built for Everette Ayers Sr. across the street from the Ebb Nell Restaurant (the present day Dockside Restaurant). The Bashor brothers started construction of the 65-foot *Inlet Princess* in January 1963, and it was launched in July 1963 for a cost of around $60,000. (Courtesy of the Bashor family.)

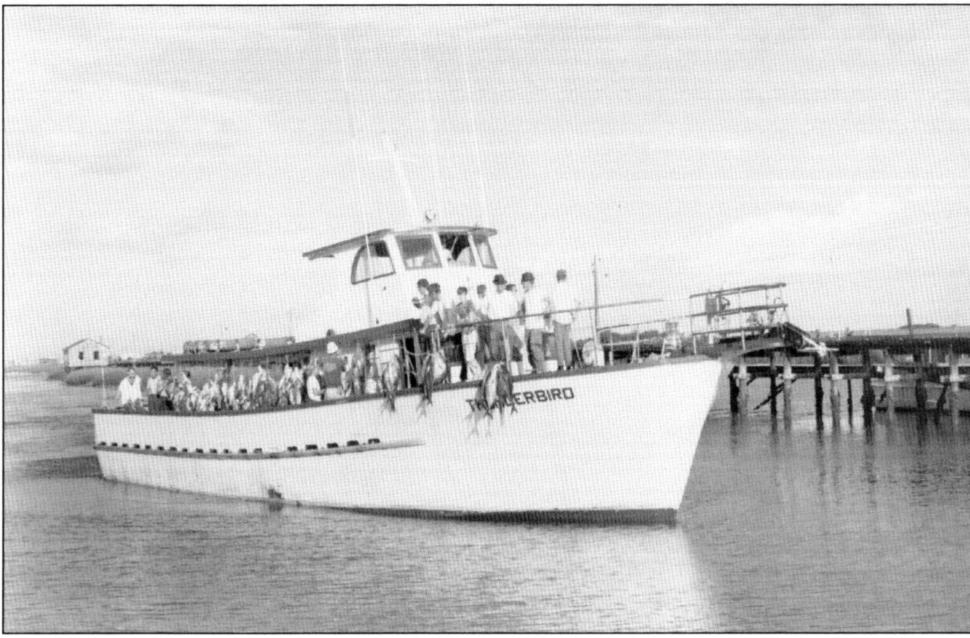

The *Thunderbird* was operated out of Alex's Marina during the 1960s by Capt. Buddy Dew, who sold it to Tommy Gaede around 1968. The *Thunderbird* was a wood hull with twin diesels that would run around 10 to 12 knots and fished the blackfish and snapper banks. Tommy leased Sam Barwick's docks at Snug Harbor and ran the *Thunderbird* and the *Tom-a-Gator* from that location in the 1970s. He was one of the first fishermen in Murrells Inlet to convert the head boats into commercial fishing boats for grouper and snapper using "bandit" reels. (Courtesy of Tommy Gaede.)

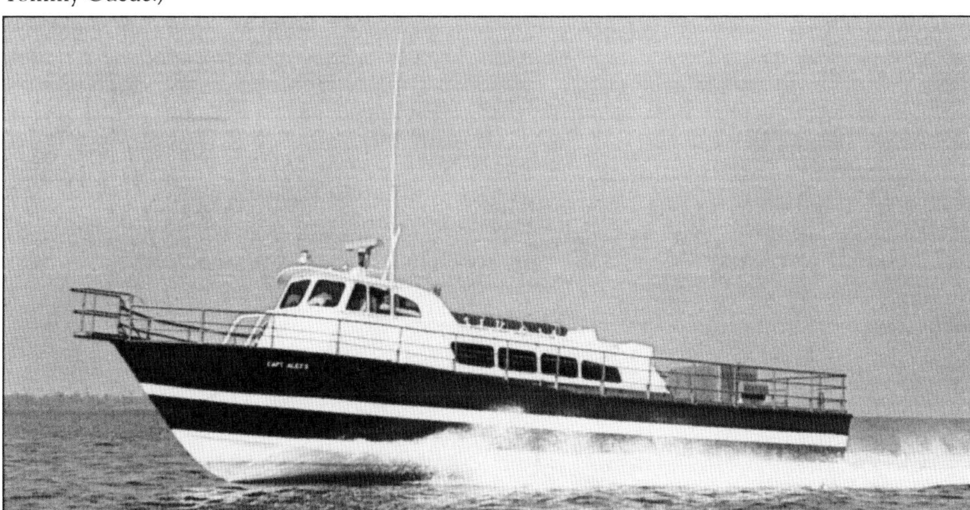

The *Captain Alex* was the first modern deep-sea fishing boat to offer one-day Gulf Stream fishing trips from Murrells Inlet. Alex Sing bought the vessel in Louisiana (it was a typical oil crew boat in the Gulf of Mexico) and started service in Murrells Inlet in 1967. With room for 41 passengers, this 65-foot aluminum-hull boat was capable of speeds up to 34 knots and allowed fishermen to drift fish in the warm waters of the Gulf Stream for new species of fish. (Courtesy of the Sing family.)

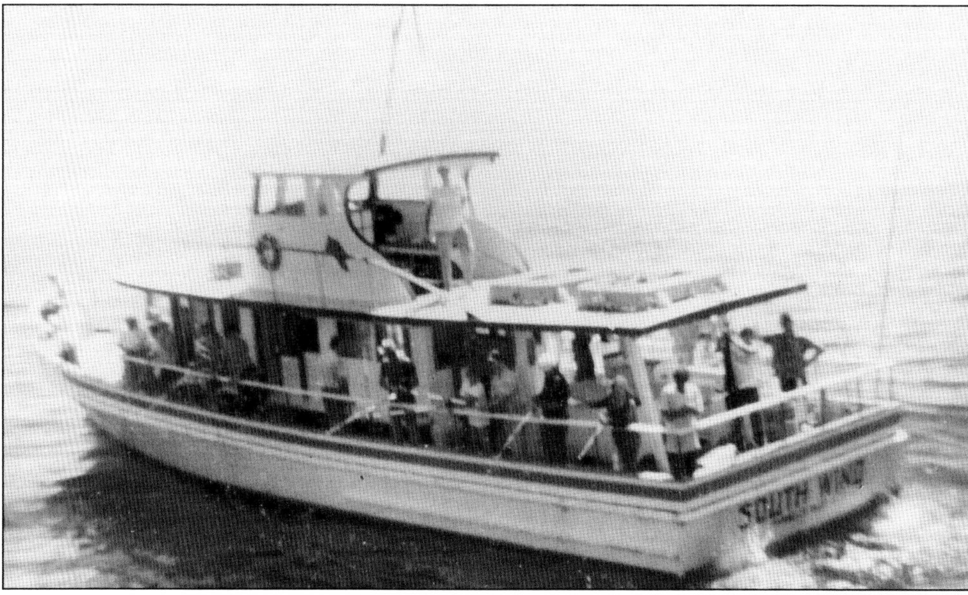

The *Southwind* was a 65-foot charter fishing boat that fished snapper banks on half-day trips out of Captain Alex's Marina. Bill James from Myrtle Beach owned the Southwind Hotel and the fishing boat and offered deep-sea fishing trips for the tourists who stayed at his hotel. Capt. Bill Moeller was one of the boat captains in the late 1960s. (Courtesy of Bill Moeller.)

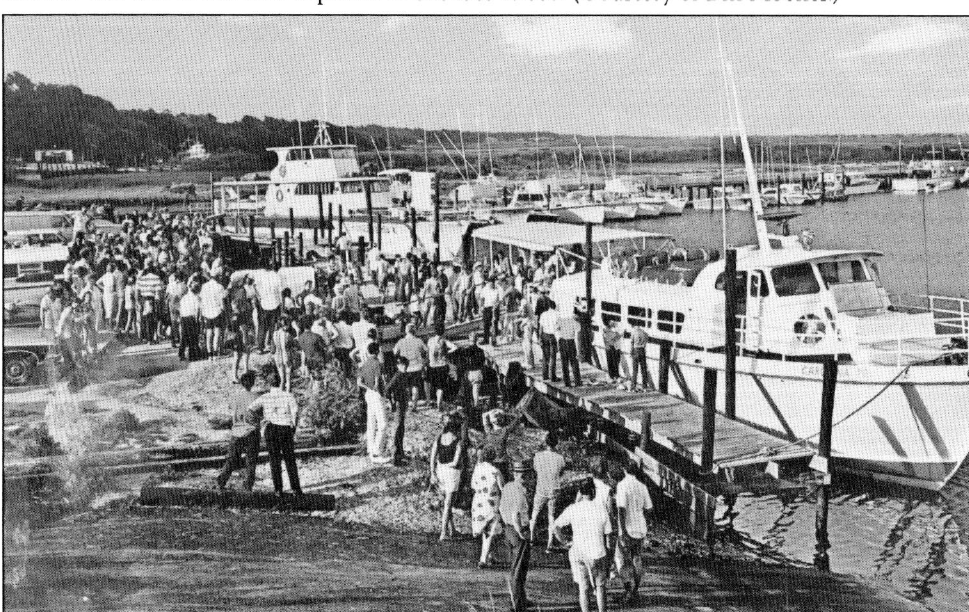

Captain Dick's Marina is shown around 1974 with a large crowd gathered to watch the charter boats arrive after a day of fishing. The *Carolina Princess* (Capt. Wayne Strickland) is shown in the foreground, and docked along the Army dock are, from left to right, the *Thunderbird II* (Capt. John Frink), the *Firebird* (Capt. Hoss Johnson), the *Firebird II* (Capt. Johnny Lewis), the *Sea Horse* (Capt. H.C. Strickland), the *Topcat* (Capt. M.G. Caughman), the *Mermaid* (Capt. Buck Kemp), and the *Playmate*. In the background beyond the Army dock are Sam Barwick's tackle shop and dock and the *Flying Fisher* (Capt. Tommy Sing). (Courtesy of the Strickland family.)

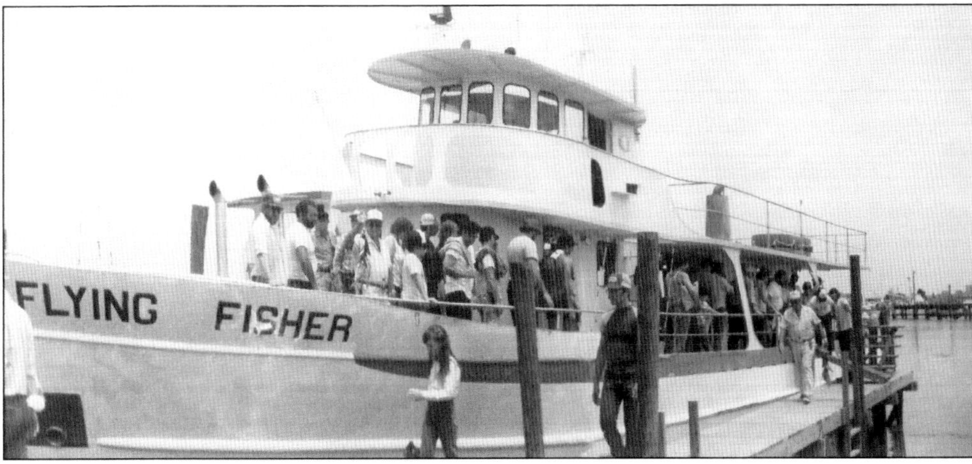

The *Flying Fisher* was a steel-hull fishing boat built in Georgetown by Thurmond Bostick and operated by Capt. Tommy Sing (one of Alex Sing Sr.'s children). The *Flying Fisher* ran half-day fishing trips to the black sea bass banks off of Murrells Inlet from Anchor Marina and Captain Alex's Marina from the 1960s to the 1980s. Guy C. Gentry Sr. is shown coming off the boat with a stringer of sea bass around 1976. (Courtesy of Guy C. Gentry III.)

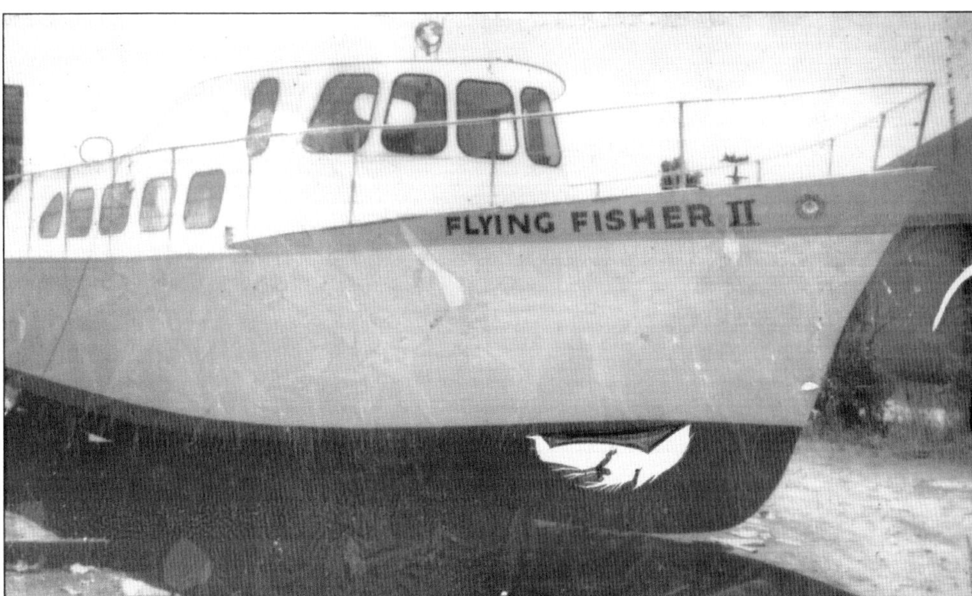

The *Flying Fisher II* was another boat that was built by Thurmond Bostick in Georgetown and operated out of Anchor Marina during the late 1960s. The *Flying Fisher II* was operated by Capt. Hoss Johnson for one season and then sold to Mike Marchant and Jack Patrick, with the name changing to *Miss South Carolina*. Due to the design of the cooling system, it was not fully utilized until after it was sold to a new owner in Texas who corrected the cooling-system design. (Courtesy of Mike Marchant.)

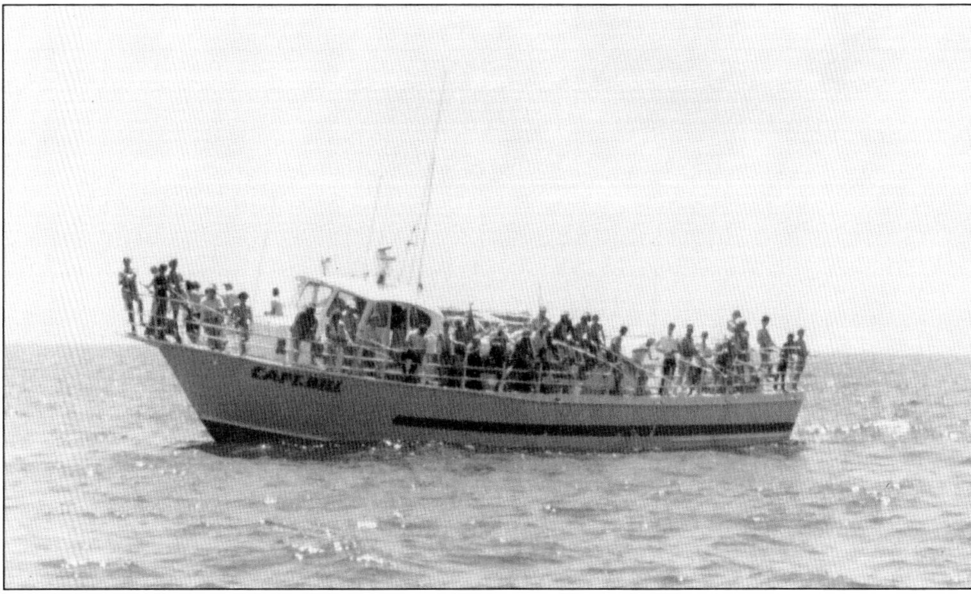

The *Captain Bill* was a 65-foot steel fishing boat that was built in Louisiana and brought into Anchor Marina around 1970 by Bill Moeller. Bill had started working on the charter boats around 1964, living at the Bay Harbor Motel with a couple of other fishermen who were working as mates on the head boats. The *Captain Bill* ran Gulf Stream fishing trips from Anchor Marina and then moved to Captain Dick's Marina around 1972 when Dick Eason and Dwayne Taylor started operations there. (Courtesy of Bill Moeller.)

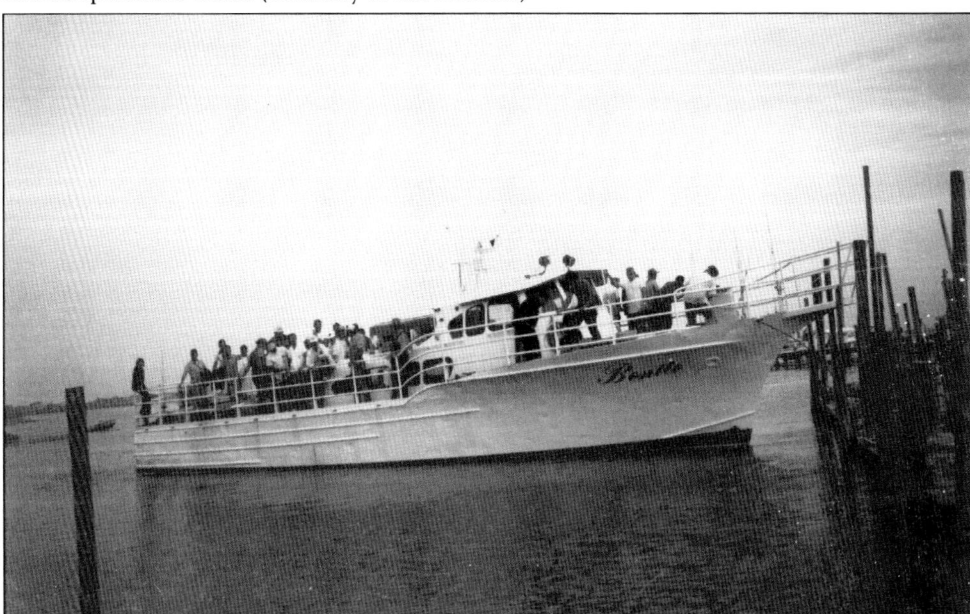

The *Bonita* was a steel-hulled fishing boat that Dick Eason, Art Flowers, and Dwayne Taylor bought in Louisiana and operated from Captain Dick's Marina in 1972. This boat was operated by several captains, including Capt. Johnny Strickland and Capt. Jimmy Stevens, during its time in Murrells Inlet for Gulf Stream fishing charters. The *Bonita* was said to be difficult to run in a downsea condition due to the hull design. (Courtesy of the Sing family.)

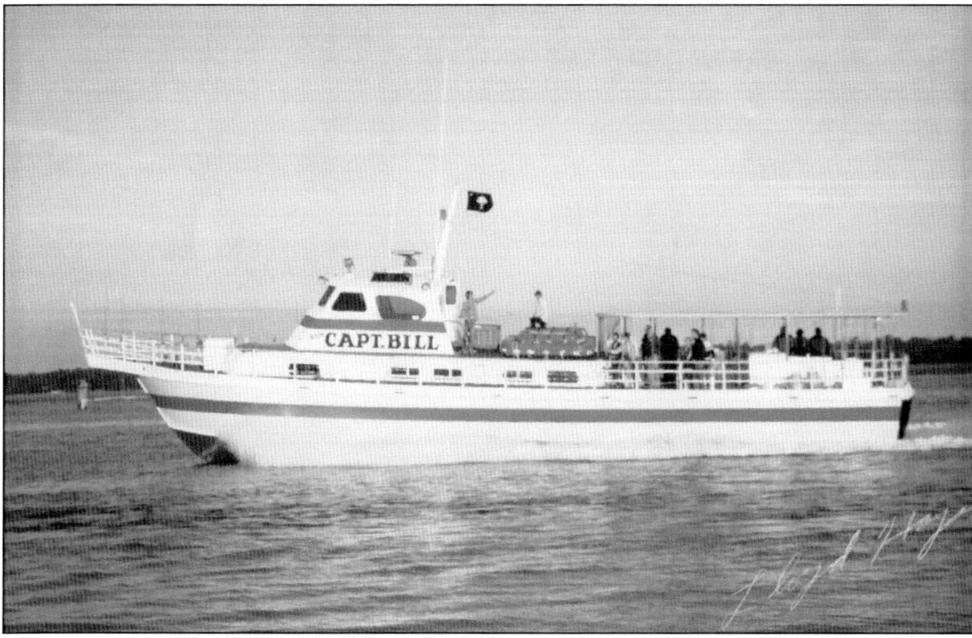

The *New Captain Bill* was a 65-foot steel fishing boat that ran Gulf Stream fishing trips from Captain Dick's Marina starting around 1974. Bill Moeller ran this boat until about the mid-1980s, when Tom Swatzel and Jerry Oakley bought the marina and several of the charter fishing boats. (Courtesy of Bill Moeller.)

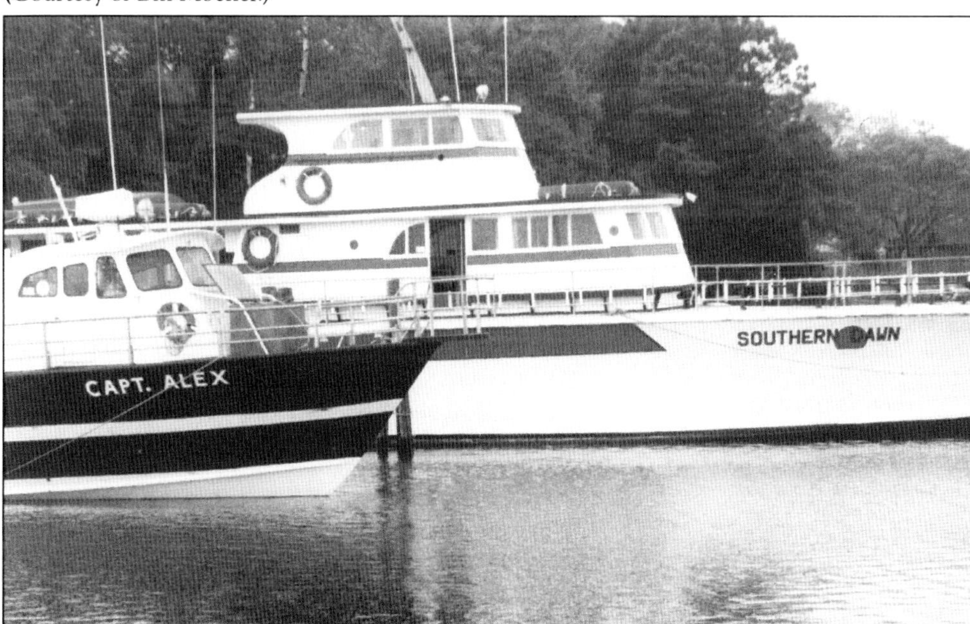

The *Captain Alex* and the *Southern Dawn*, shown in mid-1970s at Captain Alex's Marina, were purchased by Capt. Don Lash and operated during the 1970s. The *Southern Dawn* was previously named the *Hurricane* and had operated in Little River; due to the amount of water necessary to operate in and the lack of dredging in Captain Alex's Marina basin, the boat was returned to Little River after one year. (Courtesy of Don and Linda Lash.)

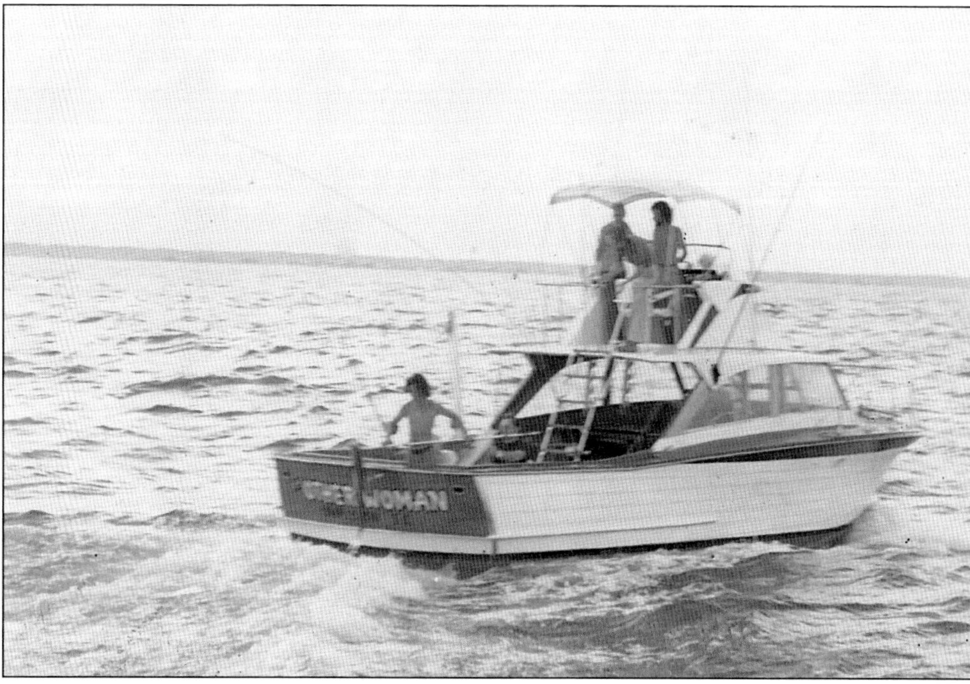

The *Other Woman* was a custom-built 32-foot Owens sportfishing boat operated by Capt. Chester Lewis around 1973. It was one of the charter fleet at Captain Dick's Marina during the 1970s, with several captains, including Danny Roberts around 1977–1978. (Courtesy of Chester Lewis.)

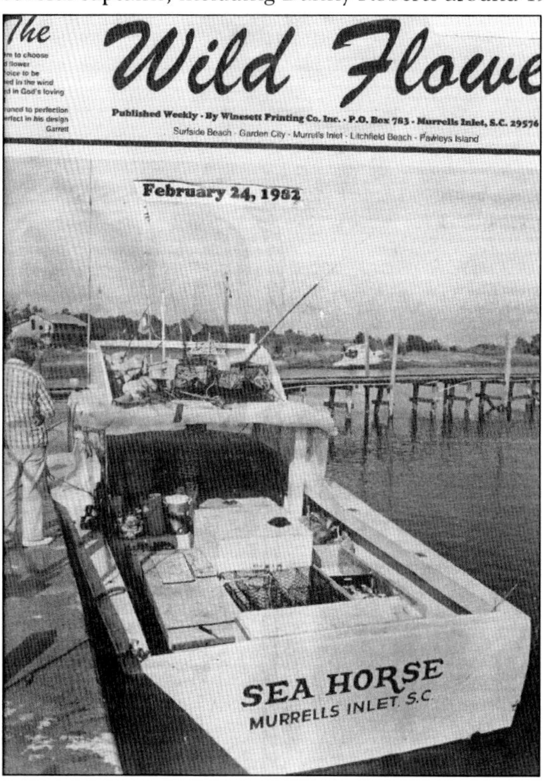

The *Sea Horse* was a custom-built 44-foot wooden boat constructed at Harkers Island, North Carolina, and brought to Murrells Inlet around 1967 by Capt. Lemuel Strickland. It operated out of Snug Harbor (Sam Barwick's marina) and Captain Alex's Marina during the 1960s and 1970s and was run by Capt. H.C. Strickland after Lemuel passed away in 1969. Shown at the dock at Captain Alex's Marina around 1982 with J.E. Perry standing on the dock and Oneal Strickland down below, the *Sea Horse* was operated as a commercial fishing boat with trapping gear for black sea bass loaded. In the background on the hill is another boat (the *Kids*) that H.C. Strickland operated during the 1960s and 1970s. (Courtesy of Garrett Winesett.)

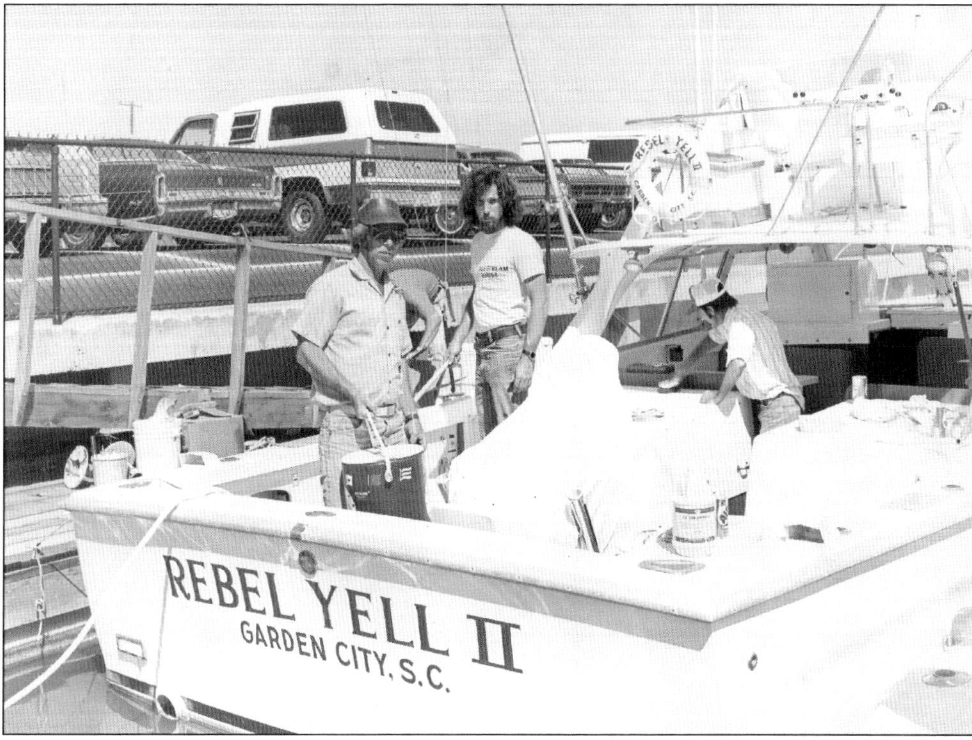

The 31-foot Bertram *Rebel Yell II* was owned by Ed Hines of Georgetown and operated by Capt. Chester Lewis out of Gulf Stream Marina. Shown at the dock in 1976 with brothers Johnny (left) and Chester Lewis (right), the *Rebel Yell II* was a contender in the billfish tournaments held in the area during the 1970s and 1980s. (Courtesy of Chester Lewis.)

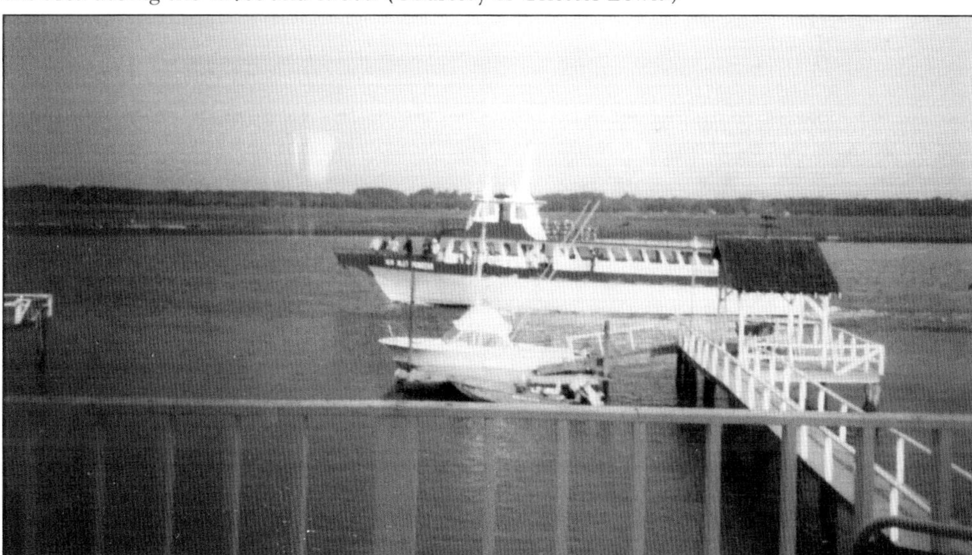

The *New Inlet Princess*, under the command of Capt. Hoss Johnson, was a daily sight in the Main Creek in Murrells Inlet, shown here passing Tom Barrineau's dock in Garden City. Hoss would sometimes make this trip a "moonlight" cruise, which would catch unsuspecting visitors by surprise if they were watching the *New Inlet Princess* pass by. (Courtesy of Tom Barrineau.)

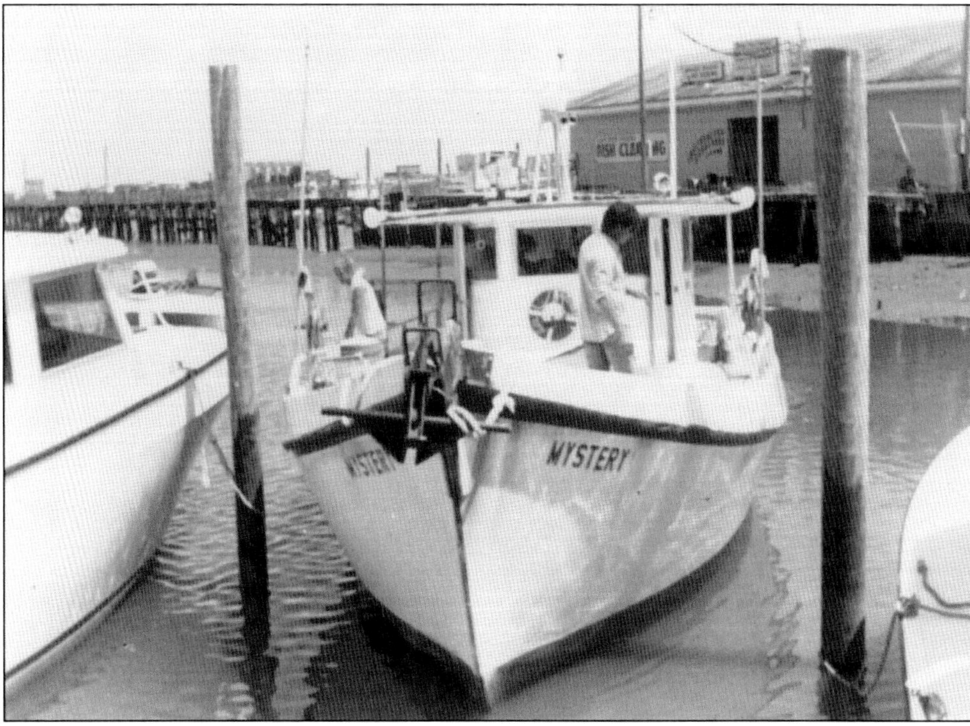

One of the commercial fishing fleet is shown docking at H&C Fisheries around 1987 (before Hurricane Hugo destroyed the docks). Dean Hair (on right) is shown aboard the *Mystery*, one of the commercial boats that fished the edge of the continental shelf to bring snapper and grouper to the seafood markets. These boats utilize "bandit" reels to drop baits into around 100–200 feet of water and catch fish on the live bottoms and ledges found offshore. (Courtesy of Dean Hair.)

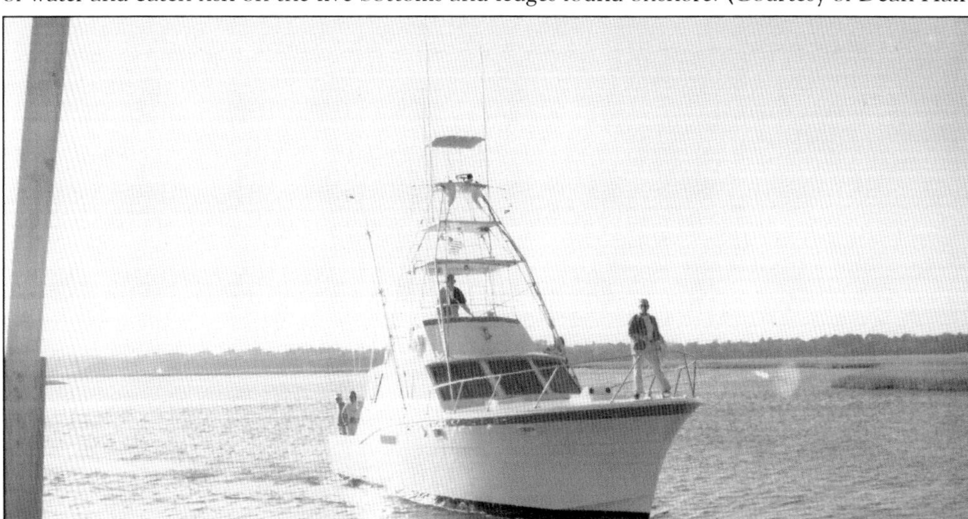

The *Partner* was a 52-foot Hatteras owned by Tom Ball and Les Morris that ran sport fishing trips from Captain Dick's Marina starting around 1977. Bill Moeller ran this boat until about the mid-1980s and was consistently catching billfish in local tournaments. Buddy Pardon was his mate during this time. (Courtesy of Bill Moeller.)

Two

CAPTAINS

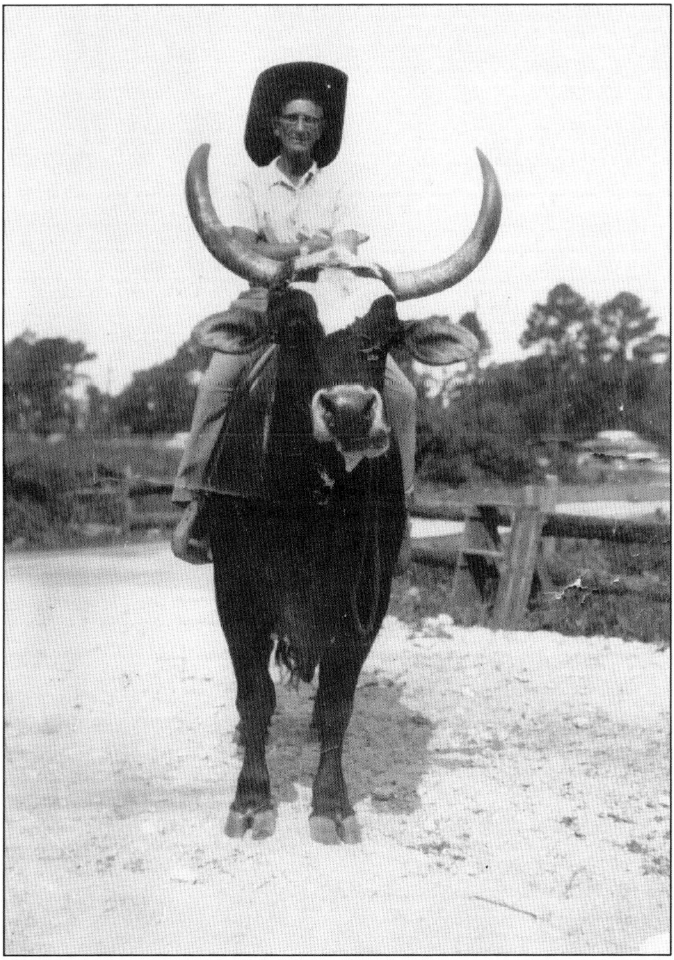

Capt. Charles Gennings Strickland Sr. (Captain Charlie) was one of the first generation of charter boat captains in Murrells Inlet, running the *Miss Olive* and the *Catherine* for Luther Smith before World War II. He was drafted into the Army Transport Service (ATS) working out of Charleston, South Carolina, to move military shipments during World War II. Two of his sons, Lemuel and H.C., ran charter boats, and numerous grandchildren and great-grandchildren still follow in his footsteps. He is shown here around 1953 on the back of Sambo, an ox that was used on his farm to plow 30 acres of fields. (Courtesy of the Strickland family.)

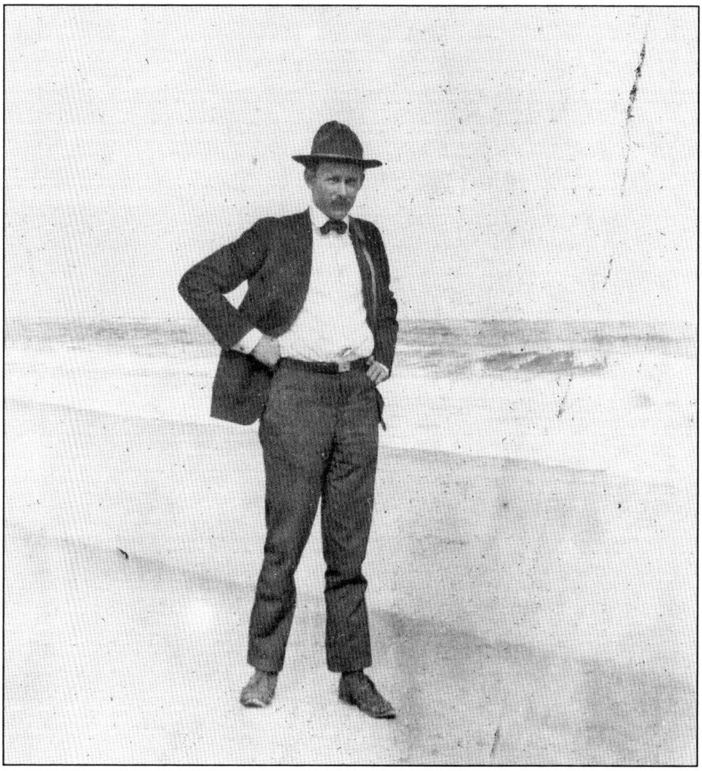

Capt. Luther Smith was the son of Henry Gilmore and Ida Odessa Smith and owned Smith's Landing, a local marina where fishermen could launch boats, pull boats out of the water on the marine railway, or go fishing on a charter boat. He ran the *Miss Catherine* and the *Ann Howe* from this site and worked with the Army to assist in the maintenance of the crash boats during World War II. (Courtesy of Dorothy Chappell.)

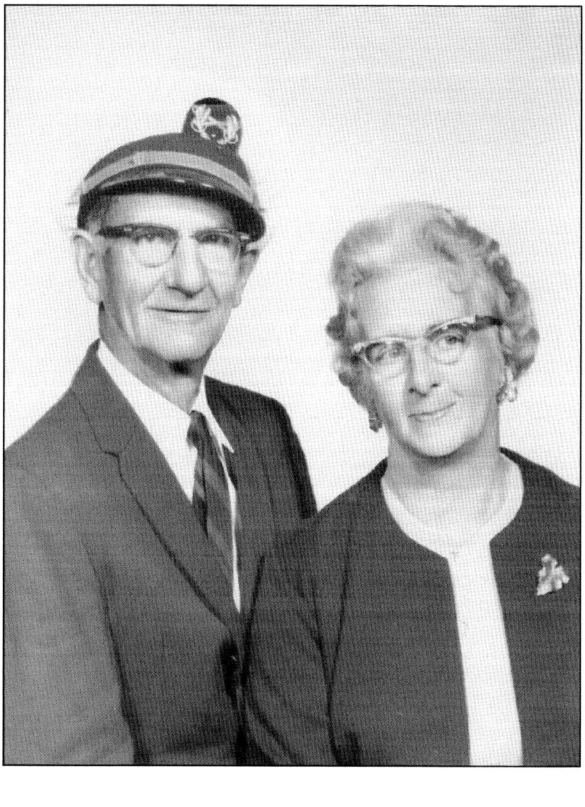

Capt. Ira Vick and his wife, Vivian, shown here in a formal portrait from their 50th anniversary, raised their family on the south end of Murrells Inlet. Captain Ira was born in the Woodland house and became a noted creek fisherman who fished gill nets for the local markets and ran charter boats, including the *Ann Howe* for Luther Smith and Mack Oliver, the *Sea Horse*, and the *Flying Squirrel*. (Courtesy of Dick Vick.)

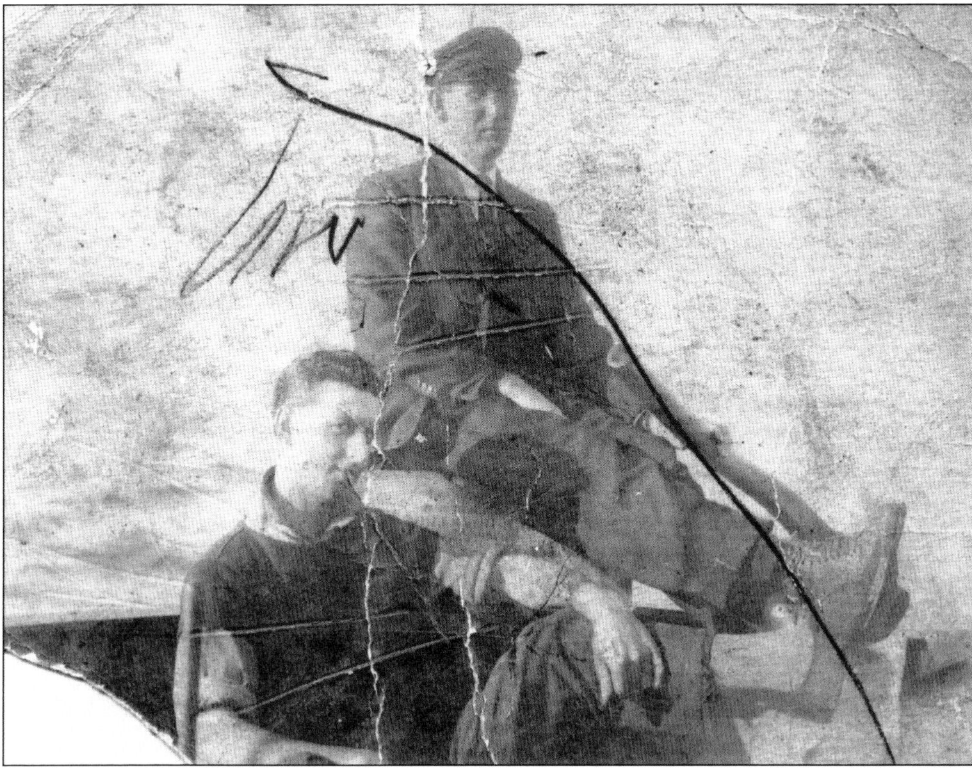

Capt. George "Son" Morse (top center) moved to Murrells Inlet from Southport, North Carolina, and was from a seafaring family. He raised a large family near the creek by present-day Morse Park and lived in a house once located where Russell's Seafood Grill is today. He is shown on an open sailing skiff around 1920 with John Causey. (Courtesy of the Morse family.)

Capt. Howard Fairfax Wesley (center) was a local outdoorsman whose nautical skills were put to work by the Army Air Force at the crash boat station in Murrells Inlet during World War II. Several local civilians were drafted into service to operate crash boats due to their knowledge of the navigation channels and the ocean bar. Shown here around 1944 on the bridge of a crash boat stationed at Murrells Inlet, he went on to be a well-known charter captain in the 1950s. (Courtesy of the Wesley family.)

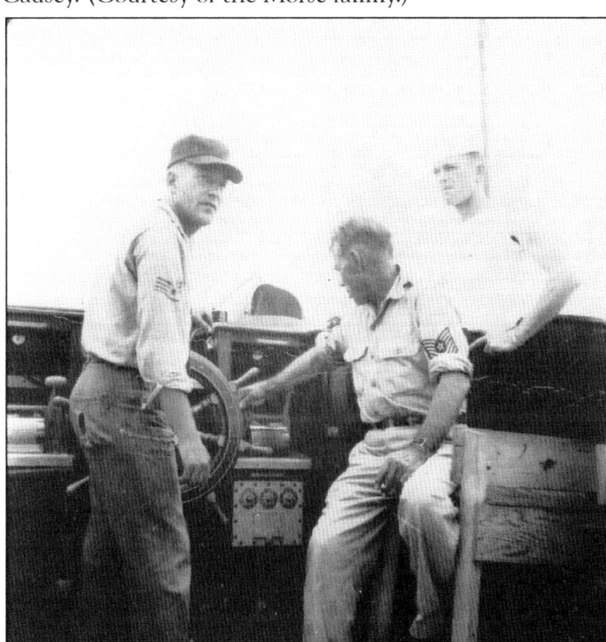

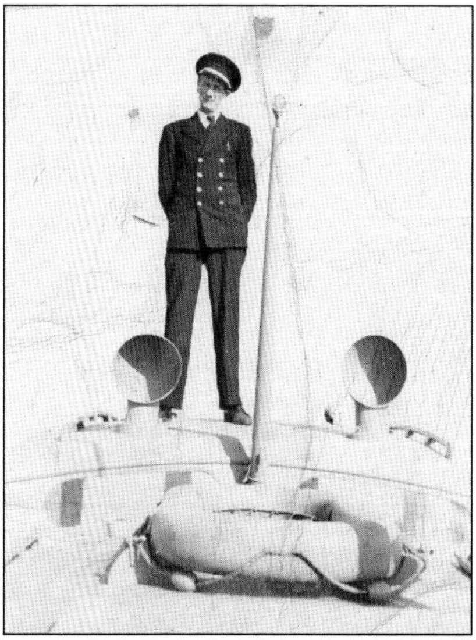

Capt. Charlie Strickland is shown in his Army Transport Service uniform from around 1943. His first fishing boat, *Miss Olive*, ran on a Palmer compression engine with a top speed of around five to six knots. Fish caught off of this boat were reeled on hand lines that wound around wooden spools; a typical offshore trip ranged around 5 to 10 miles out of Murrells Inlet in any direction to catch bottom fish (trout, sea bass, and porgies). (Courtesy of the Strickland family.)

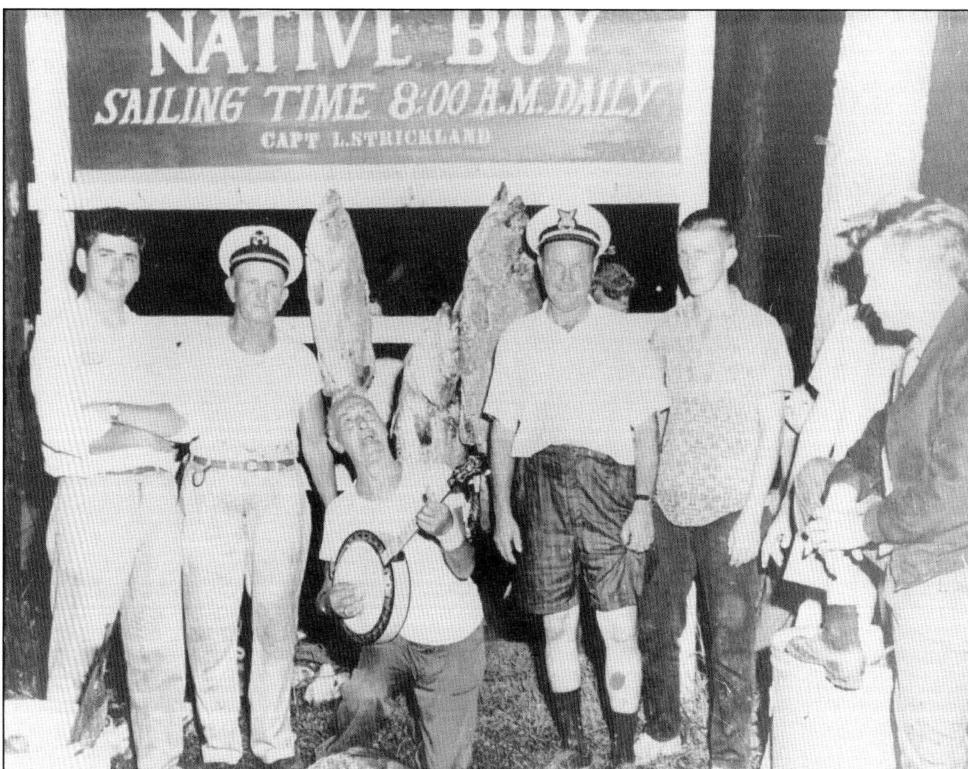

From left to right, Capt. Alex Sing Jr., Capt. Sam Worrell, "Wild Bill" Cope, Capt. Lemuel Strickland, and his son Lemuel "Bug" Strickland are pictured in front of a good catch of grouper from the *Native Boy* around 1958. A converted PT boat, the *Native Boy* was owned by Walter Christianson from Miami and was brought into Murrells Inlet for several years during the summer by Capt. Lemuel Strickland. Wild Bill Cope was an English entertainer who regularly fished on the *Native Boy* and always brought his banjo to strum and entertain the fishermen on the ride out and back in. (Courtesy of Jimmy Mayes.)

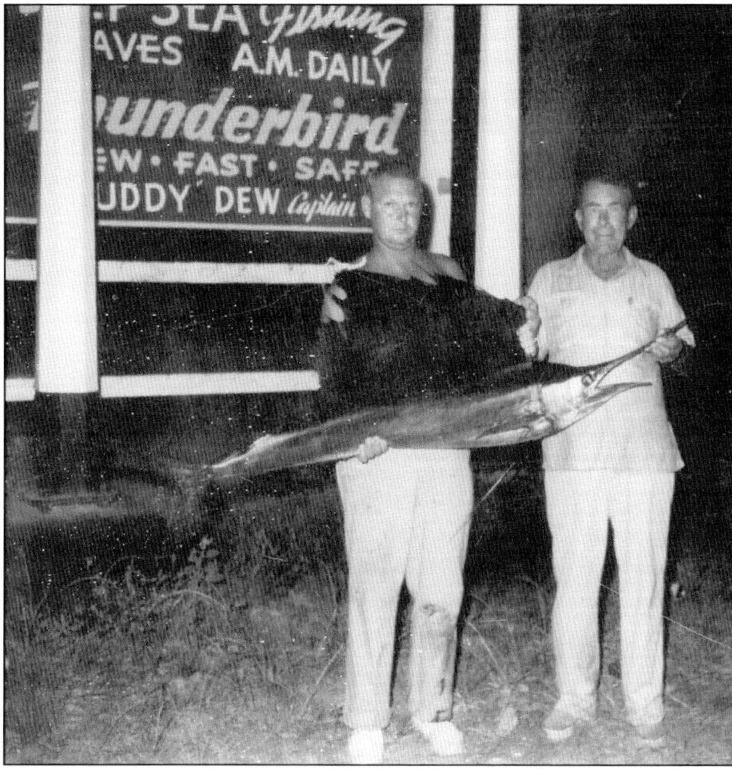

Capt. Howard F. Wesley (right) and his mate M.G. Caughman (another Murrells Inlet captain from the 1960s and 1970s) are at Captain Alex's Marina showing off a nice sailfish around 1959. Howard was one of the locals who were drafted into service for the Army Air Force (Capt. Mack Oliver also served at the crash boat station) who continued in the charter boat business after World War II. (Courtesy of the Wesley family.)

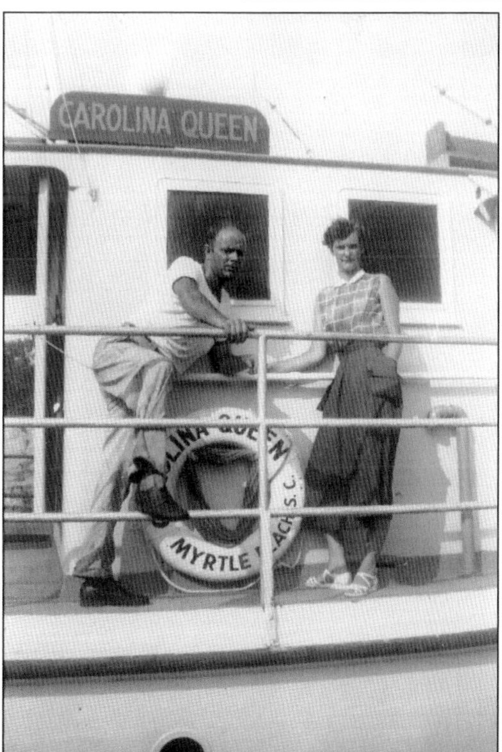

Capt. Lemuel Strickland (shown with his sister Elizabeth) was the captain of the *Carolina Queen* in the late 1950s, fishing the inshore blackfish banks off the coast. Lemuel and his father, Capt. Charlie Strickland, worked with the Army Transport Service (ATS) in Charleston during World War II, moving ships and goods along the coast. Several of his children continued in his footsteps as fishing boat captains along the East Coast. (Courtesy of the Strickland family.)

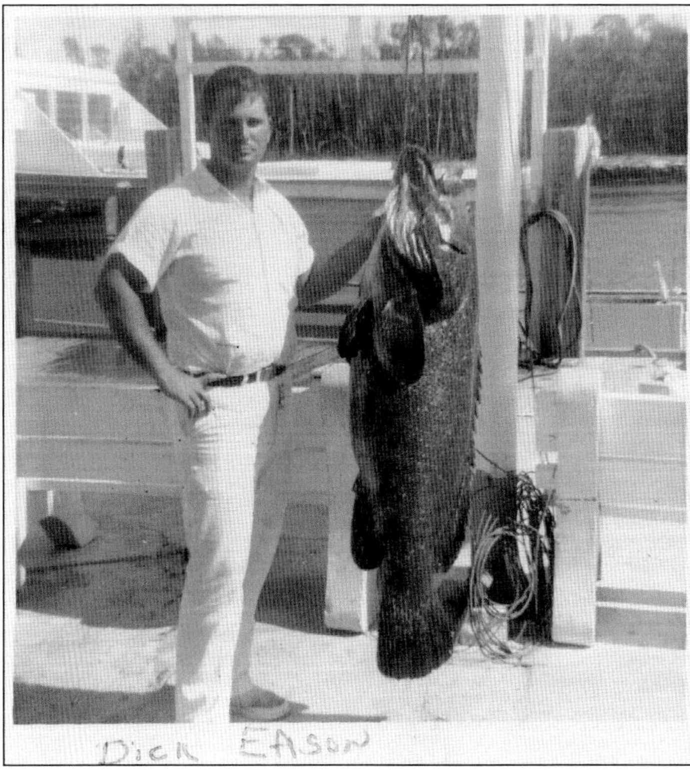

Capt. Dick Eason is shown with a nice Warsaw grouper about 1963. Dick Eason and Tommy Sing were working with Capt. Jimmy Stevens in Boynton Beach, Florida, during the winters and running charter boats in Murrells Inlet during the summers. Dick Eason operated several boats and marinas in Murrells Inlet during the 1960s and 1970s and was the original owner of Captain Dick's Marina. Dick Eason also operated the Anchor Marina prior to Captain Dick's. (Courtesy of the Eason family.)

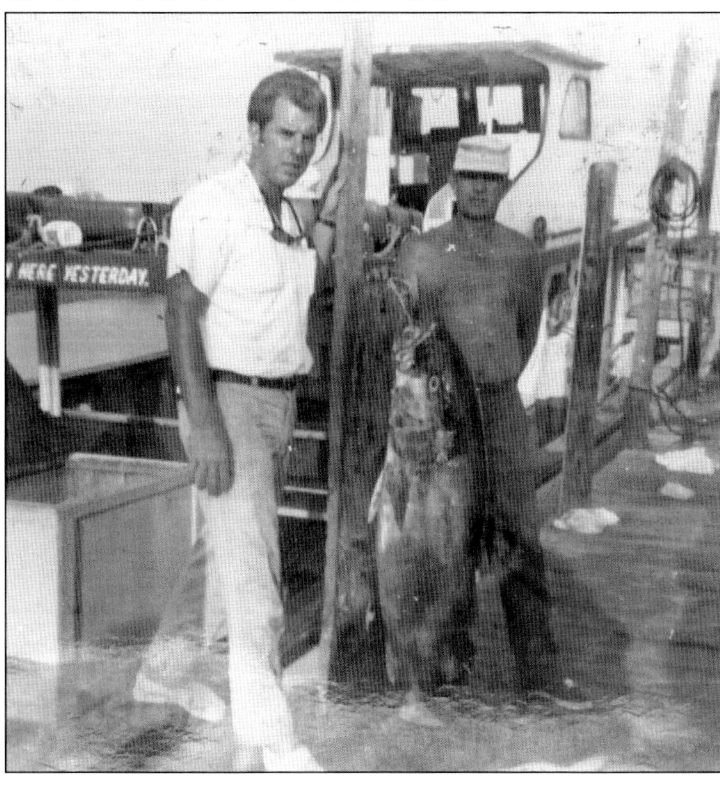

Capt. Tommy Gaede bought the *Thunderbird* from Buddy Dew around 1967 and fished the snapper banks off Murrells Inlet from Captain Alex's Marina and later from Sam Barwick's (called Thunderbird Marina at the time). He had another boat, the *Tom-a-Gator*, built for charter fishing; it was later put into service as one of the first commercial grouper/snapper boats in the area. (Courtesy of Tommy Gaede.)

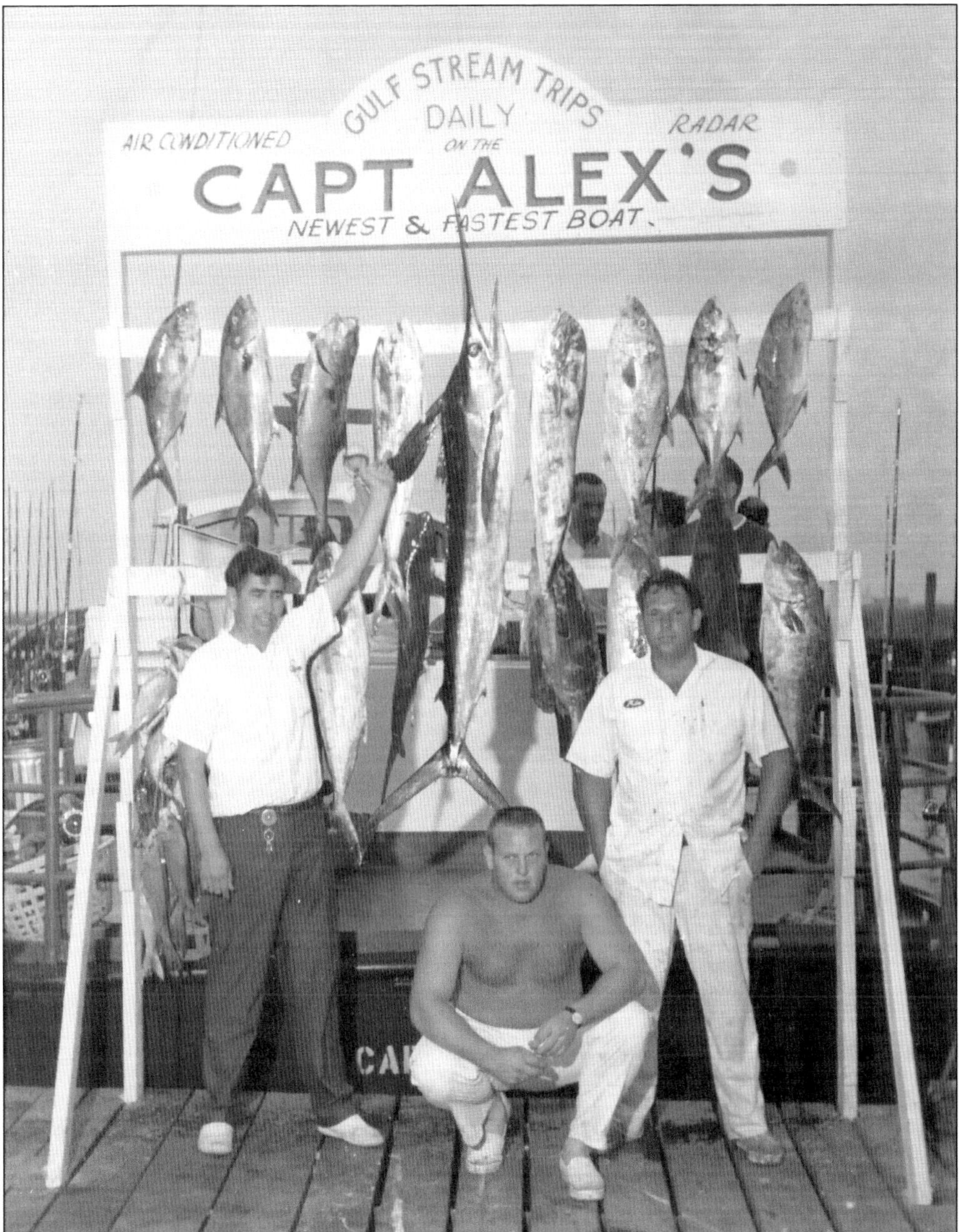

From left to right, Capts. Alex Sing, James "Hoss" Johnson, and Mike Marchant are showing off a nice catch of fish from the *Captain Alex* about 1967, shortly after the boat arrived in Murrells Inlet. Alex was a great fisherman and a showman and always attracted large crowds to the docks in the afternoons to see the variety and quantity of fish caught in the deeper Gulf Stream waters that he was able to fish during a one-day trip with this boat. (Courtesy of Mike Marchant.)

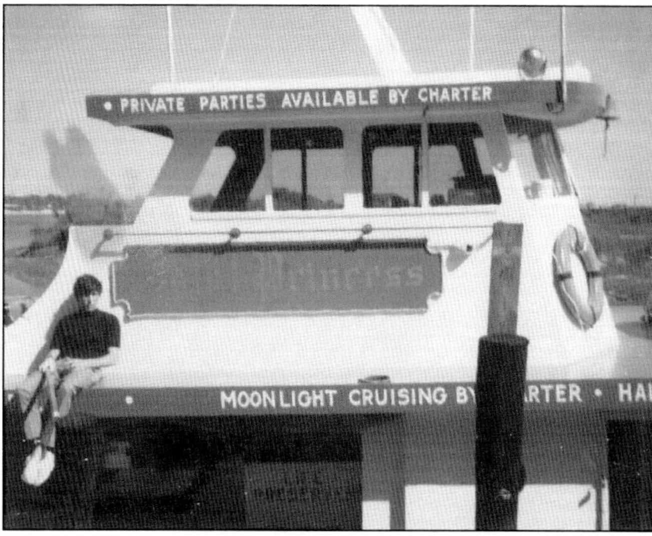

A young Chester Lewis is sitting on the top deck of the *Inlet Princess* in 1968 next to the new signs that he had painted and installed on the sides of the wheelhouse. Chester had recently completed a tour with the US Navy and came back to Murrells Inlet. He started his fishing career as a mate on the *Inlet Princess* and went on to captain many boats, including the *Rebel Yell*, the *Other Woman*, the *Linda J*, and the *Firebird II*. (Courtesy of the Eason family.)

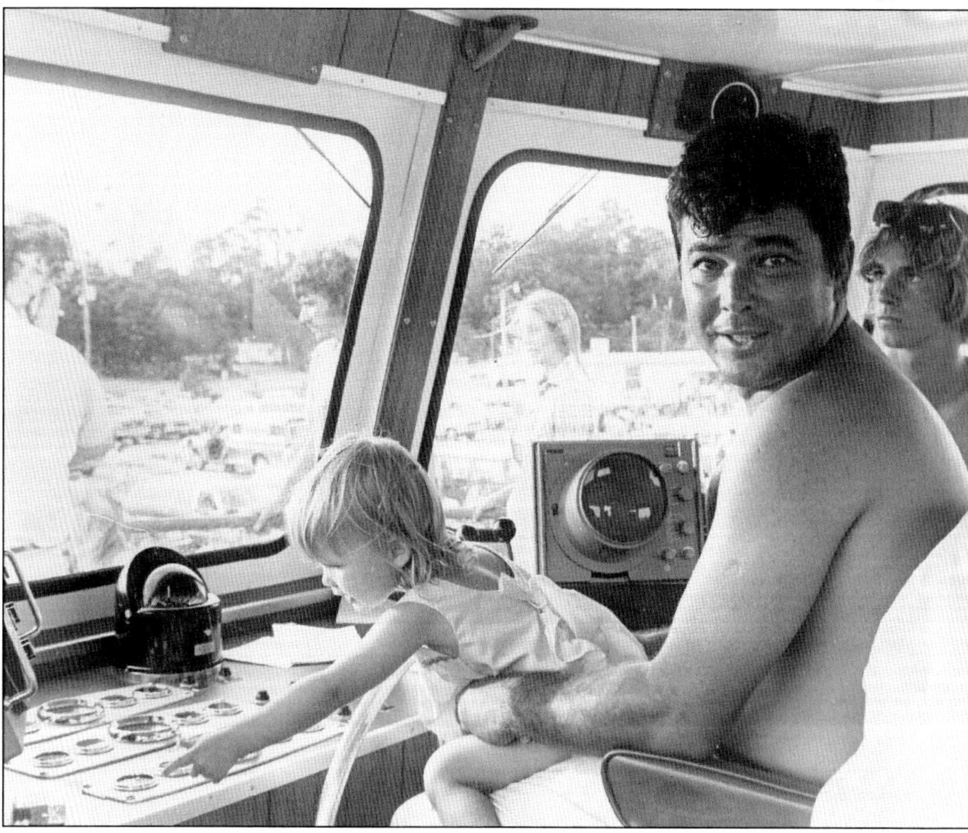

Capt. Everette Ayers is holding his daughter Regina in 1973 during the christening ceremony of the *New Inlet Princess*, with Miles Worrell standing in the background. The *New Inlet Princess* was a custom-built boat brought up from shipyards in Louisiana that became a fixture in the Murrells Inlet charter fishing industry. Everette and Capt. Hoss Johnson operated this boat from Captain Dick's Marina during the 1970s, 1980s, and 1990s, and many visitors got their first offshore experience aboard this boat. (Courtesy of the Eason family.)

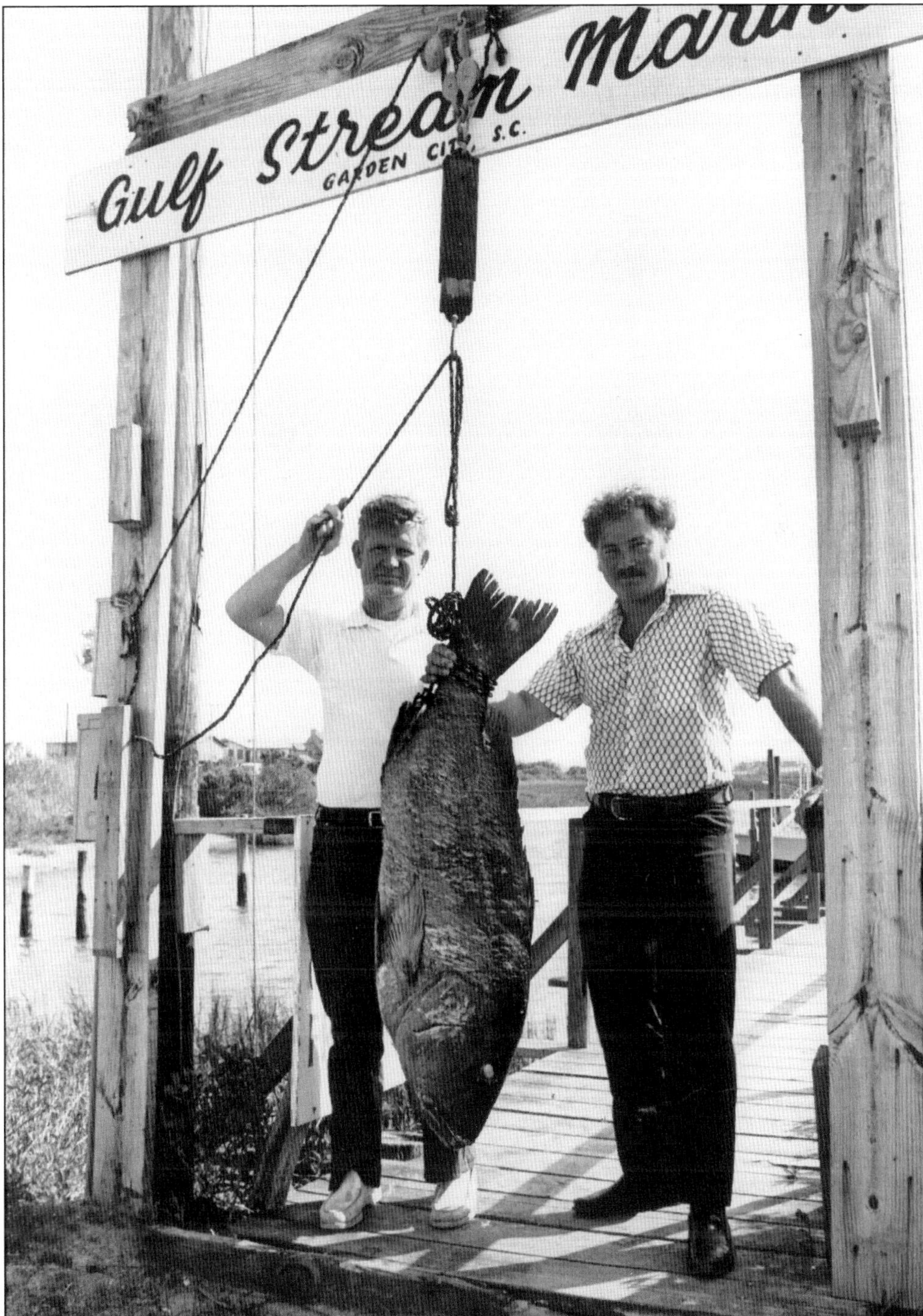

Capts. Rusty Draper (on left) and Don Lash are showing off a 123-pound cubera snapper caught during a commercial fishing trip and brought back to Gulf Stream Marina around 1974. Rusty and Don worked together on several boats during the 1960s and 1970s, and they went on to operate several of the marinas in Murrells Inlet. (Courtesy of Don and Linda Lash.)

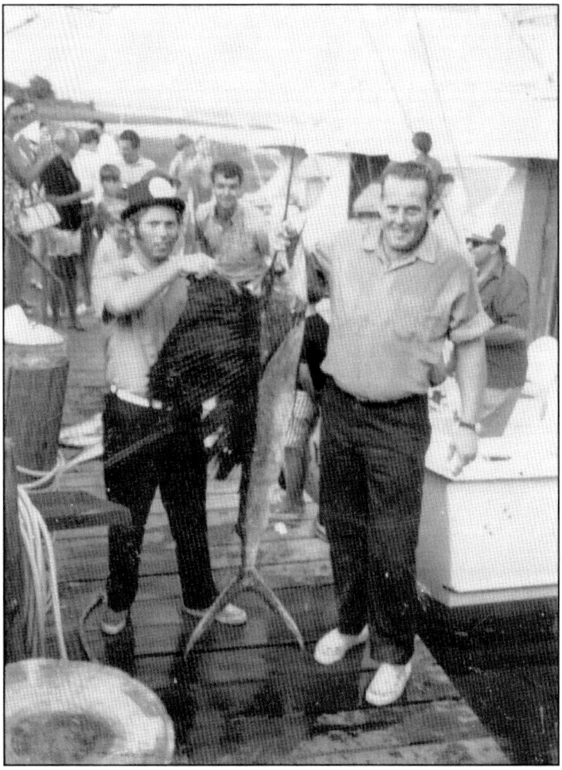

From left to right, Capt. Johnny Lewis of the *Firebird*, his mate Roger Hughes (pictured over his shoulder), and Capt. Hoss Johnson of the *Firebird II* are showing off a sailfish caught during a sportfishing charter around 1971. The *Firebird* and the *Firebird II* docked side by side at Captain Dick's next to the *Thunderbird II* and backed into their boat slips at the Army dock. (Courtesy of Jodell Johnson-Bridges.)

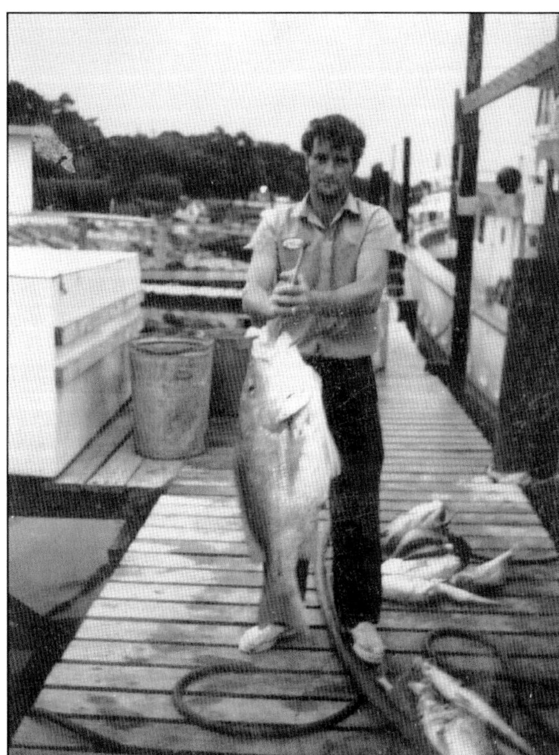

Capt. Johnny Strickland is showing off a big mule red snapper at the docks at Captain Dick's Marina around 1972. Johnny is one of Capt. Charlie Strickland's grandchildren who carried on the fishing tradition and ran the Gulf Stream trips aboard the *Carolina Princess* and the *Bonita* out of Captain Dick's Marina during the 1970s. (Courtesy of the Strickland family.)

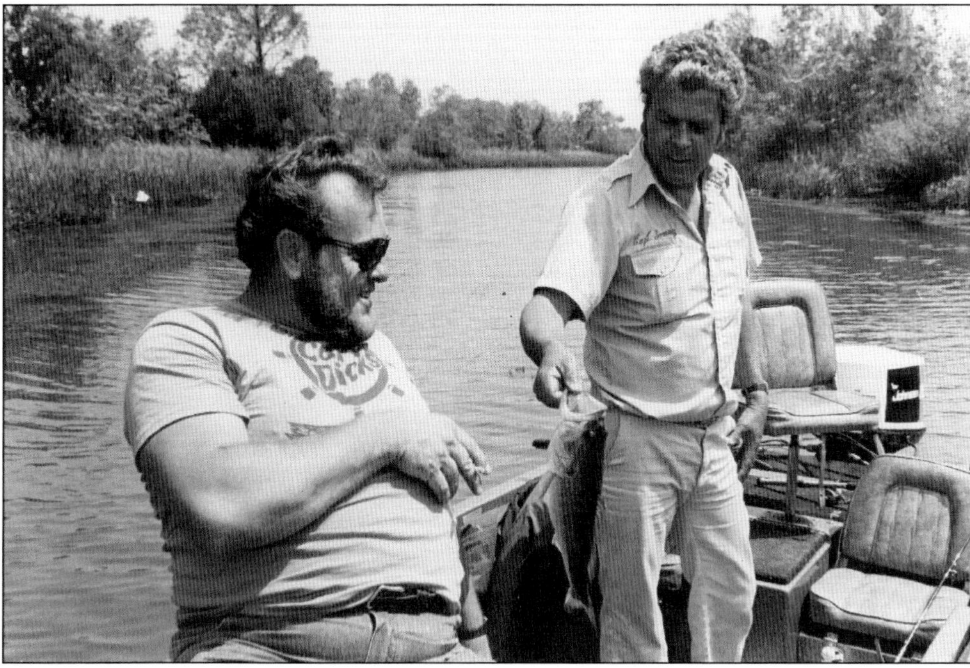

Capts. Hoss Johnson (left) and Tommy Sing (right) are out in the Waccamaw River enjoying a day off from charter fishing and catching largemouth bass in the freshwater creeks on the west side of Murrells Inlet. Captain Tommy was one of Alex Sing Sr.'s children and started as a mate on the charter boats in the early 1960s. He ran the *Flying Fisher* for many years out of Anchor Marina. Hoss Johnson was another creek rat who went from mate to captain on numerous boats but was best known for his time on the *New Inlet Princess*. (Courtesy of Jodell Johnson-Bridges.)

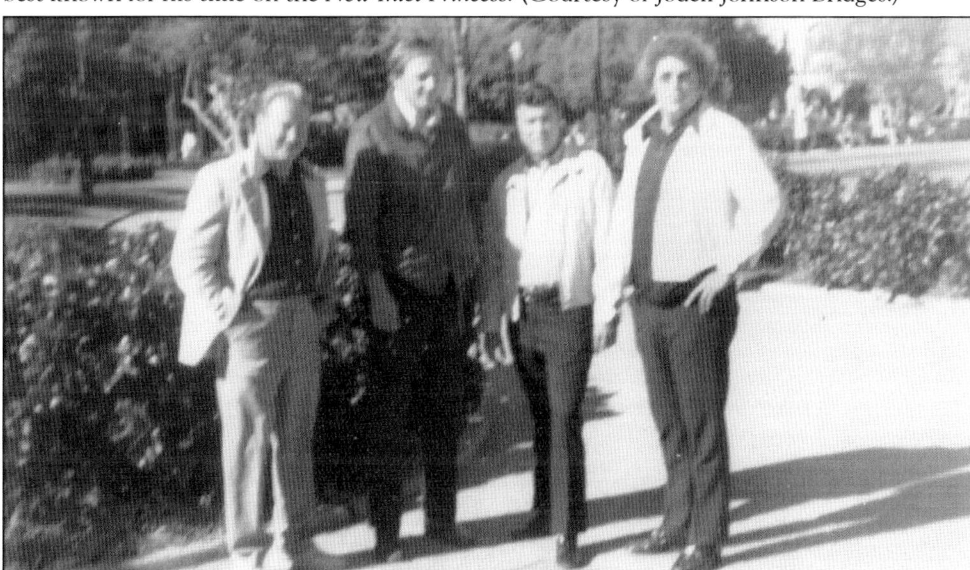

Capts. Don Lash, Bill Moeller, and Everette Ayers Jr. with Robin Loud are shown from left to right at a fishing exposition show in New Orleans around 1977; Hoss Johnson was taking the picture. Don Lash traveled from South Florida to meet the Murrells Inlet delegation at the expo near downtown New Orleans. (Courtesy of Robin Loud.)

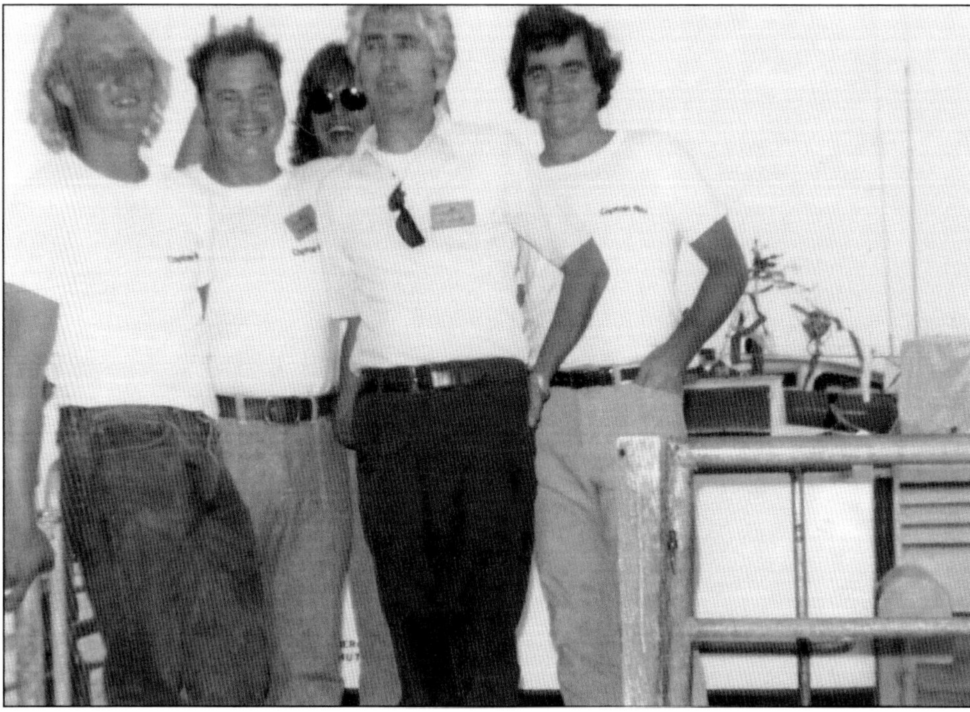

From left to right, Blondie Jennings, Don Lash, Homer Raquels, Alex Sing, and Jimmy Mayes are pictured on the back of the *Captain Alex* in 1977 during the dedication ceremony for the proposed Murrells Inlet jetties. Prior to the construction of the jetties, charter boats were subject to the tides and shifting sandbars for safe passage into the ocean and the return back to the docks in the afternoons. (Courtesy of Don and Linda Lash.)

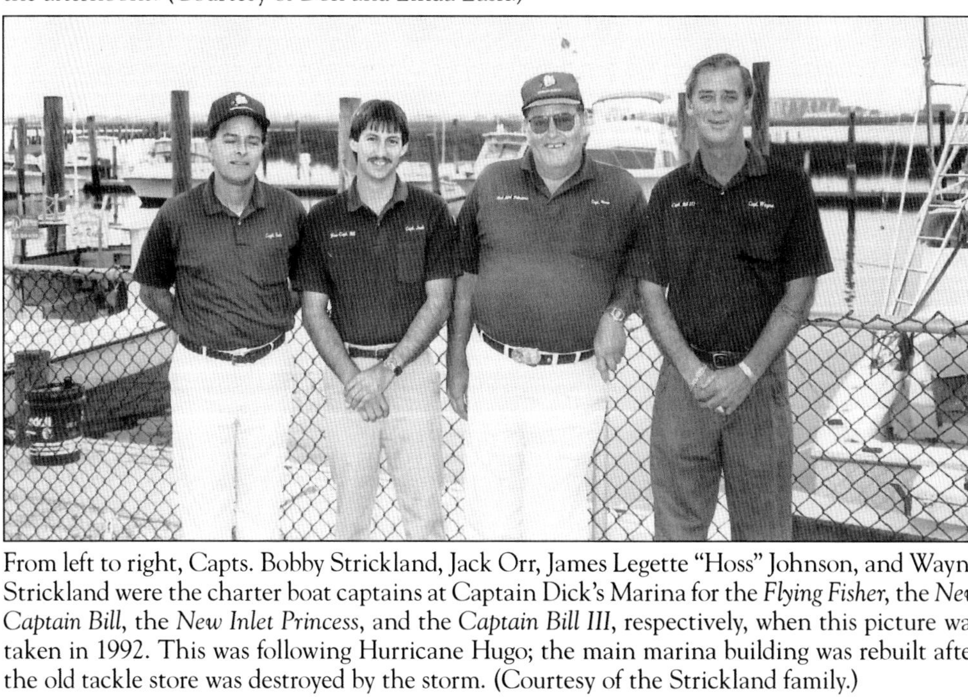

From left to right, Capts. Bobby Strickland, Jack Orr, James Legette "Hoss" Johnson, and Wayne Strickland were the charter boat captains at Captain Dick's Marina for the *Flying Fisher*, the *New Captain Bill*, the *New Inlet Princess*, and the *Captain Bill III*, respectively, when this picture was taken in 1992. This was following Hurricane Hugo; the main marina building was rebuilt after the old tackle store was destroyed by the storm. (Courtesy of the Strickland family.)

Three

Creek Rats

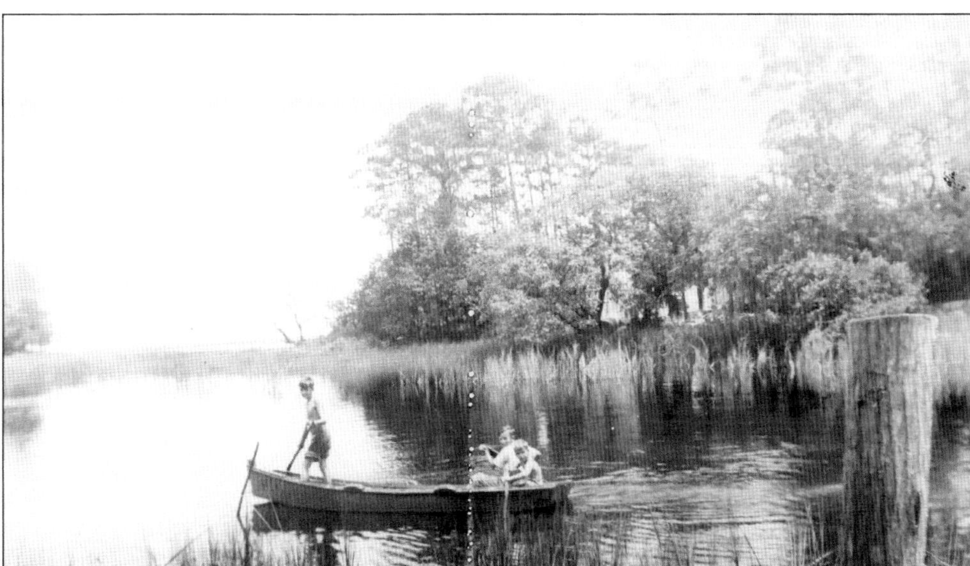

Wesley Gordon (standing in front) and, from left to right in the stern, cousins Jack and Terry Simpson (visiting from Pennsylvania) are seen paddling a wooden skiff in the marsh behind Herman Gordon's house around 1940. The creek-front road that preceded Highway 17 ran along the tree line in the background and crossed over the marsh beside the Grant property, using wood planks to support the cars from sinking in the mud. (Courtesy of Taryn Gordon Wilson.)

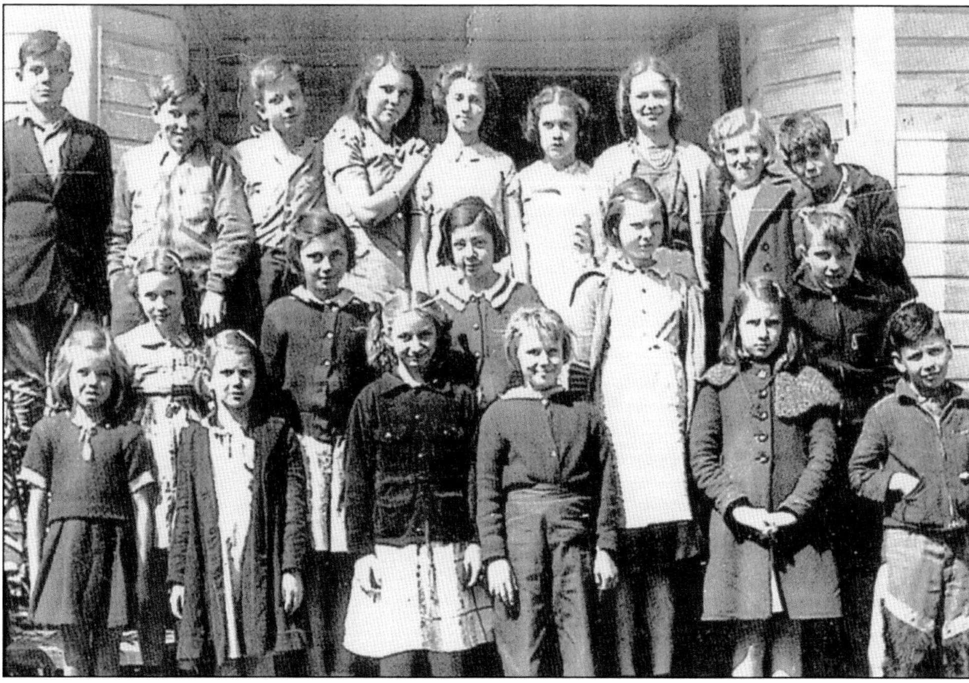

This photograph of the students of Murrells Inlet Elementary School in 1938 is a who's who of Murrells Inlet history. They are, from right to left, (first row) Alex Sing, Shirley Vick, Margaret Milligan, Edith Bashor, Alzata Cowart, and unidentified; (second row) Jack Eason, Juanita Sessions, Barbara Vick, Gladys Smith, and Maxine Oliver; (third row) Lauren Byrd, Dorothy Stiller, ? Wilson, Inez Legette, Ester Martin, ? Smith, Junior Vick, James Sing, and J.K. Smith. (Courtesy of Dick Vick.)

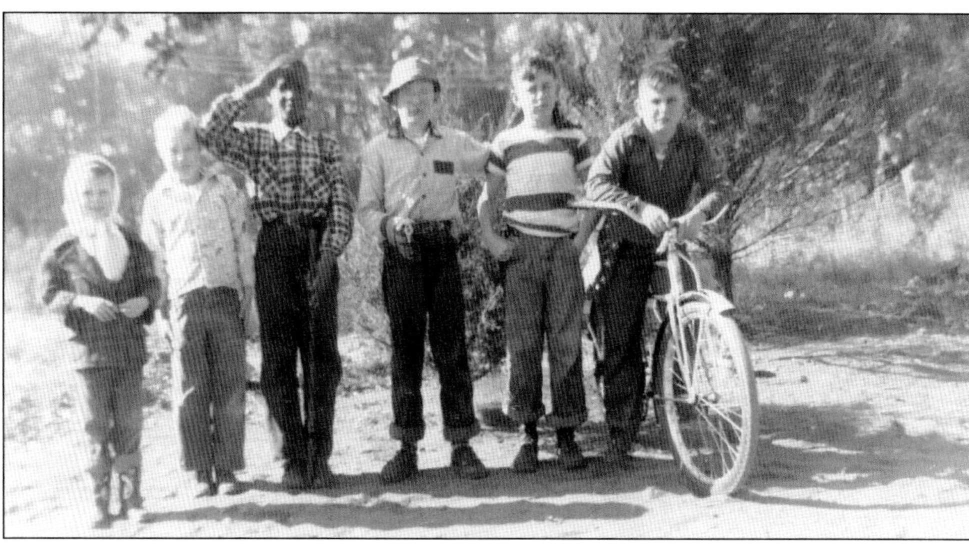

A group of creek rats at Bay Harbor includes, from right to left, Dick Eason, Ronnie Eason, Billy Gasque Jr., Roosevelt Pickett, Harry Outlaw, and Brenda Eason around 1950. The Bay Harbor site was a central gathering place for the neighbors, including the food store, the restaurant, the oyster roast, and the hotel, which had a sun porch across the front with one of the first televisions in the inlet. (Courtesy of the Eason family.)

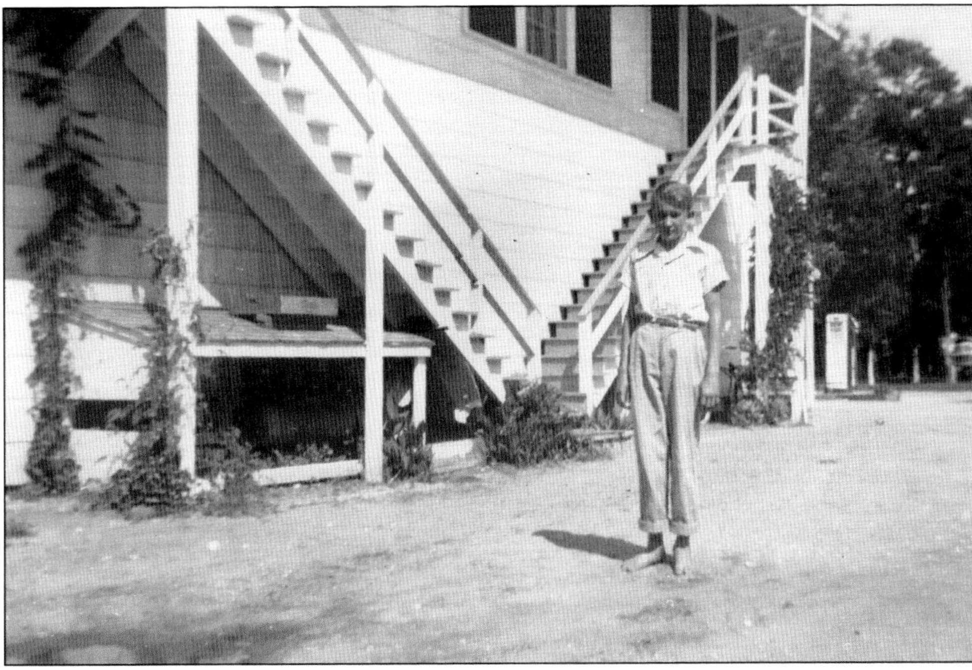

A young Wallace Lee stands beside the steps of the Bay Harbor Motel around 1950. Wallace Lee and Ronnie and Dick Eason were usually found together around Bay Harbor when they were not out in the creek. Wallace Lee, son of Eford and Pearl Lee, stayed around Murrells Inlet and became well known for his seafood restaurants. (Courtesy of the Eason family.)

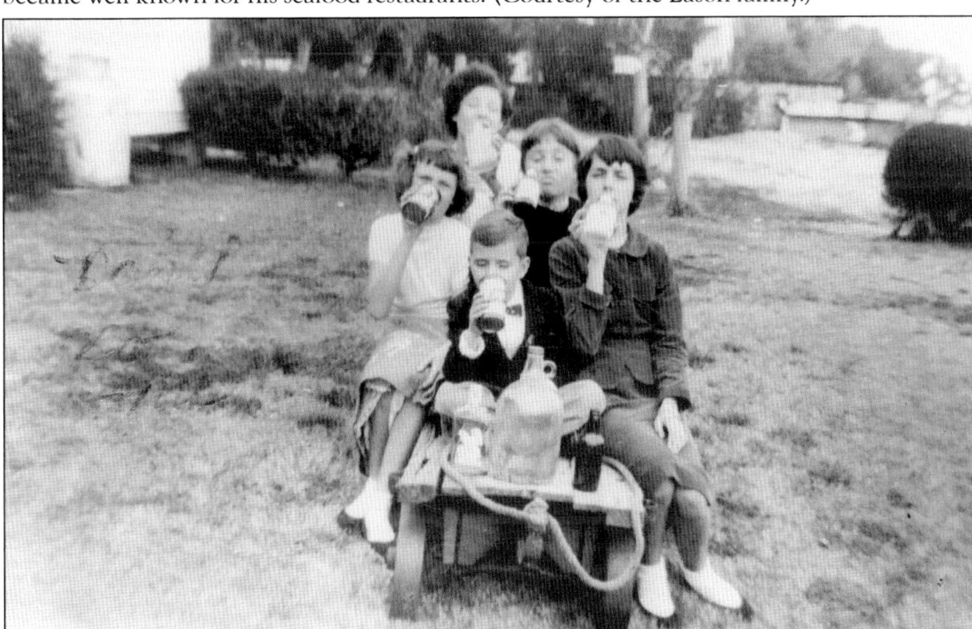

From left to right, Brenda Eason, Carolyn Eason, Frankie Eason, Judith Bashor, and May Padgett are setting a bad example with some empty beer cans and liquor bottles they had cleaned up from around Bay Harbor in 1954. The picture has a hand-written caption of "don't do this" on the front. (Courtesy of the Eason family.)

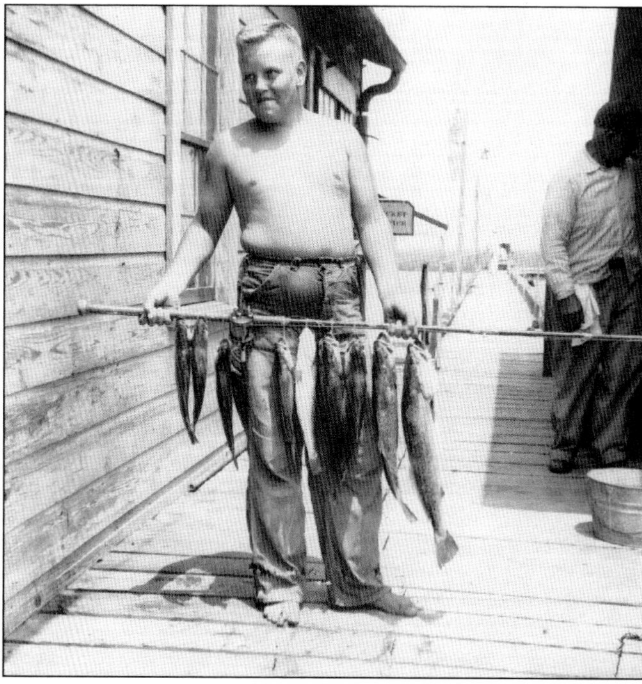

James Legette "Hoss" Johnson is showing off a nice catch of trout caught off the Army dock around 1960. The FFA took back over the lodge and sold tickets for the fishing pier at the house on the pier that had been used as a radio room and oil storage. Hoss was a natural fisherman in the saltwater and freshwater creeks as well as the ocean and fished the waters around Murrells Inlet his entire life. (Courtesy of Jodell Johnson-Bridges.)

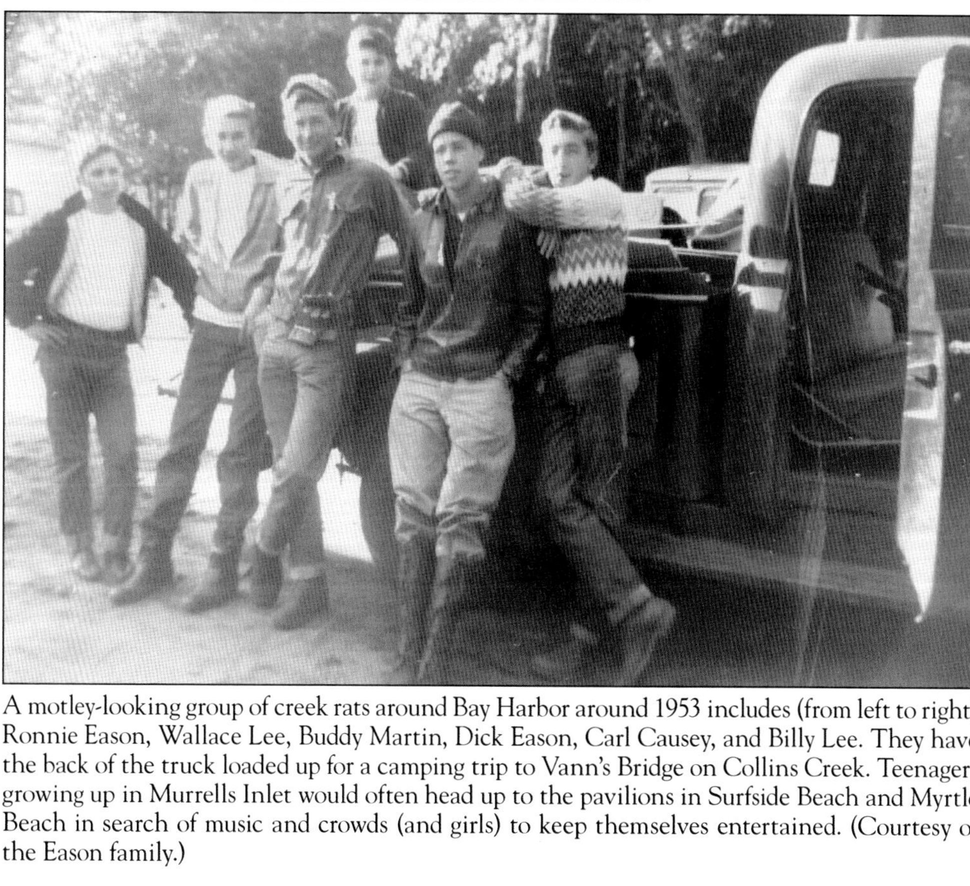

A motley-looking group of creek rats around Bay Harbor around 1953 includes (from left to right) Ronnie Eason, Wallace Lee, Buddy Martin, Dick Eason, Carl Causey, and Billy Lee. They have the back of the truck loaded up for a camping trip to Vann's Bridge on Collins Creek. Teenagers growing up in Murrells Inlet would often head up to the pavilions in Surfside Beach and Myrtle Beach in search of music and crowds (and girls) to keep themselves entertained. (Courtesy of the Eason family.)

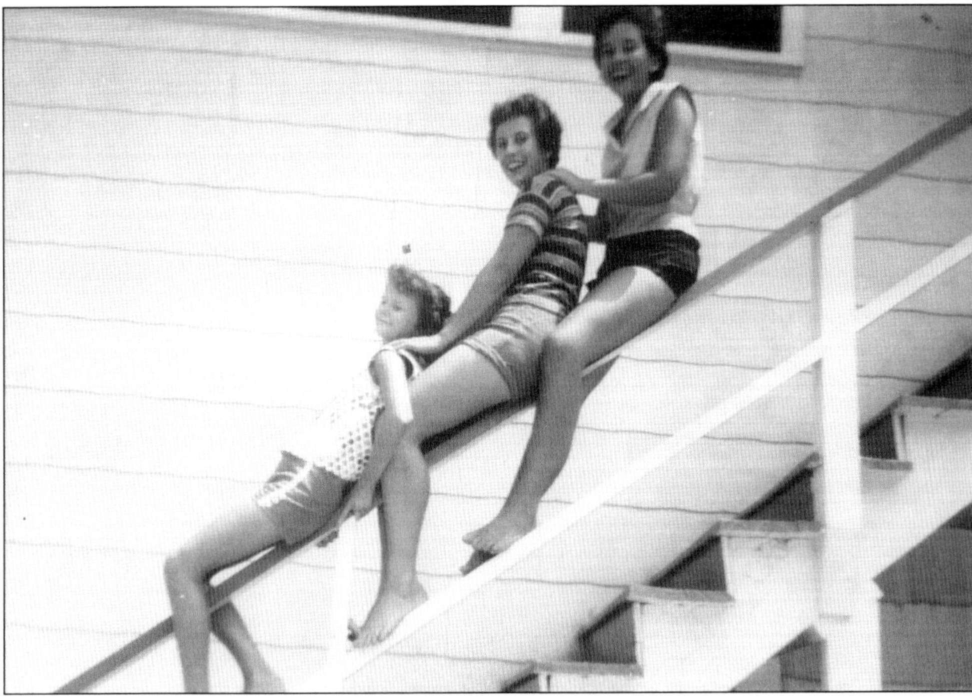

From left to right, Brenda Eason, Annie Laurie Suggs, and Betty Sing pose on the side stairs leading up to the Bay Harbor Motel in 1956. The Sing and Eason families lived across the street from each other and were always working and playing together. (Courtesy of the Eason family.)

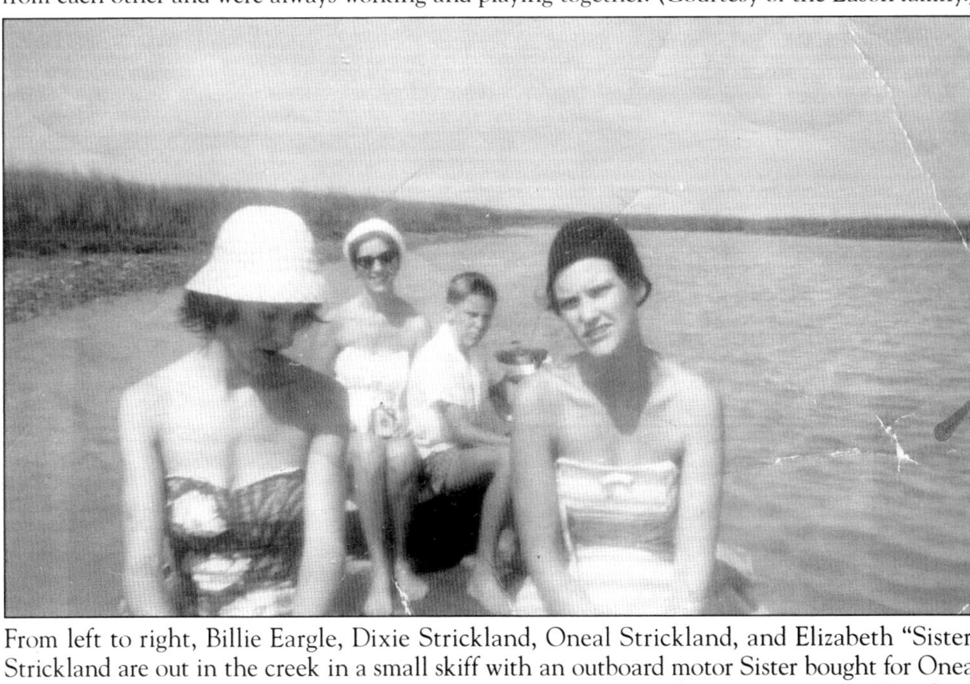

From left to right, Billie Eargle, Dixie Strickland, Oneal Strickland, and Elizabeth "Sister" Strickland are out in the creek in a small skiff with an outboard motor Sister bought for Oneal around 1953, shortly after she graduated from the Baptist Hospital nursing program. Oneal was a well-known creek rat who could always find enough fish or shrimp to fill the cooler and passed his love of the creek to the next generation. (Courtesy of the Strickland family.)

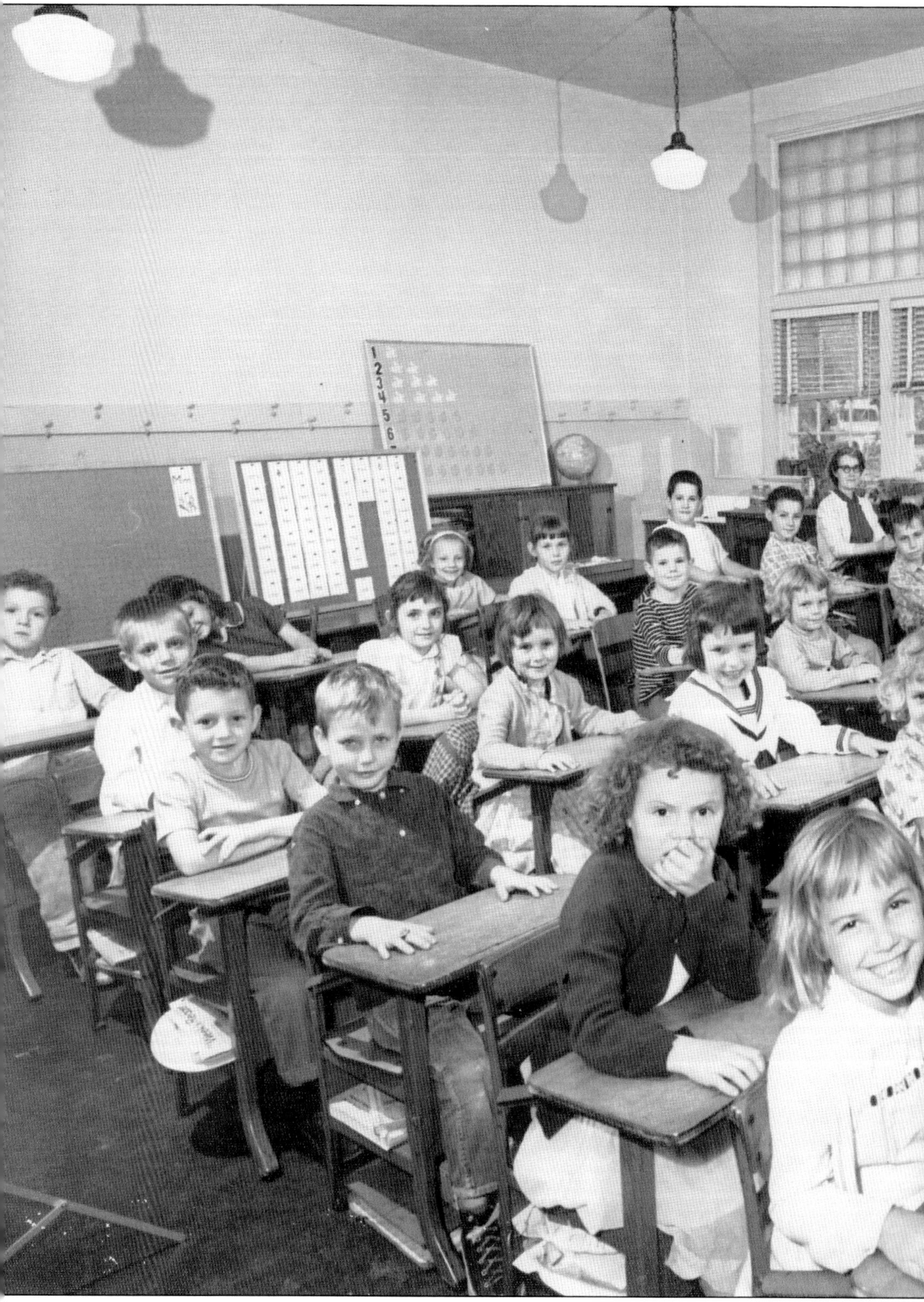

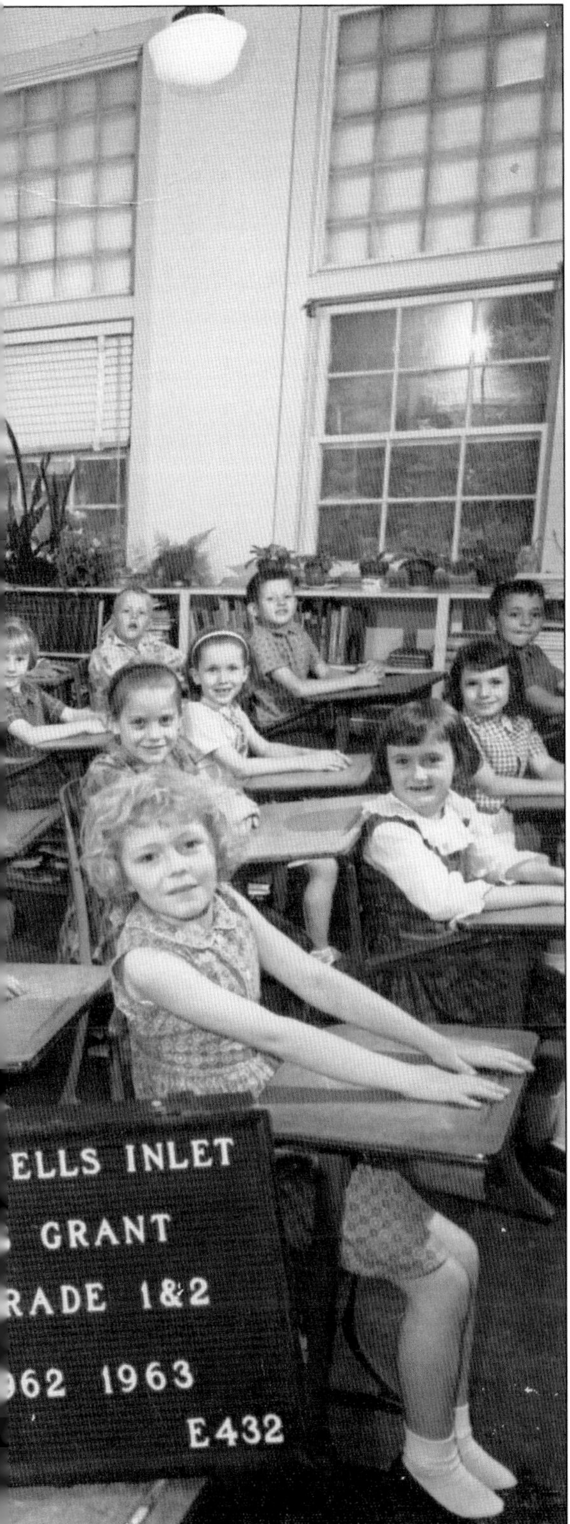

Murrells Inlet Elementary School first- and second-grade classes in 1963 include, from front to back, (first row) Julie Jarven, Geneva Carter, unidentified, Kenny Carter, Albert Todd, and John Carter; (second row) Doris Hughes, Debra Jordan, Cindy Sing, Gila Mae Lowes, unidentified, Betty Kersey; (third row) Pam Miller, Joyce Tarbox, Taryn Gordon, Denise Eaddy, Ken Collins, Gail Morse, and Rhonda Collins; (fourth row) unidentified, Peggy England, Arlene Jones, Odell Todd, unidentified, and Roland Pierce; (fifth row) Randy Goins, Bradley Chadwick, Johnny Brown, Victor Todd, Joe Gordon, and teacher Thelma Grant. (Courtesy of the Gordon family.)

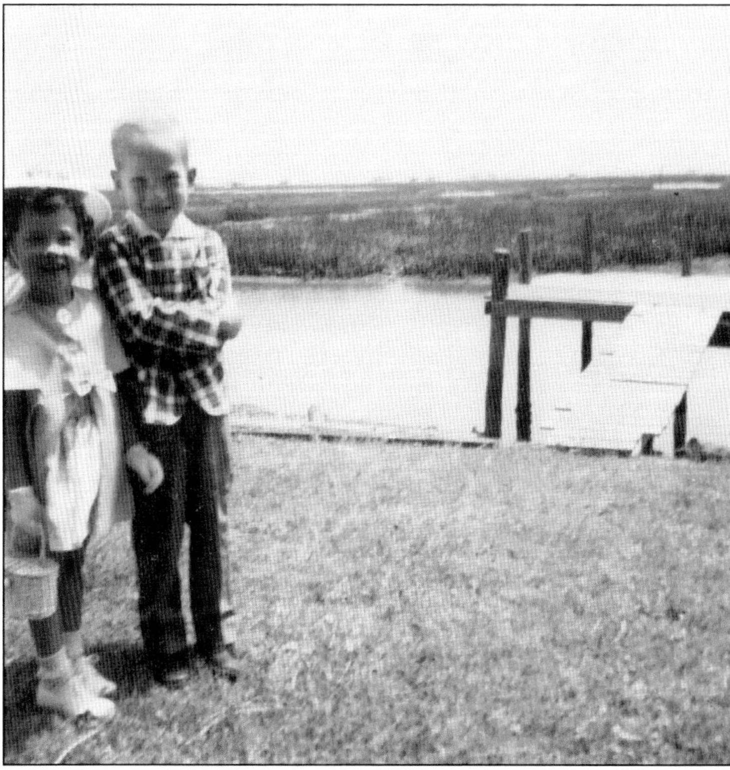

Tookie Chandler and Tom Hora are dressed in their Easter suits in 1963 along the creek near Genevieve Willcox Chandler's house. The Chandler family lived with Genevieve next to Anchor Marina and grew up playing and working in this section of the creek. Genevieve's brother Clarke Willcox Jr. was living in the Hermitage (just to the north) at this time. (Courtesy of Tookie Chandler Jones.)

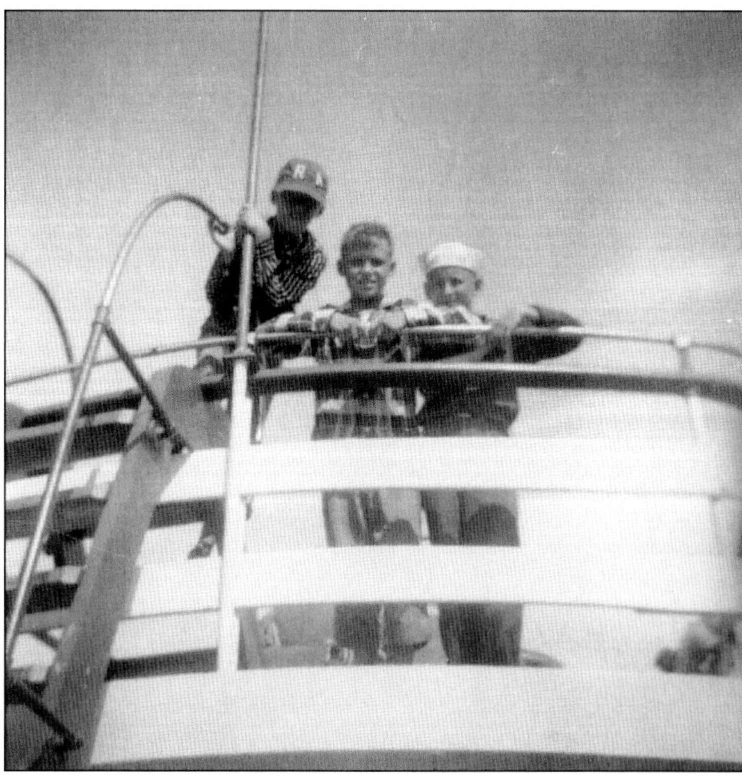

From left to right, Jerry Wells, Randall Wells, and their cousin Steven Foy are on the upper deck of the *Thunderbird* during a fishing trip to the blackfish bottoms off Murrells Inlet in 1960. They went fishing with their great-uncle Homer Wells. (Courtesy of Jerry Wells.)

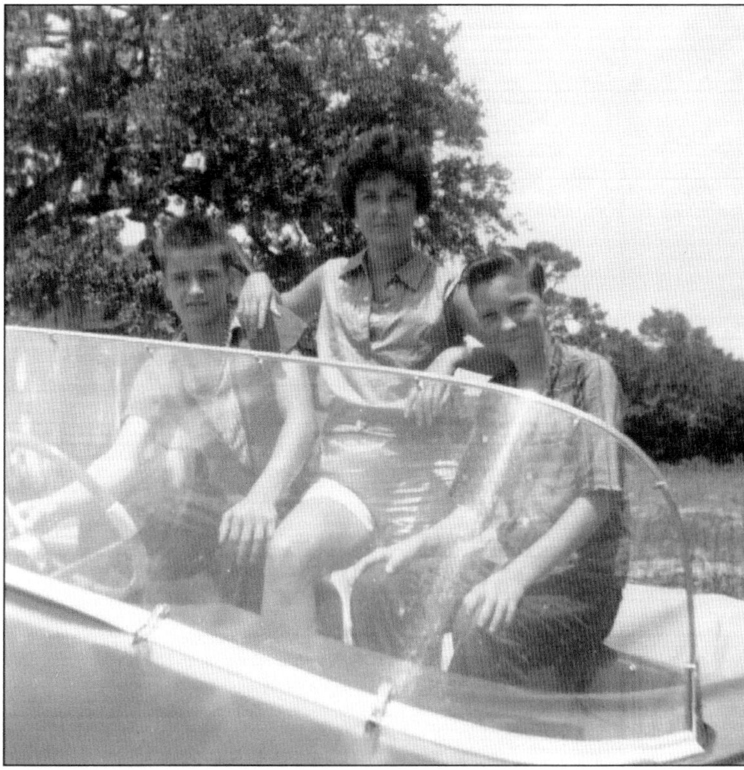

From left to right, Johnny, Sissy, and Oneal Strickland are sitting in Charlie Strickland's new red fiberglass boat behind their house on the creek around 1960. The boat was ordered from Western Auto and featured a Ted Williams outboard motor. Charlie's family lived in the house he purchased from the Gordons on the creek next door to his brother Lemuel. (Courtesy of the Strickland family.)

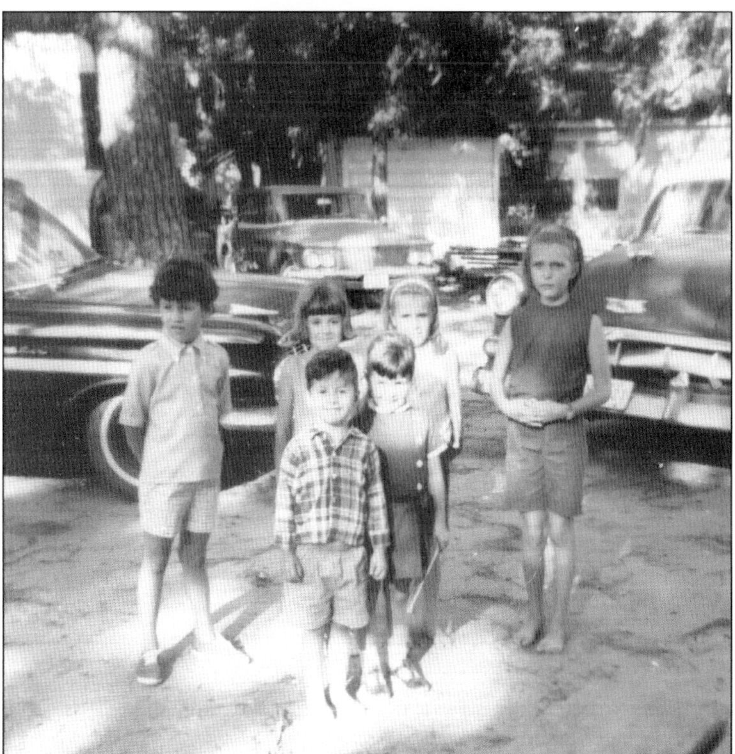

From left to right, Jennifer, Sandra, and Alexander Sing, Carol Eskridge, and Ann and Loretta Strickland play behind Alex's Marina around 1967. Ann and Loretta's father, H.C. Strickland, lived next-door to Alex's, and the neighborhood children could usually be found playing around the docks during the summertime. (Courtesy of the Sing family.)

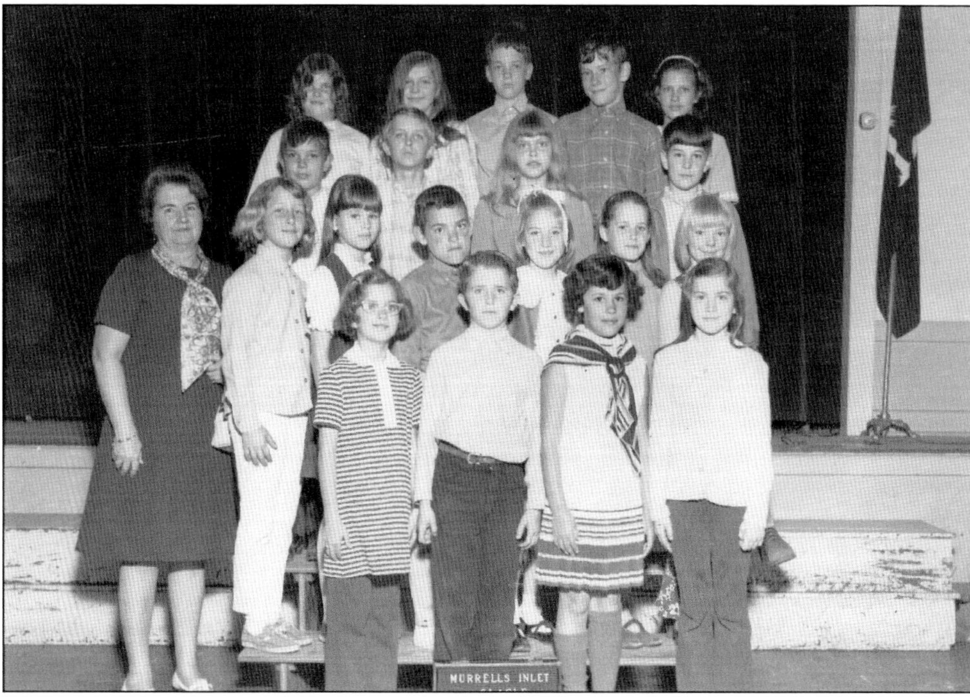

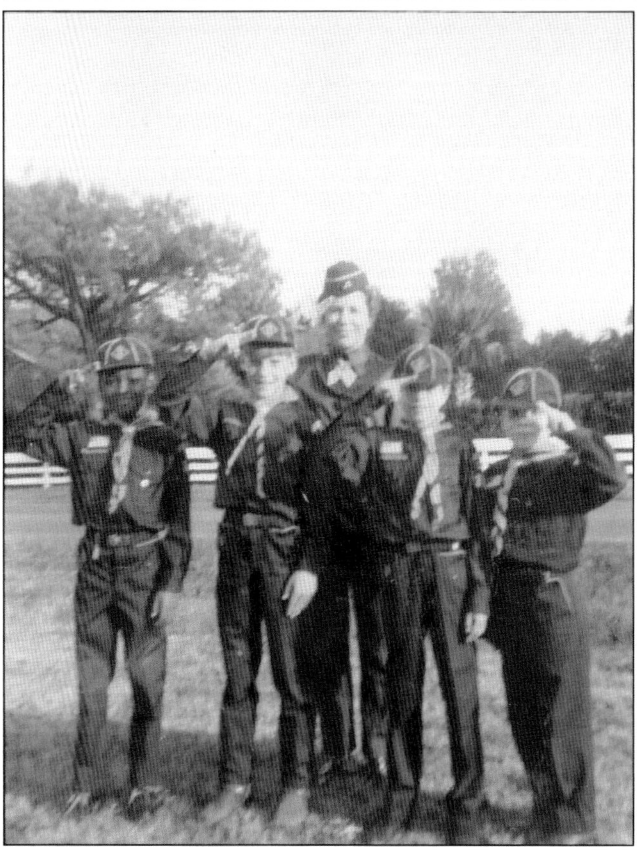

The fourth-grade class at Murrells Inlet Elementary in 1974 included, from left to right, (first row) Kathy Lee, Clinton Brown, Jennifer Sing, and Frankie Scott; (second row) teacher Inez Turbeville (substituting for Mrs. Slagle), Maria Ferranti, Angie Sing, Robin Tyson, Tammy Jones, unidentified, and Donna Meyers; (third row) Neil Kersey, Michael Todd, unidentified, and Clay Pierce; (fourth row) Debbie Swords, Susan Todd, Chris Mahaffey, unidentified, and Celeste McDowell. (Courtesy of the Sing family.)

In 1972, Joanne Welch and her Cub Scout den, including, from left to right, Anthony Bromell, Wes Gordon, Douglas Whitehead, and Glenn Welch, are standing in the front yard of Wagon Wheel Farms by Highway 17. (Courtesy of the Welch family.)

Four

FAMILIES

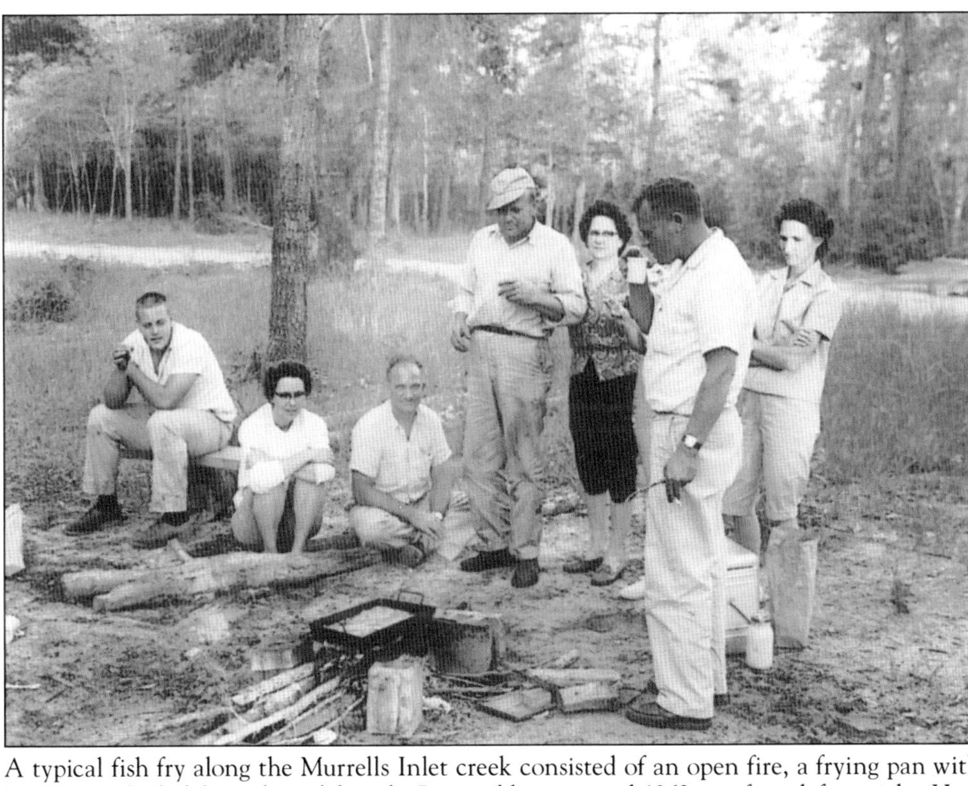

A typical fish fry along the Murrells Inlet creek consisted of an open fire, a frying pan with hot grease, fresh fish, and good friends. Pictured here around 1962 are, from left to right, Hoss Johnson, Pearline and Jesse Murdock, Remear and Gladys Hughes, J. Wesley Sr., and Ola Mae Hughes. (Courtesy of Joyce Hughes Brett.)

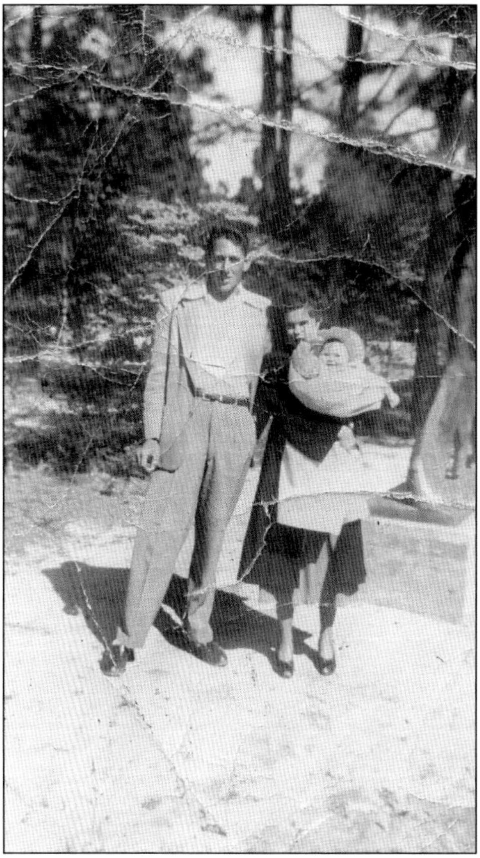

Clarence "Beau" and Margaret Morse, holding their oldest daughter, Judy, are shown during an outing to Brookgreen Gardens around 1949. Clarence and Margaret raised five daughters at their home on the creek where the present-day Morse Park is located. Clarence was one of George and Mae Morse's children who was raised on the creek fishing and harvesting shellfish. George and Mae Morse lived across the street from the site of the oyster roast that Clarence operated from the 1950s through the 1980s. (Courtesy of the Morse family.)

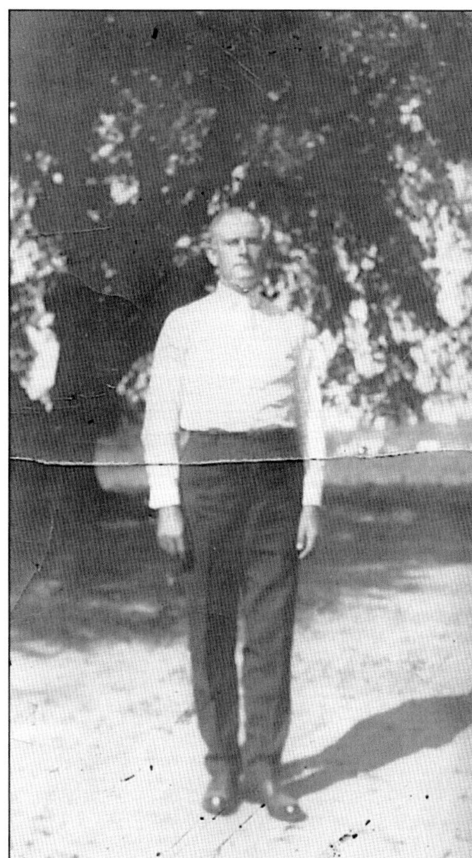

Thomas Mobley Chandler Sr. was the patriarch of the Chandler family in Murrells Inlet and worked as the caretaker for Wachesaw Plantation in the 1930s. He was married to Genevieve Willcox, a well-known author and artist who worked with the WPA project to preserve oral history of the area. Her father was Clarke A. Willcox Sr., who had purchased Wachesaw Plantation in 1910 and sold the property in 1930 to William A. Kimbel. (Courtesy of Tookie Chandler Jones.)

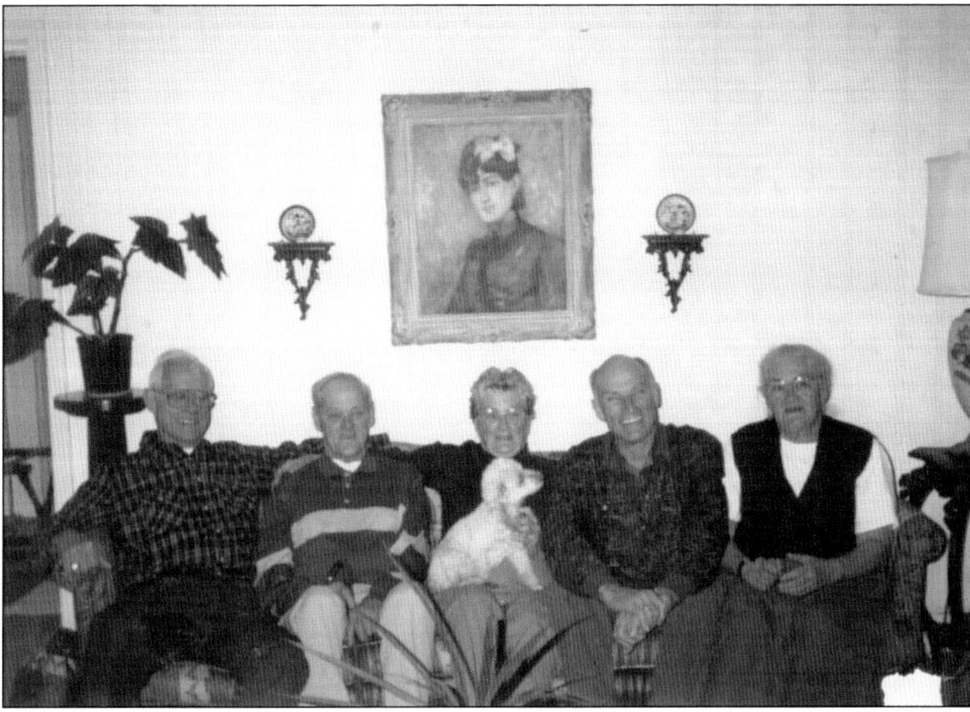

The children of Thomas Mobley Chandler Sr. and Genevieve Willcox Chandler are seated under a painting of their grandmother Mary Anna Ashe Moore Willcox, wife of Clarke A. Willcox Sr. Shown in this 1993 picture are, from left to right, Joe Chandler, Tommy Chandler Jr., June Hora, Bill Chandler, and Genevieve "Sister" Peterkin. (Courtesy of Tookie Chandler Jones.)

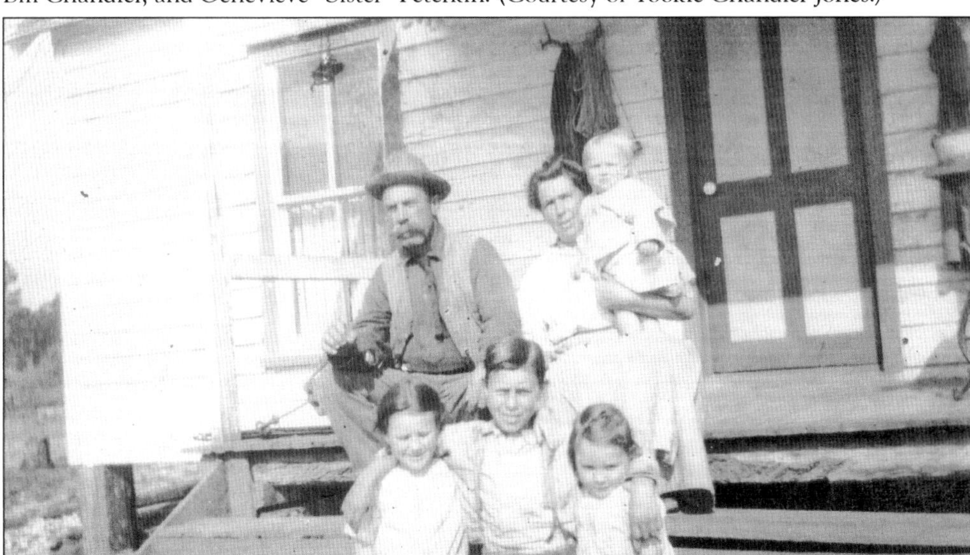

Paul Herbert Wesley is pictured with his wife, Hannah Matthews (holding Alice), and Ruth, Howard, and Jean seated below from left to right. Paul left New York in a covered wagon around 1900 headed south to find a place to settle down, and two of the children (Mae Morse, not shown, and Howard) were born along the way to Conway, South Carolina. They moved to Murrells Inlet around 1910, and Paul was the census enumerator in 1920. (Courtesy of the Wesley family.)

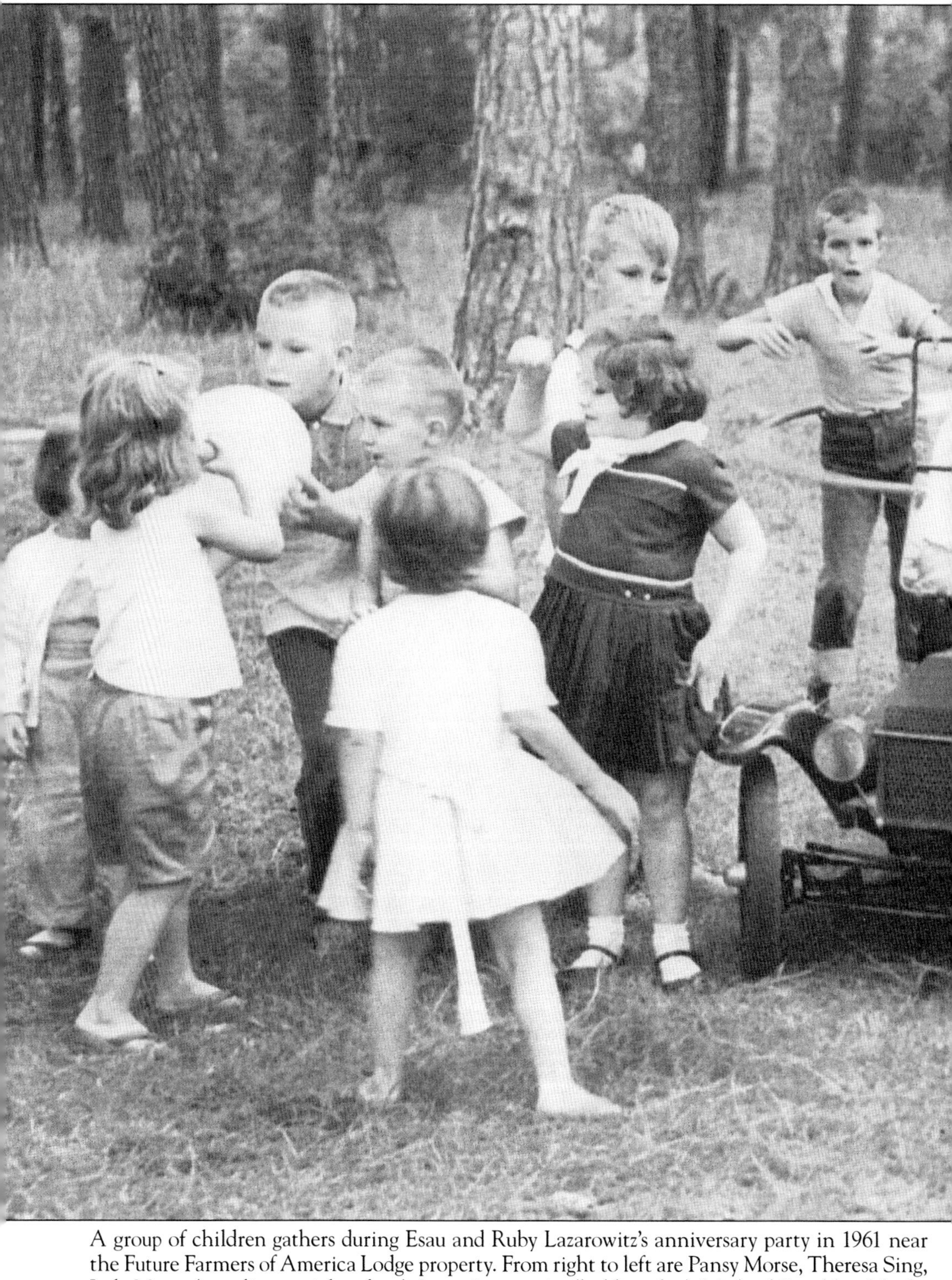

A group of children gathers during Esau and Ruby Lazarowitz's anniversary party in 1961 near the Future Farmers of America Lodge property. From right to left are Pansy Morse, Theresa Sing, Judy Morse (standing to right of car), Larry Lazarowitz (holding dog), Michael Strickland (right front of car), Janie Strickland, Phyllis Kitrell (in car), Jimmy Strickland (with hula hoop), Edna

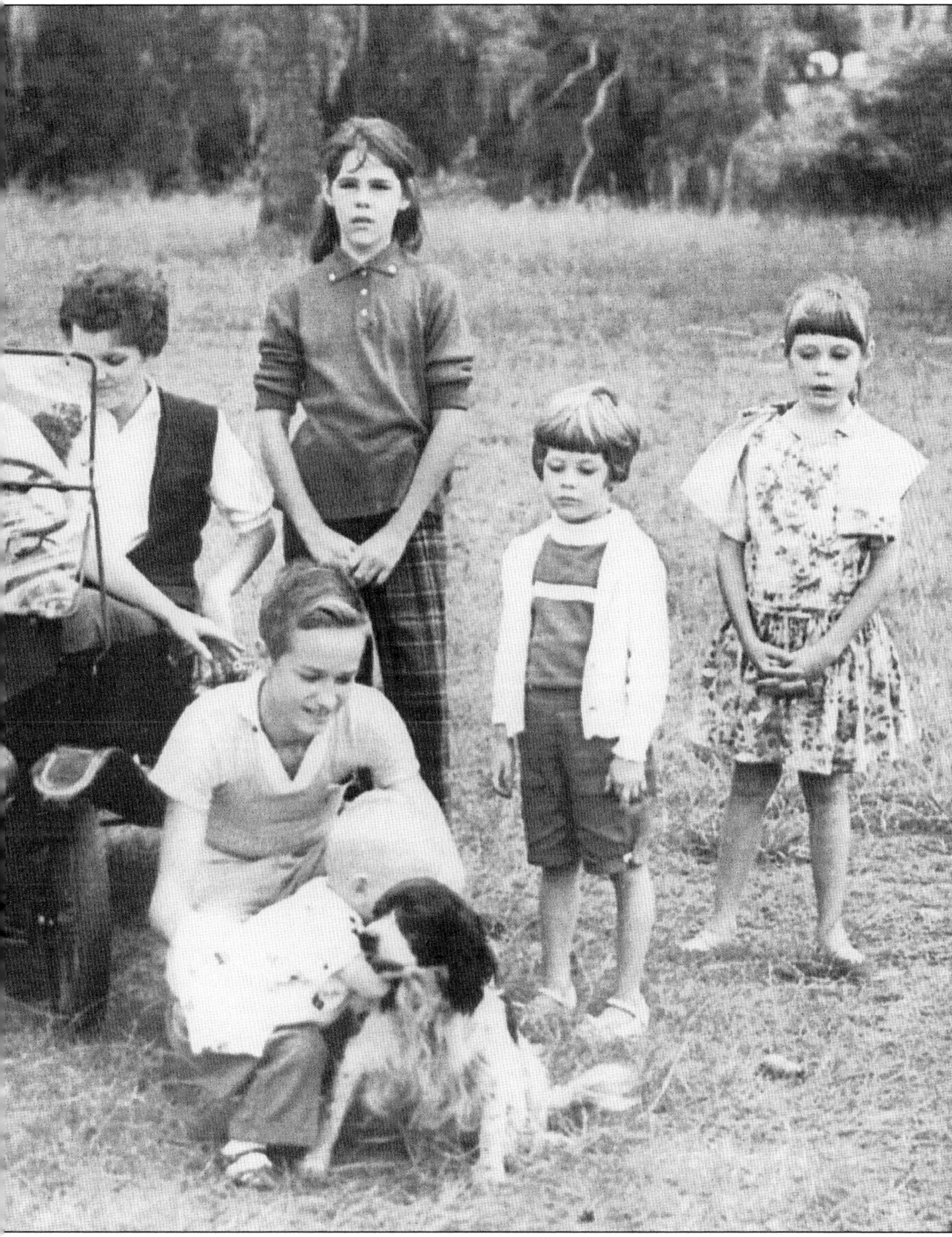

Mae Lazarowitz (left of the car), Eric Eason (behind Edna Mae), and Keith and Eddie Strickland (on right with balloon). Esau owned the Model T go-cart, and he allowed Mike (his next-door neighbor) to take it out and drive it on special occasions. (Courtesy of the Sing family.)

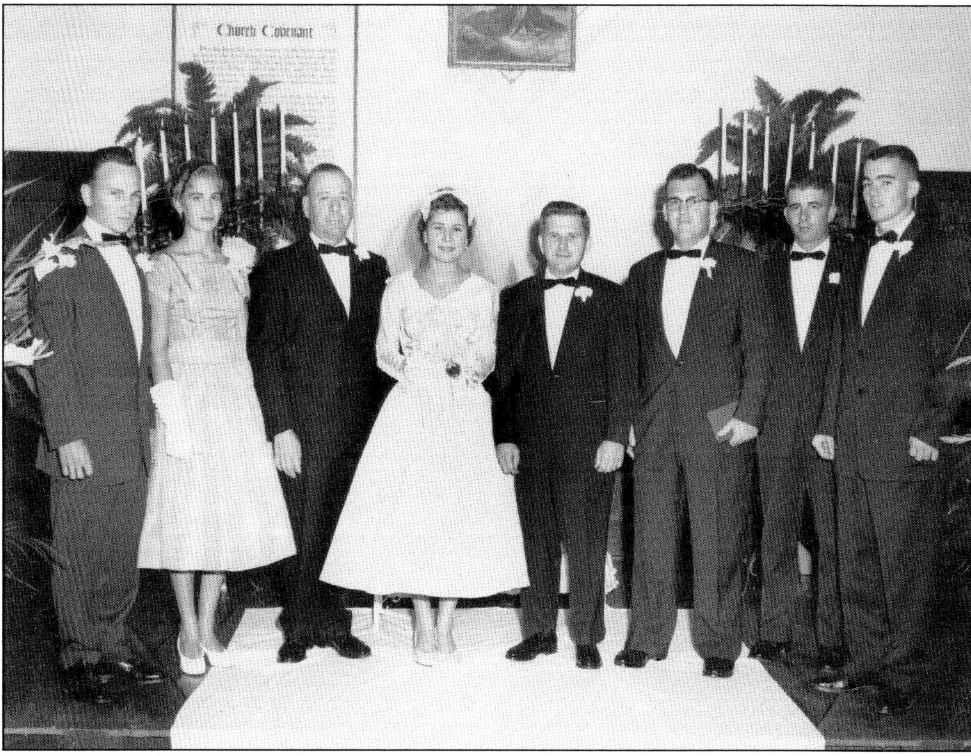

Here is a wedding photograph from Charles and Joanne Welch's wedding at Collins Creek Baptist Church in 1957. Pictured are, from left to right, Jimmy Murdock, Rae Wesley, Joe Clardy Sr., Joanne and Charles Welch, Rev. Bob Hyatt, Farrell Welch, and Jimmy Marsh. (Courtesy of Wesley family.)

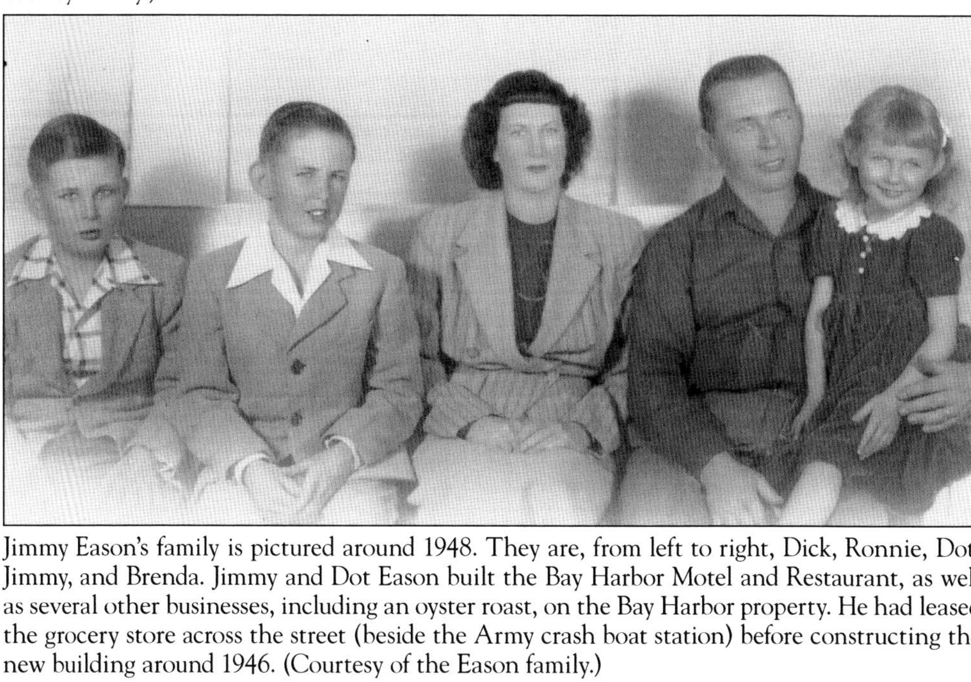

Jimmy Eason's family is pictured around 1948. They are, from left to right, Dick, Ronnie, Dot, Jimmy, and Brenda. Jimmy and Dot Eason built the Bay Harbor Motel and Restaurant, as well as several other businesses, including an oyster roast, on the Bay Harbor property. He had leased the grocery store across the street (beside the Army crash boat station) before constructing the new building around 1946. (Courtesy of the Eason family.)

Herman and Aleene Gordon are seen celebrating their 25th wedding anniversary in their home on Murrells Inlet in October 1958 with sons Wesley and Wayne (right). Herman Gordon owned and operated numerous businesses in Murrells Inlet, including grocery stores, fish houses, and the Western Auto. (Courtesy of the Gordon family.)

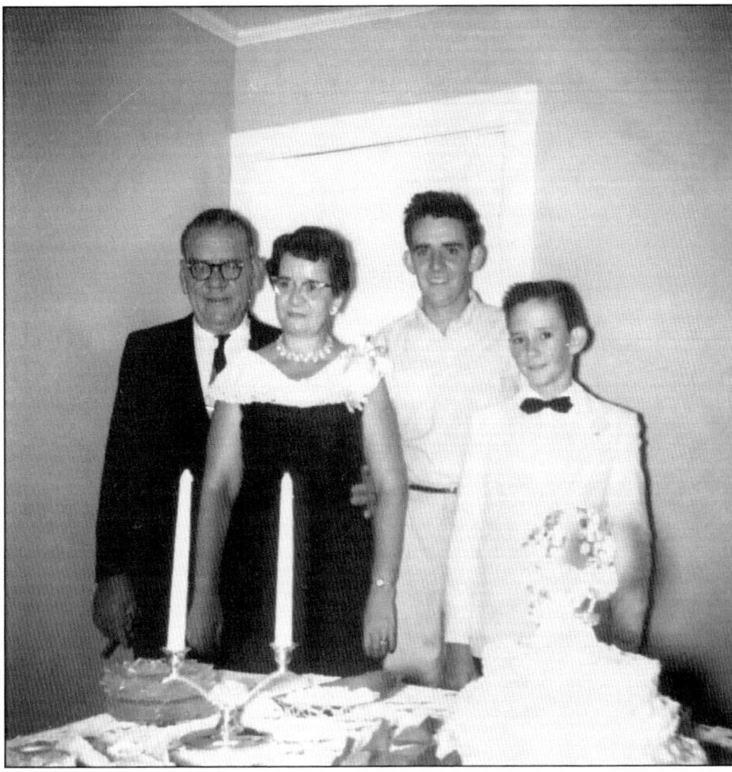

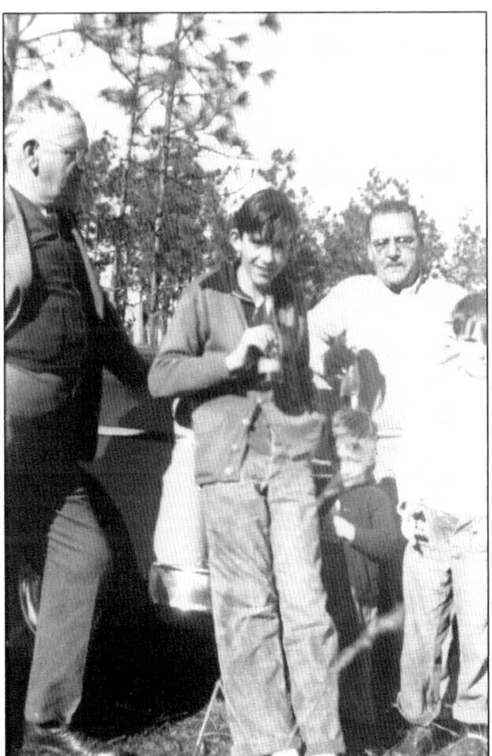

From left to right, John Gordon Sr., Wesley Gordon, Wayne Gordon, John Gordon Jr., and Gerald Gordon are taking a soda break around 1948. John Gordon Sr. was a barber from Mullins, South Carolina, who opened a barbershop in Murrells Inlet and lived in a house by the Baptist church on William Dallas Avenue that he bought from Charlie White. (Courtesy of the Gordon family.)

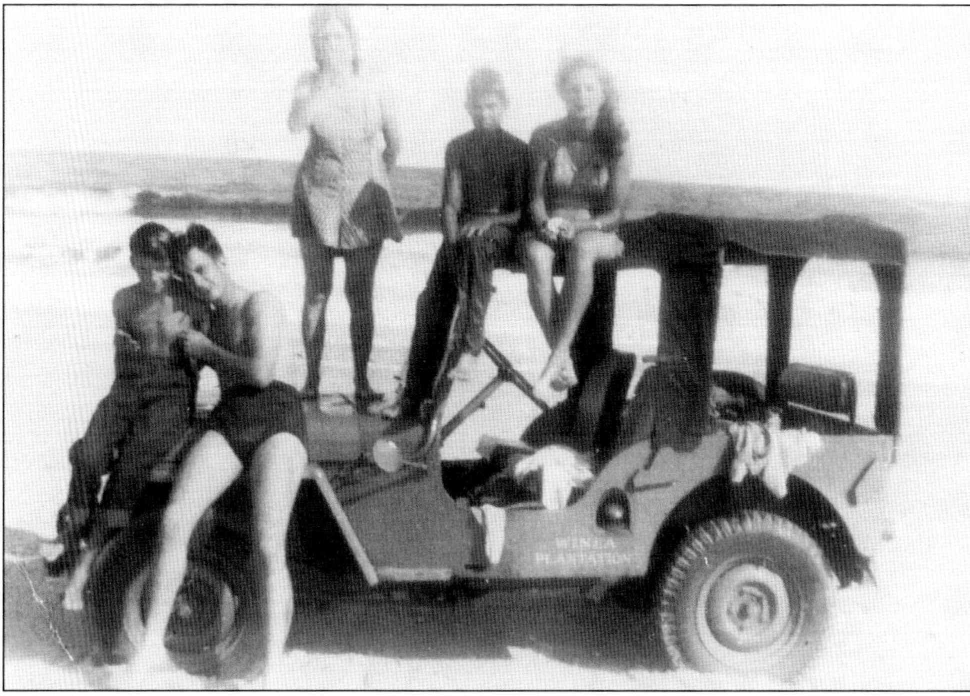

The children of Ira Vick are sitting on the beach in Litchfield around 1947 on a jeep from Winea Plantation, which was where Ira worked as a caretaker. Pictured shortly after Junior returned from service with the Navy are, from left to right, Billy, Junior, Barbara, Jimmy, and Shirley Vick. (Courtesy of Dick Vick.)

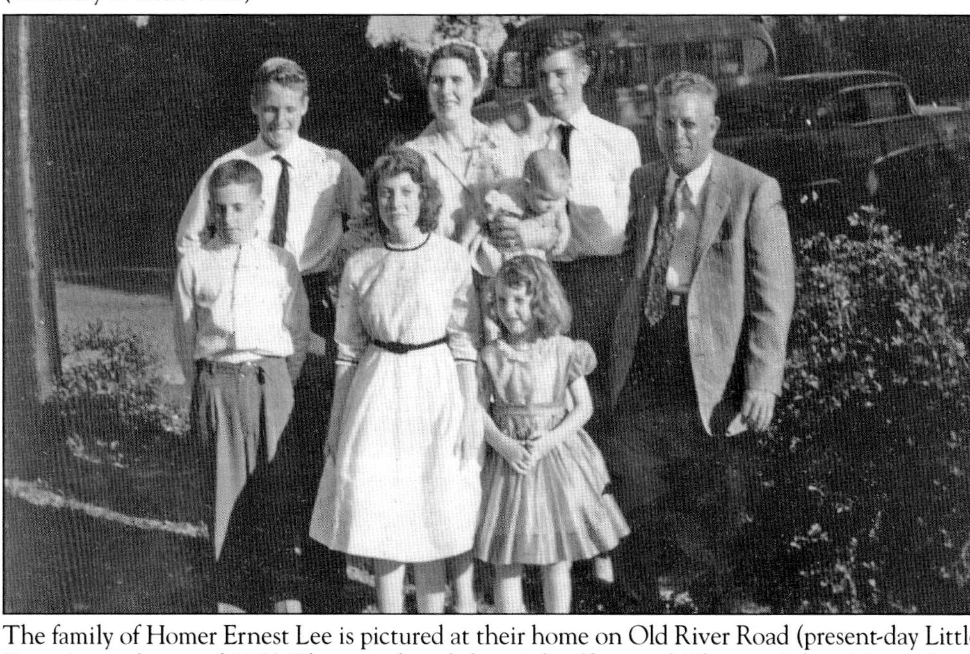

The family of Homer Ernest Lee is pictured at their home on Old River Road (present-day Little Tony Avenue) around 1955. They are, from left to right, (first row) Thomas Aiken, Norma Jean, and Joyce Elaine; (second row) Daniel Alvin, Juanita Smith, Theresa Kay, Homer Ernest Jr., and Homer Ernest Lee Sr. (Courtesy of Jean Strickland.)

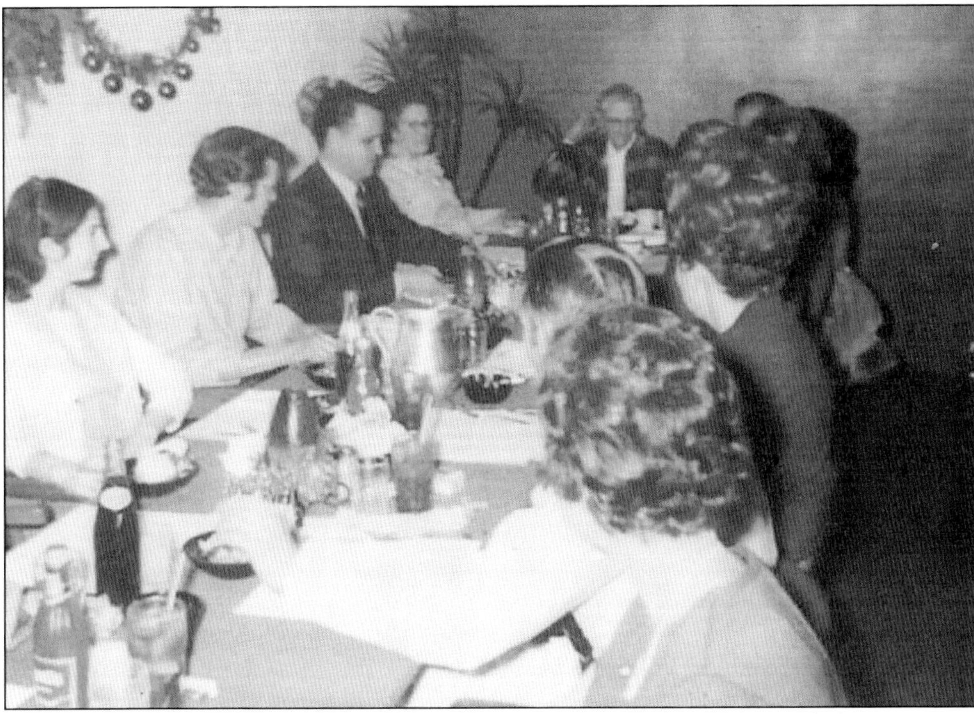

Capt. Charlie Strickland and family eat supper at Bay Harbor Restaurant around Christmas 1969, including (clockwise from left) Dolores and Oneal Strickland; Johnny and Dixie Feagin; Grace, Charlie, Charlie Jr., Honey, Glenda, and Al Strickland; and Sister Menger. This dinner was in honor of Charlie and Grace's 50th wedding anniversary. (Courtesy of the Strickland family.)

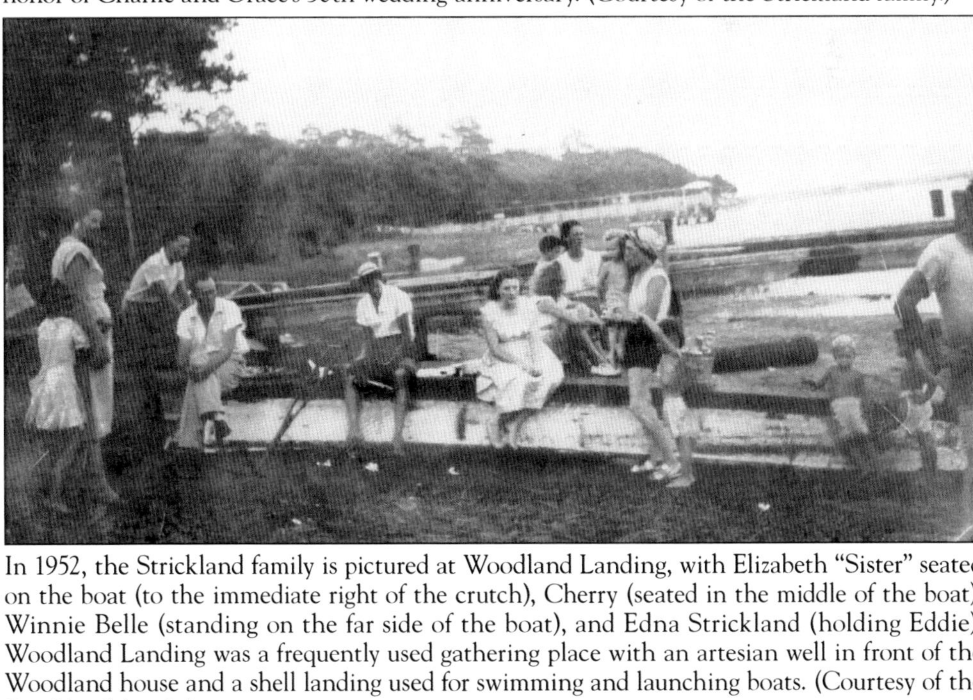

In 1952, the Strickland family is pictured at Woodland Landing, with Elizabeth "Sister" seated on the boat (to the immediate right of the crutch), Cherry (seated in the middle of the boat), Winnie Belle (standing on the far side of the boat), and Edna Strickland (holding Eddie). Woodland Landing was a frequently used gathering place with an artesian well in front of the Woodland house and a shell landing used for swimming and launching boats. (Courtesy of the Strickland family.)

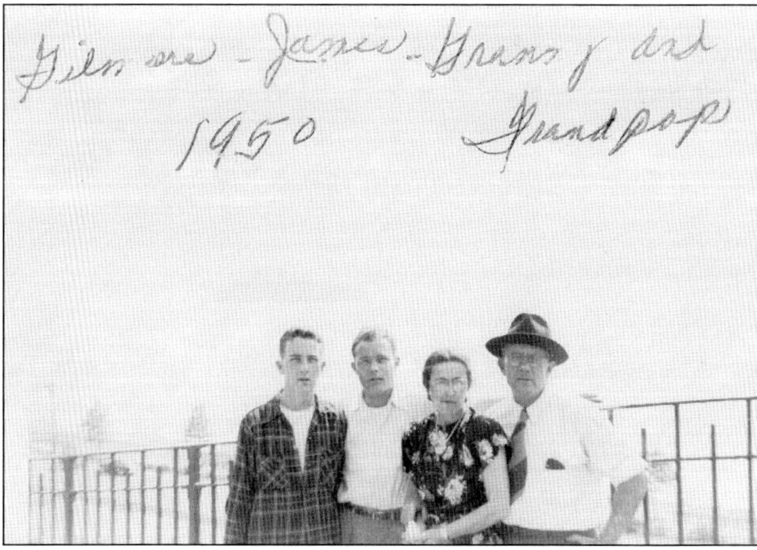

Henry Gilmore and Ida Smith bought Sunnyside around 1910 and raised a family there, including Luther, Nan, Ashby Gilmore, and Mary Walker Smith. Pictured here are, from right to left Ashby Gilmore, Pearly, James, and Gilmore Smith. (Courtesy of the Smith family.)

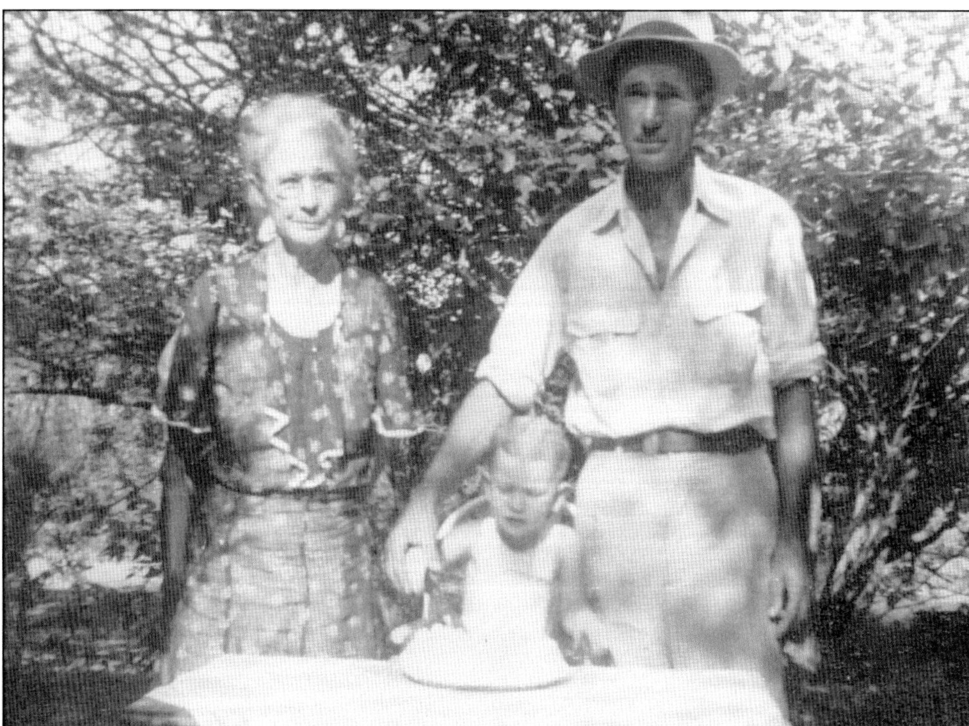

Three generations of Vereens, including Florence Elizabeth Marlow Vereen, Sam Gordon Vereen Jr., and Sam Gordon "Sonny" Vereen Sr., are at the family farm near Collins Creek celebrating Sam Jr.'s second birthday. Sonny was one of Samuel Permenter Vereen's eight children. (Courtesy of the Vereen family.)

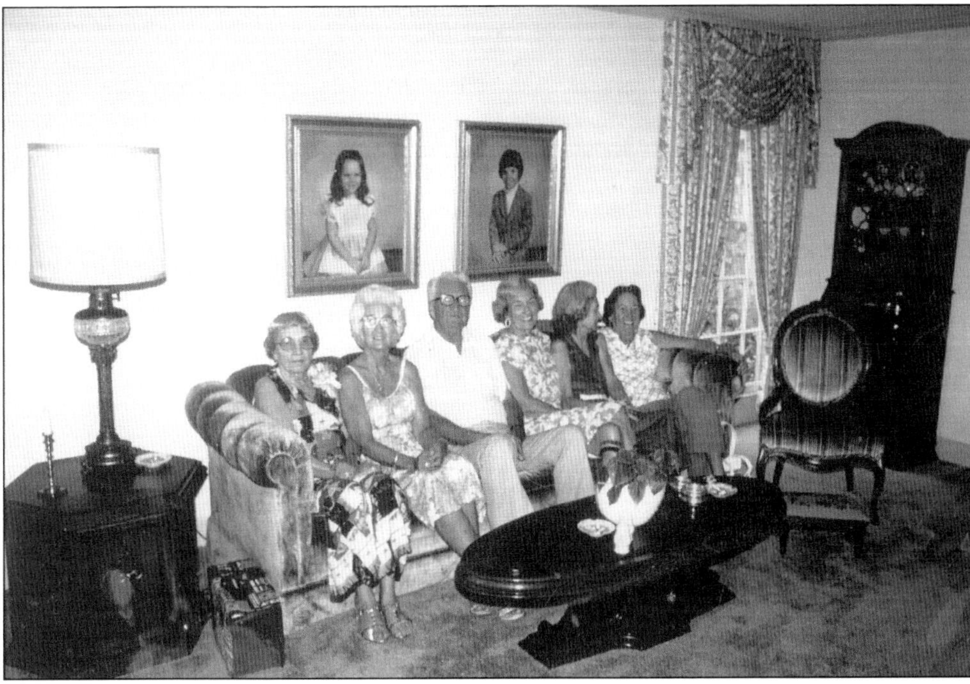

The children of Ernest B. "Bossy" Vereen in a family photograph are, from left to right, Elouise "Nudge" Edwards, Inez Stalvey, Ernest Barry Vereen, Geneva Loud, Elizabeth "Monk" Eason, and Rebecca "Becky" Shirley. His children all lived in the Garden City area on land passed down from John F. Vereen, whose children included Bossy, Sam Permenter, Gordon, Benny, Lucy, and Joseph. (Courtesy of Robin Loud.)

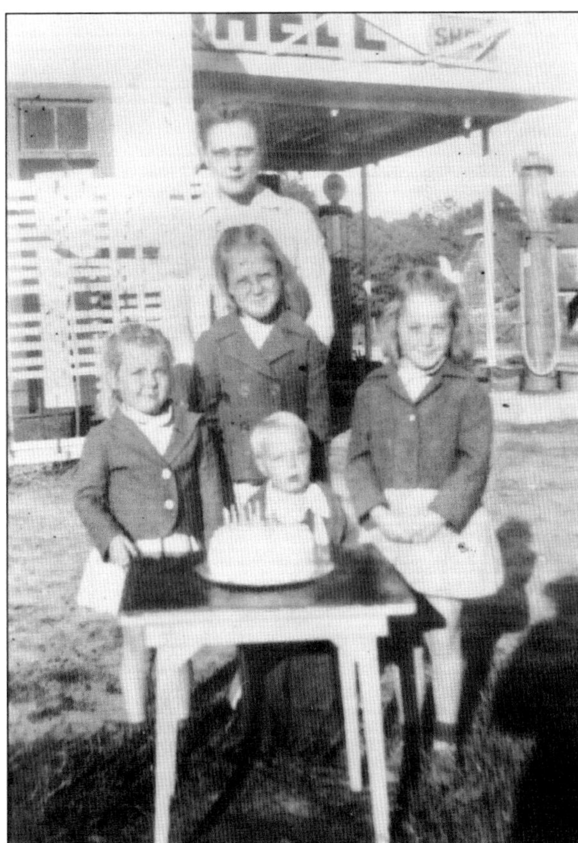

Sam Outlaw's family from about 1945 included his wife, Lessie; daughters, from left to right, Shirley, Clara, and Sammie Jean; and son Harry. Sam was in the Merchant Marines during World War II, and his family lived in the Shell station building that is now Lees Inlet Kitchen. Sam built the Ocean Highway Garage on land purchased from Joe Parker when he returned home from the war. (Courtesy of the Lee family.)

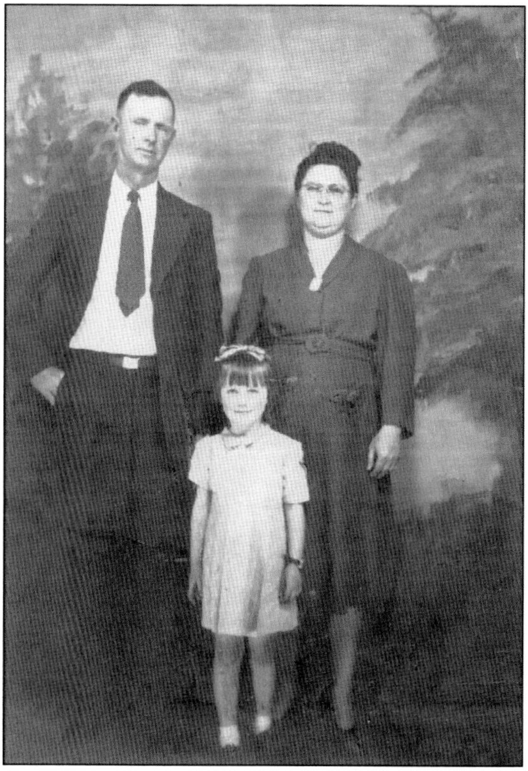

Andrew Hobson "Captain Hobby" and Bertie Nance are pictured with their youngest daughter, Lorraine (other children included Harvey, D.J., Paul, Lucille, Velma, and Margarite). Hobby was a commercial fisherman and used haul seines to harvest the large schools of fish that would migrate along the beach every fall. (Courtesy of Lorraine Nance Rowe.)

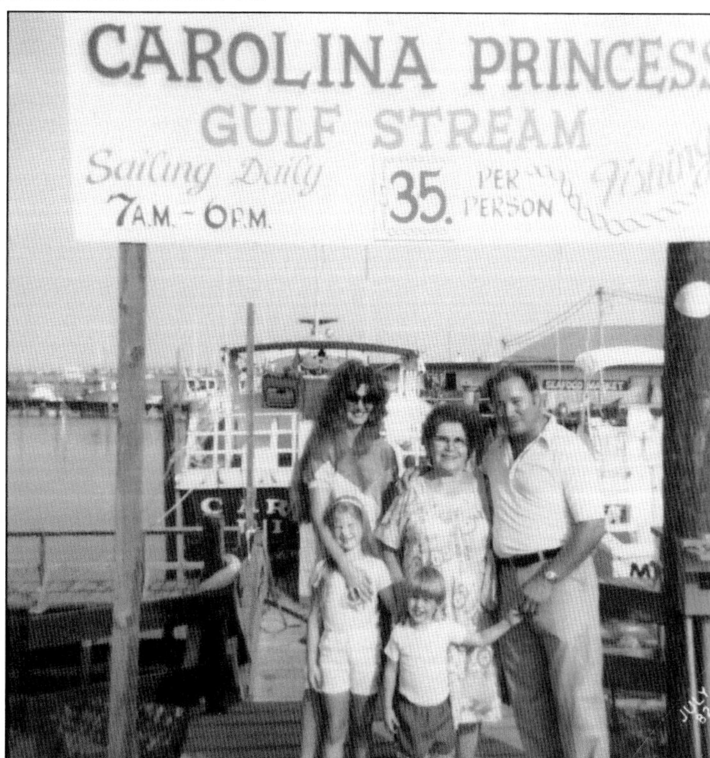

Don Lash and his family, including his grandmother Anna Zavla; his wife, Linda; and his children Dawn and Nick, are pictured at the docks at Captain Alex's Marina when he was running it around 1982. Linda is the daughter of Juanita Sessions Collins, who was married to Capt. Jimmy Stevens. (Courtesy of Don and Linda Lash.)

Five

Fishermen

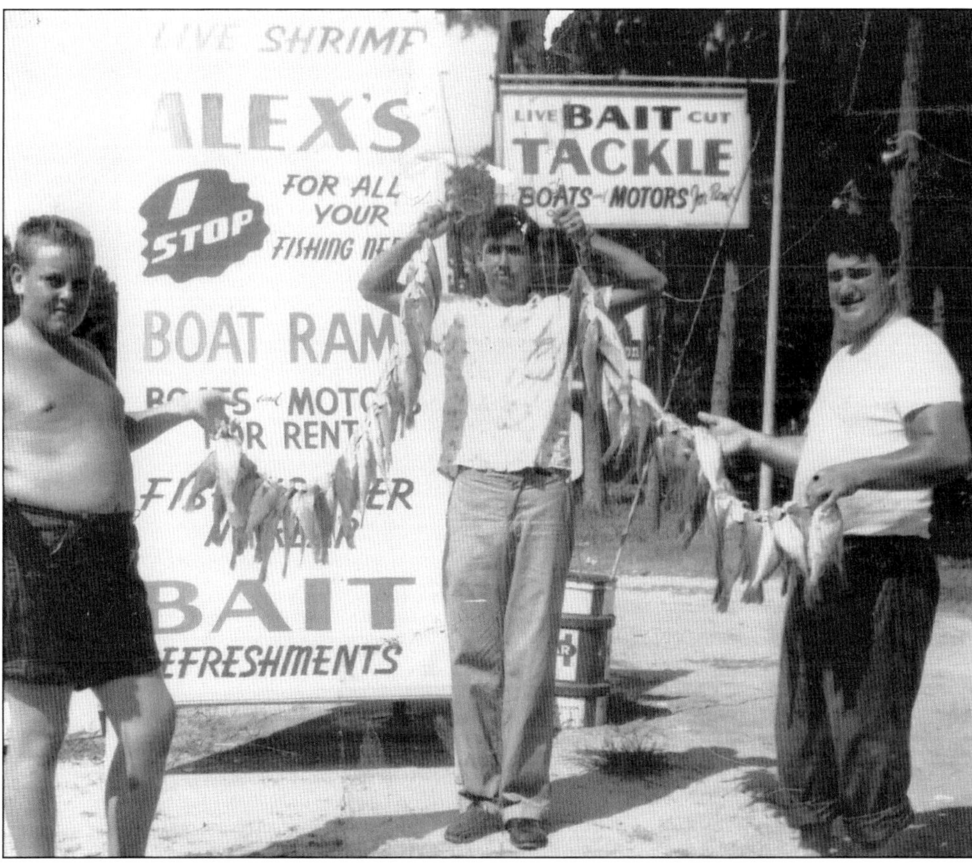

From left to right, Hoss Johnson, Alex Sing, and an unidentified fisherman show off a stringer of spots and croakers caught during the fall run around 1964. Fishermen could get guides for any type of fishing trips at Captain Alex's Marina and come back with a large catch because of the availability of fish and the knowledge of the guides. (Courtesy of the Sing family.)

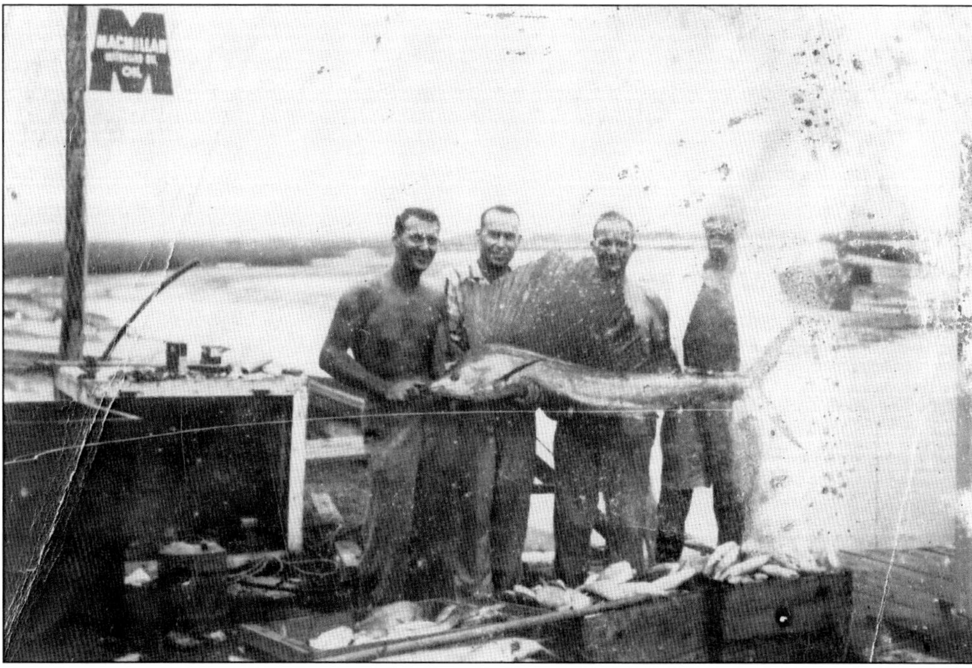

From left to right, M.G. Caughman, Paul Patrick, Wesley Hughes Sr., and Mr. Massey are shown holding a sailfish caught about the *Miss Octavia* around 1958. This was the first reported landing of a sailfish in Murrells Inlet and a precursor of the big game sportfishing that followed in the 1960s. (Courtesy of the Caughman family.)

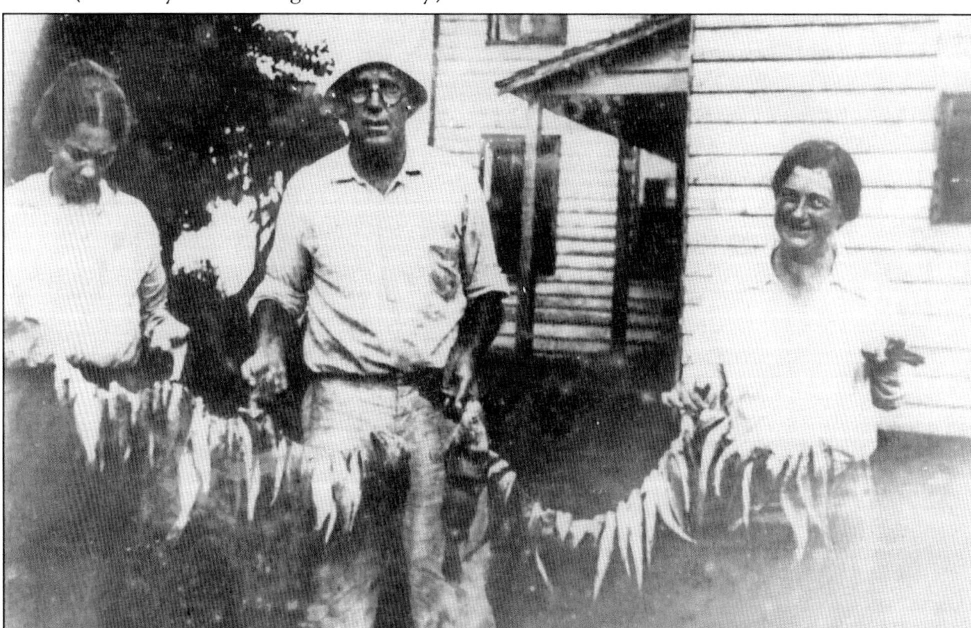

Since the late 1800s, the King family have owned a vacation home beside Oliver's Lodge called King's Krest, and Gracie Johnson King, Joe King, and Lena Cowan are shown here from left to right with a nice catch of spots, trout, and drum in a photograph from the mid-1930s. (Courtesy of the King family.)

Unidentified fishermen are pictured with a nice catch of spottails and trout in front of Sam Barwick's Tackle Shop, which moved in the north side of the Bay Harbor Motel beside Jimmy Eason's store in the mid-1950s. Sam Barwick worked for Luther Smith before he opened his first tackle shop. Sam had two other tackle shop locations, one behind the Bay Harbor when he first started and the last one on the creek near where Drunken Jacks is located. (Courtesy of the Eason family.)

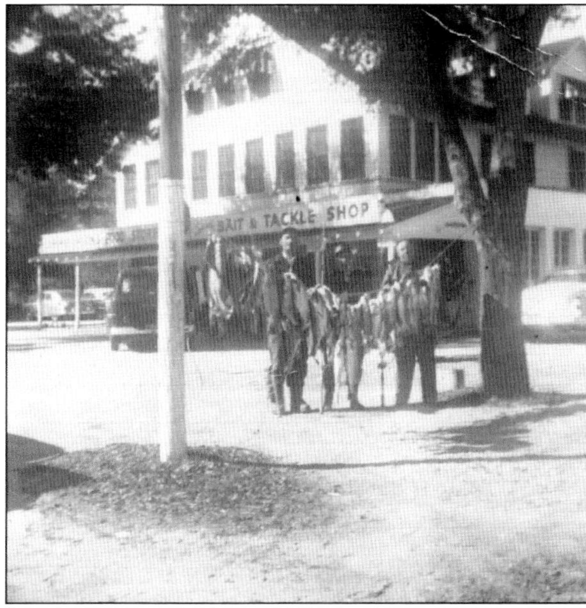

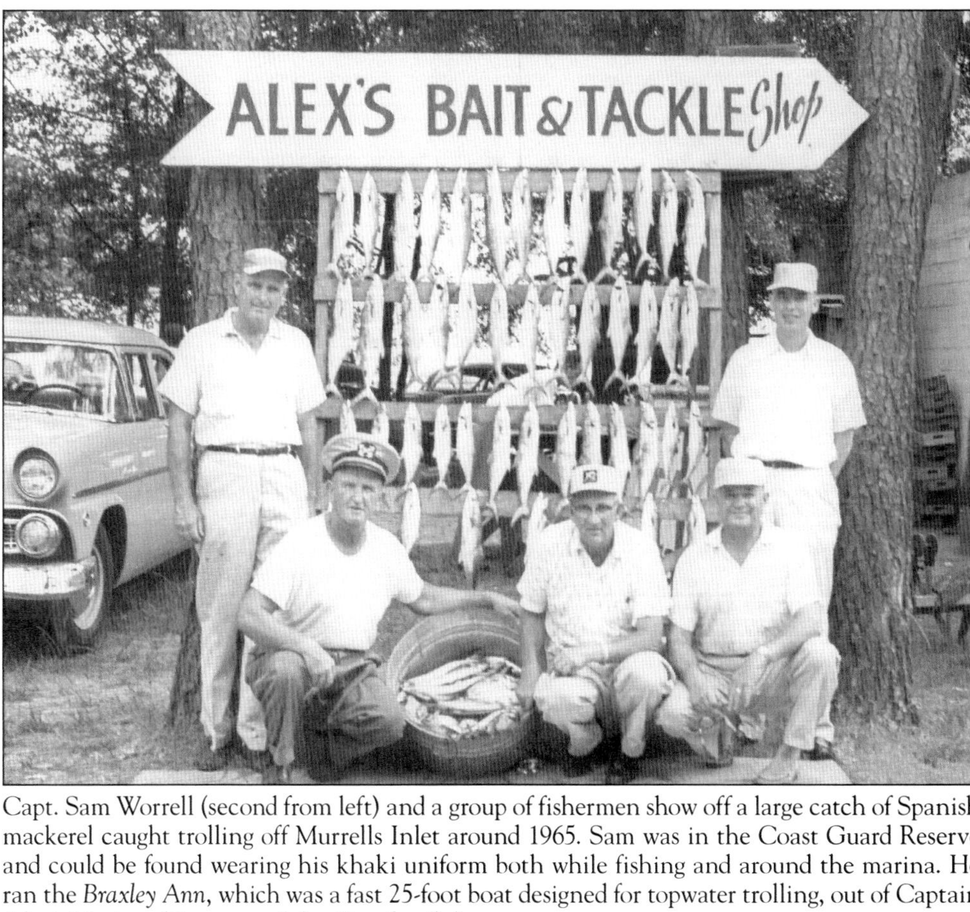

Capt. Sam Worrell (second from left) and a group of fishermen show off a large catch of Spanish mackerel caught trolling off Murrells Inlet around 1965. Sam was in the Coast Guard Reserve and could be found wearing his khaki uniform both while fishing and around the marina. He ran the *Braxley Ann*, which was a fast 25-foot boat designed for topwater trolling, out of Captain Alex's Marina. (Courtesy of the Sing family.)

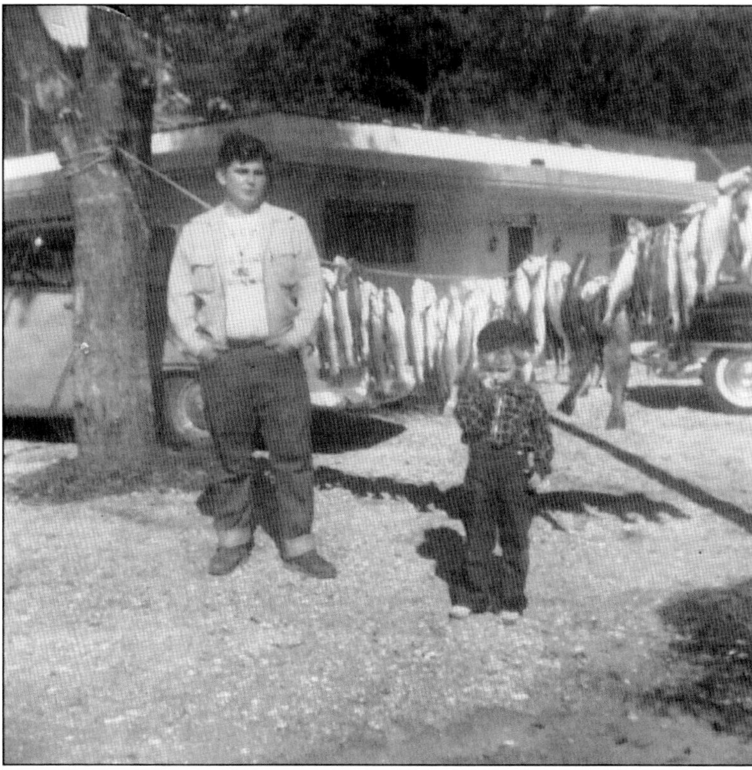

Dick Eason is shown with a big catch of trout at Bay Harbor around 1956. Dick is one of Jimmy and Dot Eason's children and was an avid fisherman, later operating several boats and marinas in Murrells Inlet, including Captain Dick's Marina, which he opened around 1971. (Courtesy of the Eason family.)

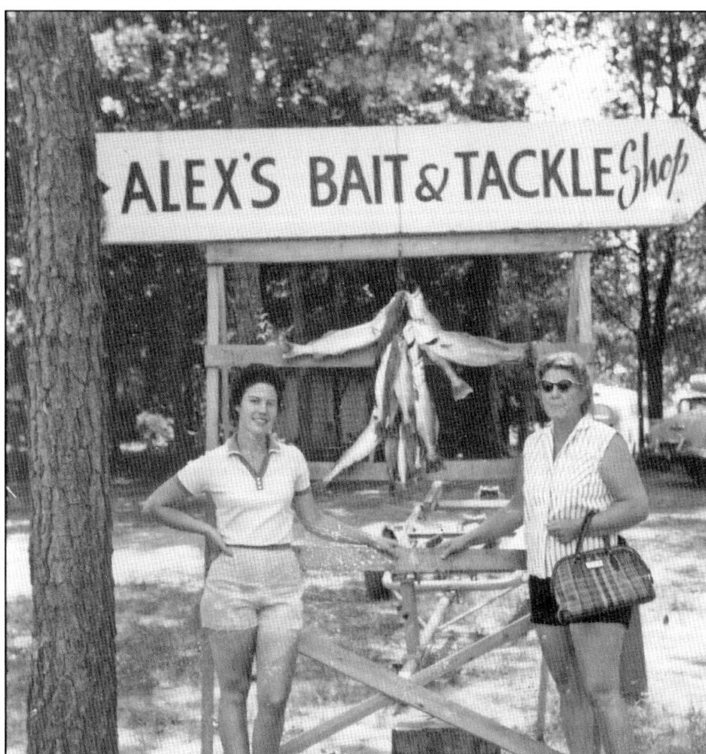

Betty Jo Sing (left) and Miriam Stroupe pose with a large catch of trout around 1967 at Alex's Marina. Betty Jo was married to Alex Sing and helped build the business into one of the hubs of the Murrells Inlet fishing scene. She was also an accomplished angler who could compete with anyone else in the creek. (Courtesy of the Sing family.)

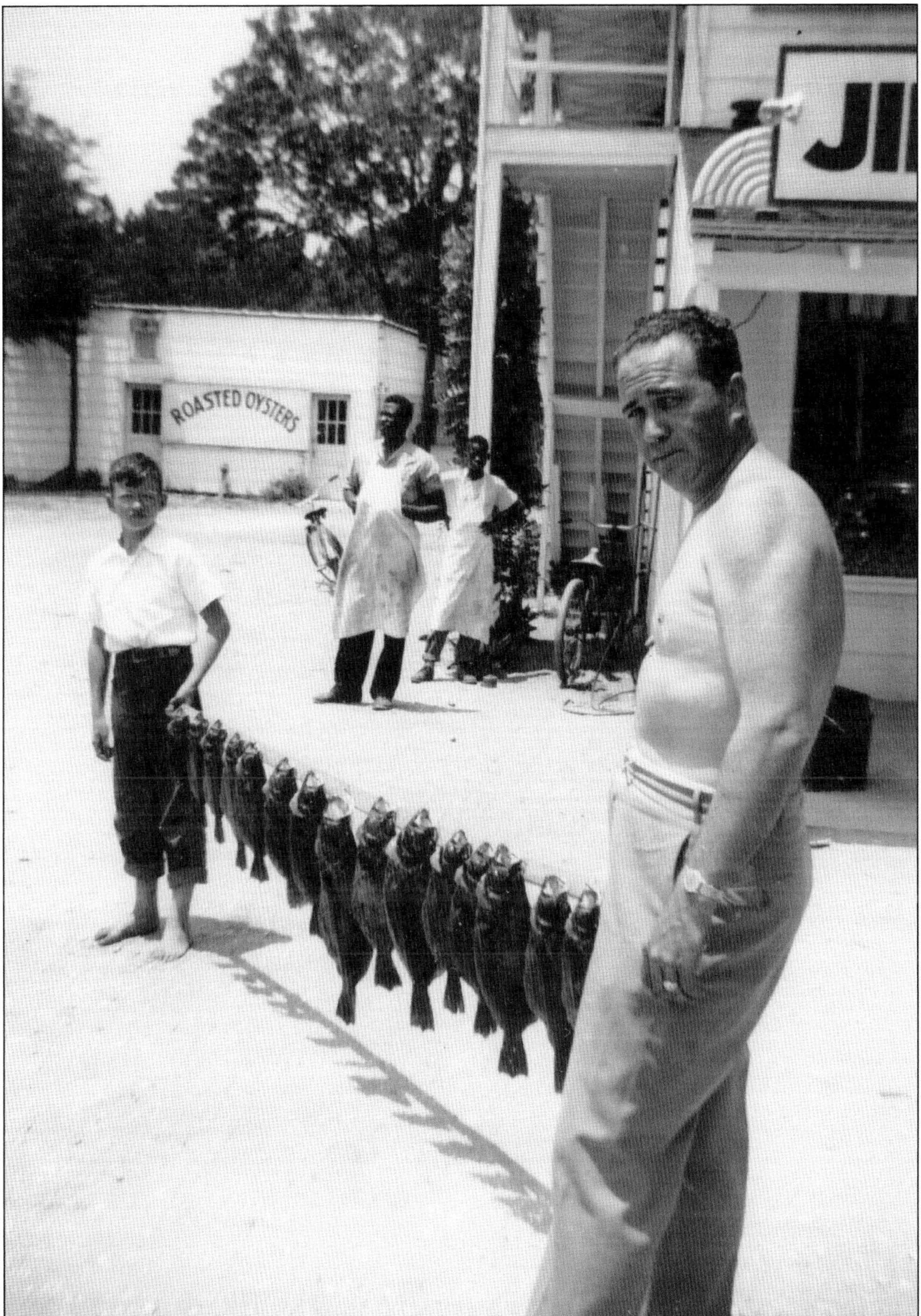

From right to left, Jimmy Eason, Robert Alston, and Wilson and Billy Gasque Jr., shown at Bay Harbor Store around 1958, are holding a board with a nice catch of flounder. In the background is the Bay Harbor Oyster Roast, where diners would line up at community tables and the oysters were cooked on sheets of metal and shoveled onto the tables. (Courtesy of the Eason family.)

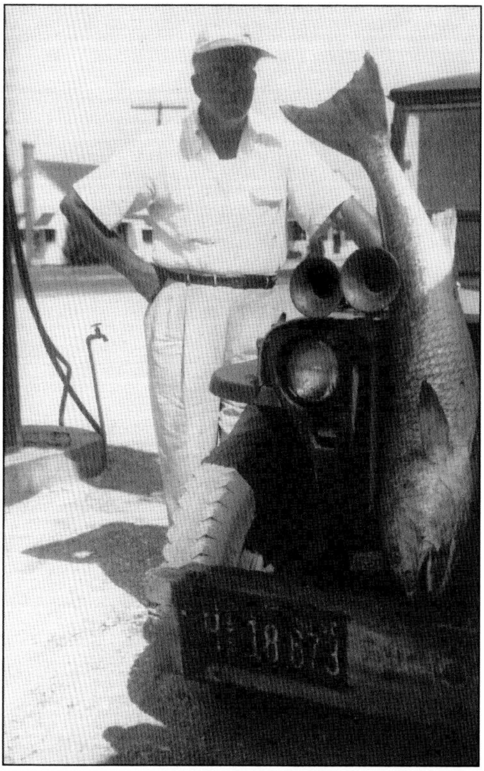

Charles Edwards was married to Elouise "Nudge" Vereen and operated several businesses, including a gas station, the Garden City Motor Court, and the Garden City Grill near the Garden City causeway and Highway 17. He is shown at the gas station around 1950 with a large spottail bass caught surf fishing in Garden City. (Courtesy of Robin Loud.)

From left to right, M.G. Caughman, Howard Wesley and an unidentified fisherman pose with a nice catch of dolphin, king mackerel, amberjack, and a sailfish caught trolling offshore from Murrells Inlet around 1960. M.G. was reported to catch a sailfish almost every year during August off of Myrtle Beach and bring it back into Murrells Inlet. (Courtesy of the Wesley family.)

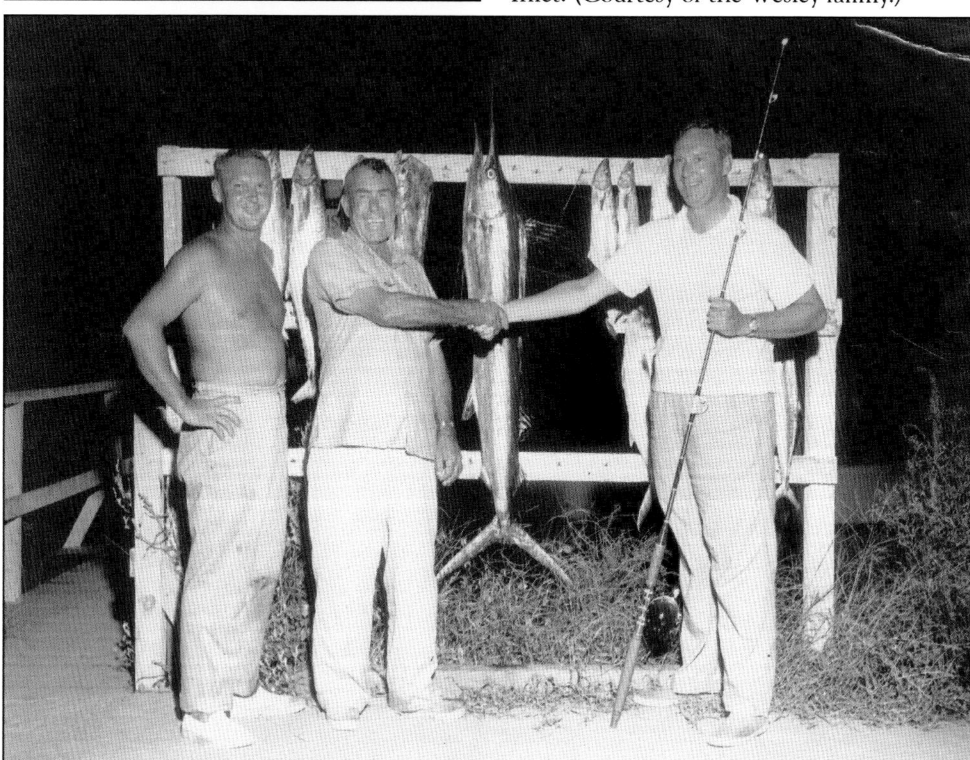

Farrell Welch (brother of Charles Welch) shows off a stringer full of trout, spottail bass, and flounder caught in Murrells Inlet around 1970. This picture was taken behind Charlie's house at Wagon Wheel Farms, with the old office in the background. (Courtesy of the Welch family.)

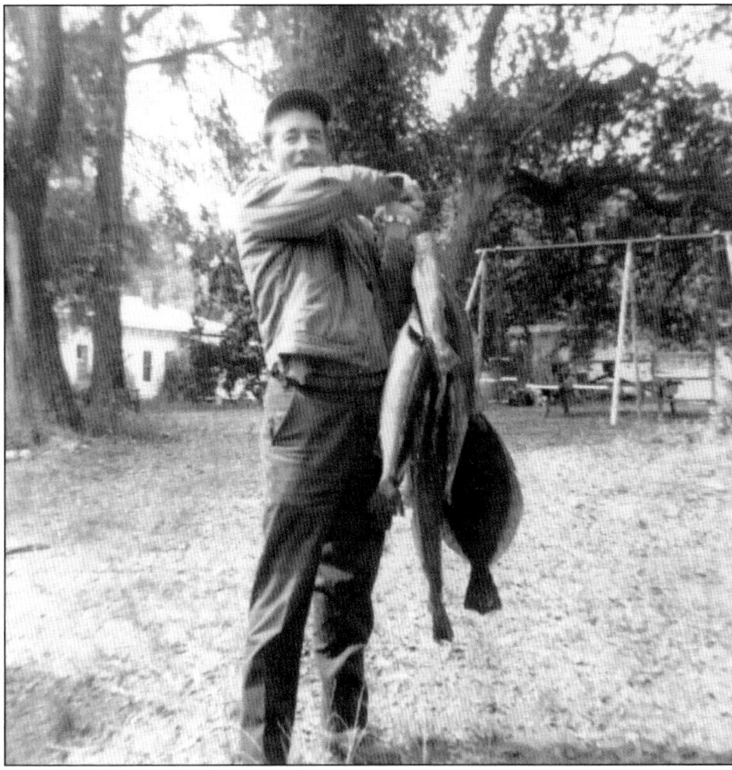

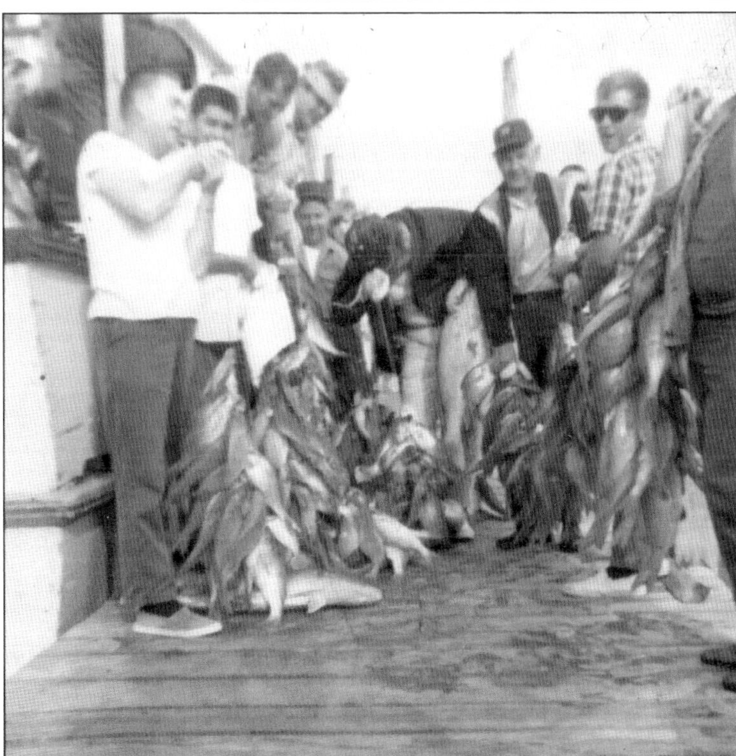

A group of fishermen with stringers full of snapper is pictured in June 1969 after a day of fishing offshore with Capt. Tommy Gaede on the *Thunderbird*. Catches like this were common, and tourists would gather at the docks every afternoon to watch the boats unload their catch. (Courtesy of Tommy Gaede.)

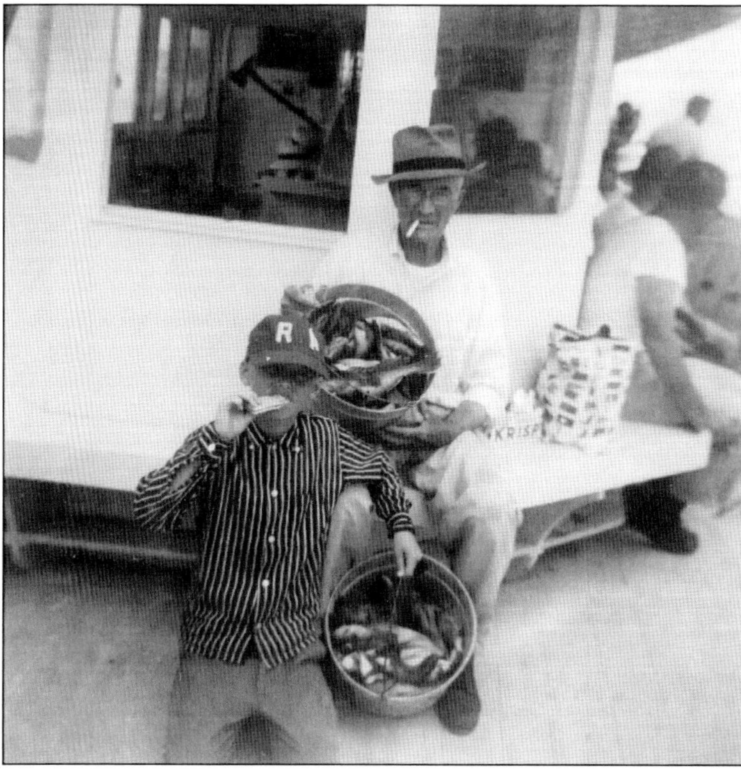

Jerry (on left) and Homer Wells show off a basket of black sea bass caught aboard the *Inlet Princess* during a fishing trip in August 1963. Homer's son Sanford Wells was a fishing boat captain during the 1950s, running the *Miss Octavia* out of Murrells Inlet. (Courtesy of Jerry Wells.)

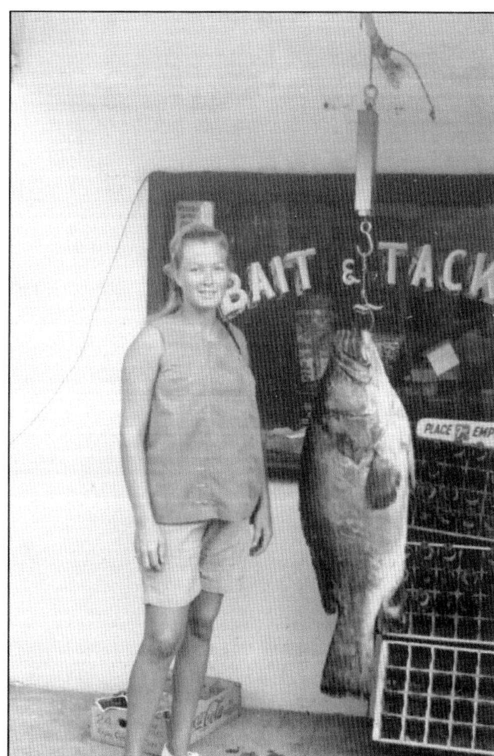

Linda Malnow from Spartanburg, South Carolina, was a waitress at Bay Harbor Restaurant around 1968 and is shown with a large grouper caught by Mike Marchant on the *Captain Alex* in front of Captain Alex's Marina (Courtesy of Mike Marchant.)

Mike Marchant, a mate on the *Captain Alex* in the late 1960s, is shown cleaning a grouper caught during an offshore fishing trip around 1968 while a crowd of onlookers observes the fish that were brought in that day. Mike started off as a mate and went on to run several boats in Murrells Inlet during his time. (Courtesy of Mike Marchant.)

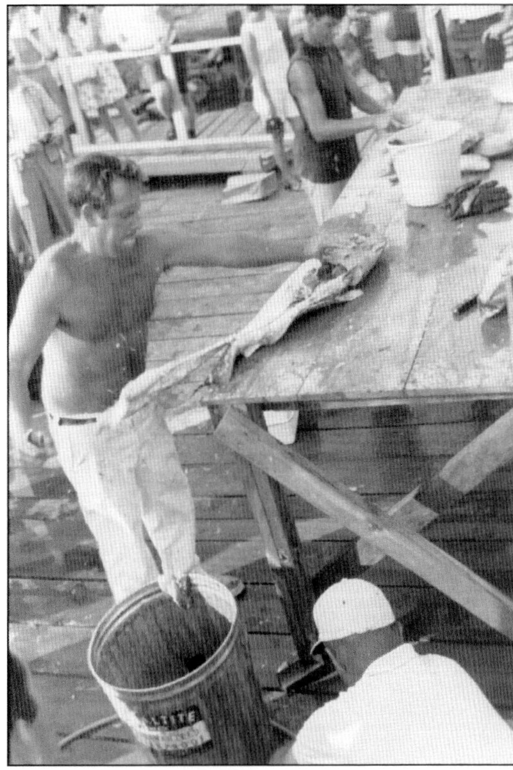

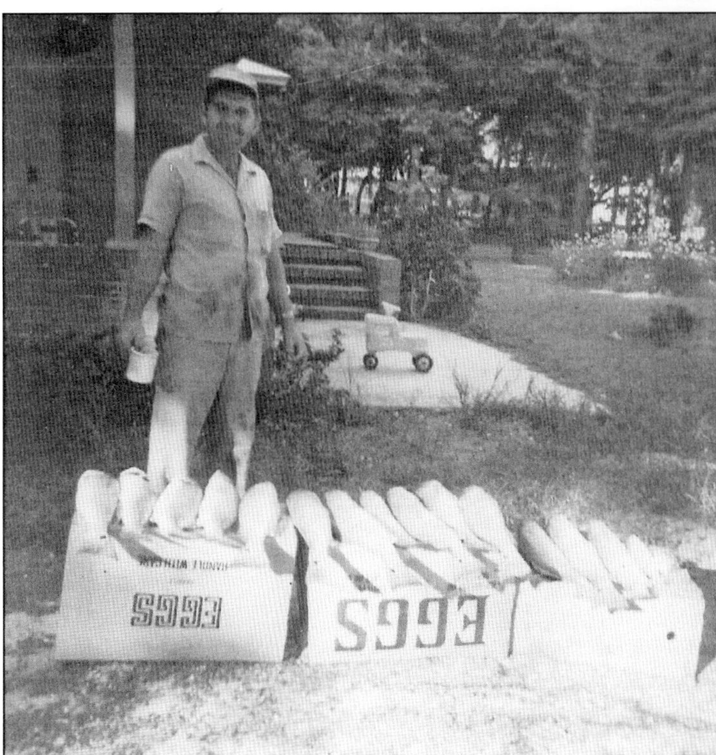

Charlie Welch looks pretty happy with 14 nice spottail bass (red drum) caught during a fishing trip in September 1966. Charlie came to Murrells Inlet in the 1950s to operate Wagon Wheel Farms (a poultry farm) and raised chickens for meat and laying hens for fresh eggs. He lived in this house at the top of the hill on the farm for over 30 years before moving into the house on the creek across the street that he purchased from Dick Eason. (Courtesy of the Welch family.)

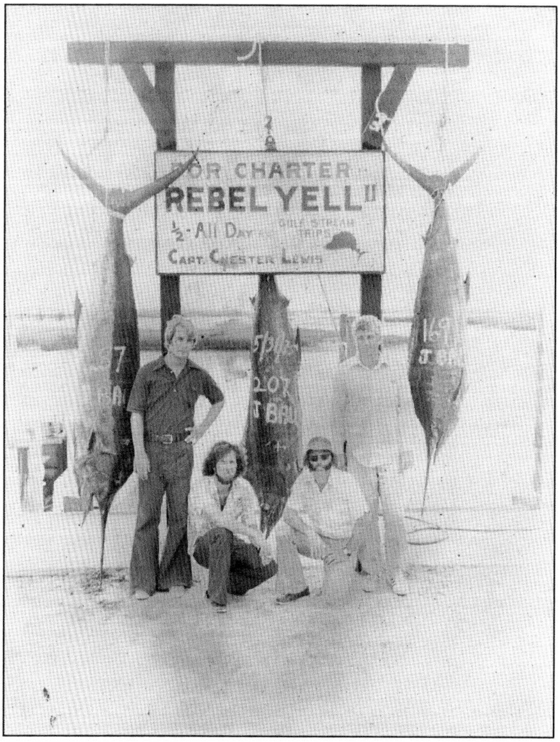

From left to right, Johnny Ball, Capts. Chester and Johnny Lewis, and mate Larry Smith are showing off three blue marlin caught on the fishing boat *Rebel Yell II* during the Pabst Blue Ribbon Tournament held at the Gulf Stream Marina in 1975. (Courtesy of Chester Lewis.)

From left to right, Johnny Vereen, Capt. Bill Moeller (kneeling), Furman Long, Sam Vereen (kneeling on right), Mike Edwards, and mate Buddy Pardon are in front of a blue marlin caught on the fishing boat *Partner* during the Pabst Blue Ribbon tournament at Gulf Stream Marina in 1979. (Courtesy of Bill Moeller.)

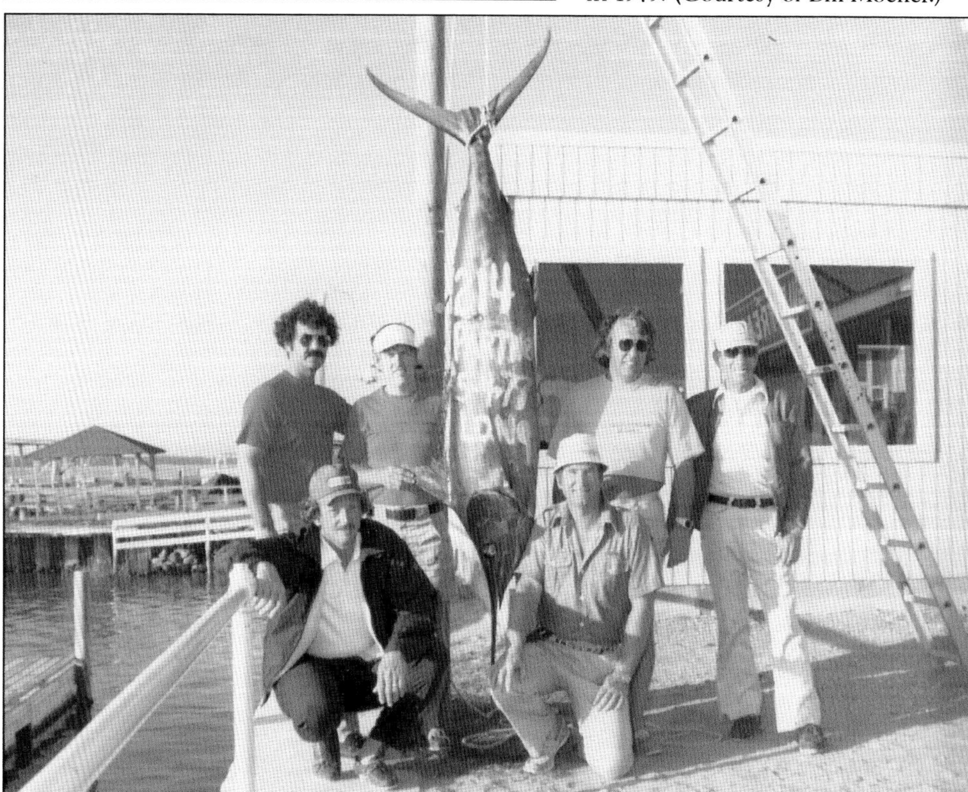

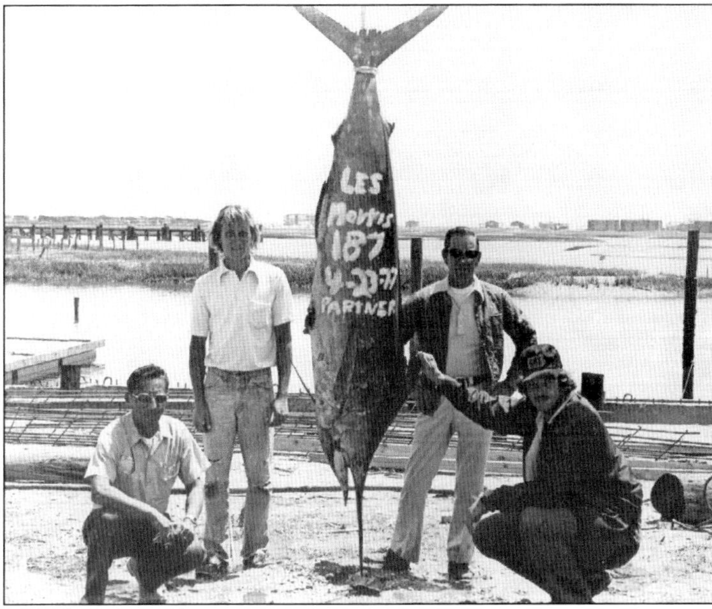

From left to right, Frank Sarvino, Charley Hanson, Buddy Pardon, and Bill Moeller are pictured with a blue marlin caught on the sport fishing boat *Partner* at Captain Dick's Marina during a tournament in April 1977. The concrete seawall in the background was being constructed at this time to replace the wood bulkhead that was installed around 1971. (Courtesy of Bill Moeller.)

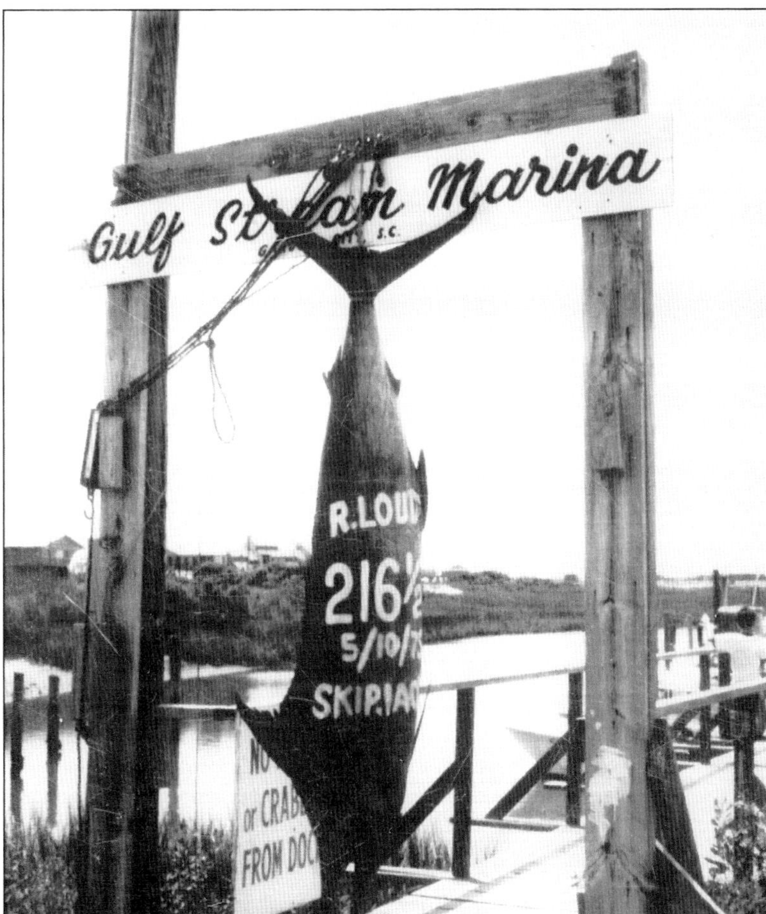

Robin Loud caught a blue marlin while on board the *Skipjack* during the first trip of the year to the Gulf Stream. The 25-foot Bertram *Skipjack* was owned by Robin and Mike Edwards, originally bought from Dick Burnside. (Courtesy of Robin Loud.)

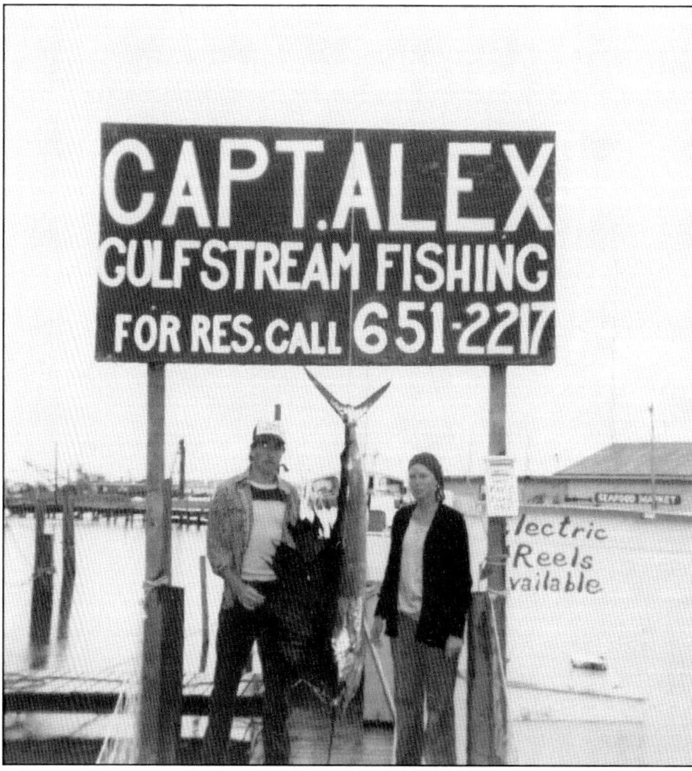

A couple that went fishing aboard the *Captain Alex* brought back a nice sailfish during a trip with Capt. Don Lash around 1977. Don purchased the boat and marina in 1975 and operated that location until 1982. (Courtesy of Don and Linda Lash.)

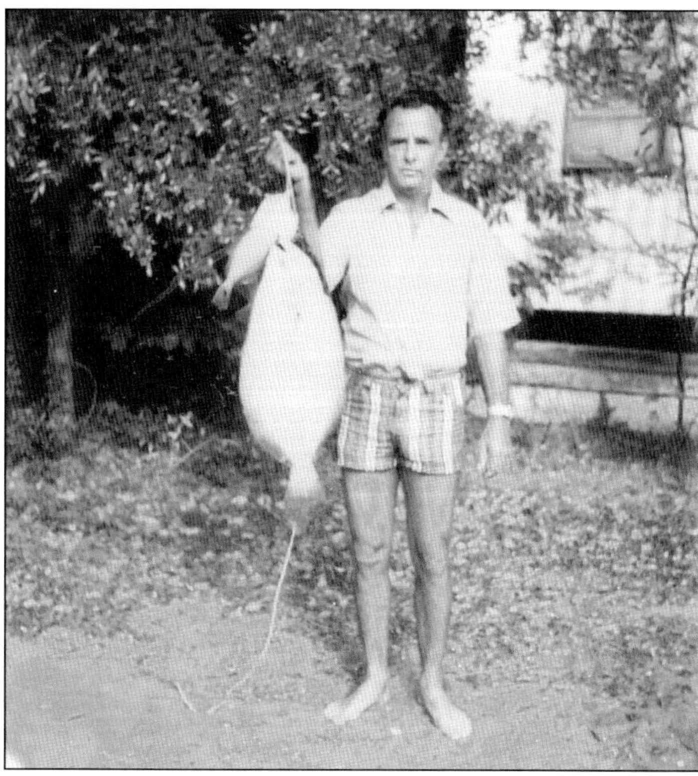

Dick Vick shows off a stringer of fish caught in Murrells Inlet in 1974, including a 13-pound flounder. Dick was one of Capt. Ira Vick's five children and learned to fish the creeks of Murrells Inlet with Captain Ira. Dick came home to Murrells Inlet after a 20-year career with the Navy and was named after local doctor Dick Willcox (one of Clarke Willcox Sr.'s children), known at the time by his neighbors as "Bubba Dick." (Courtesy of Dick Vick.)

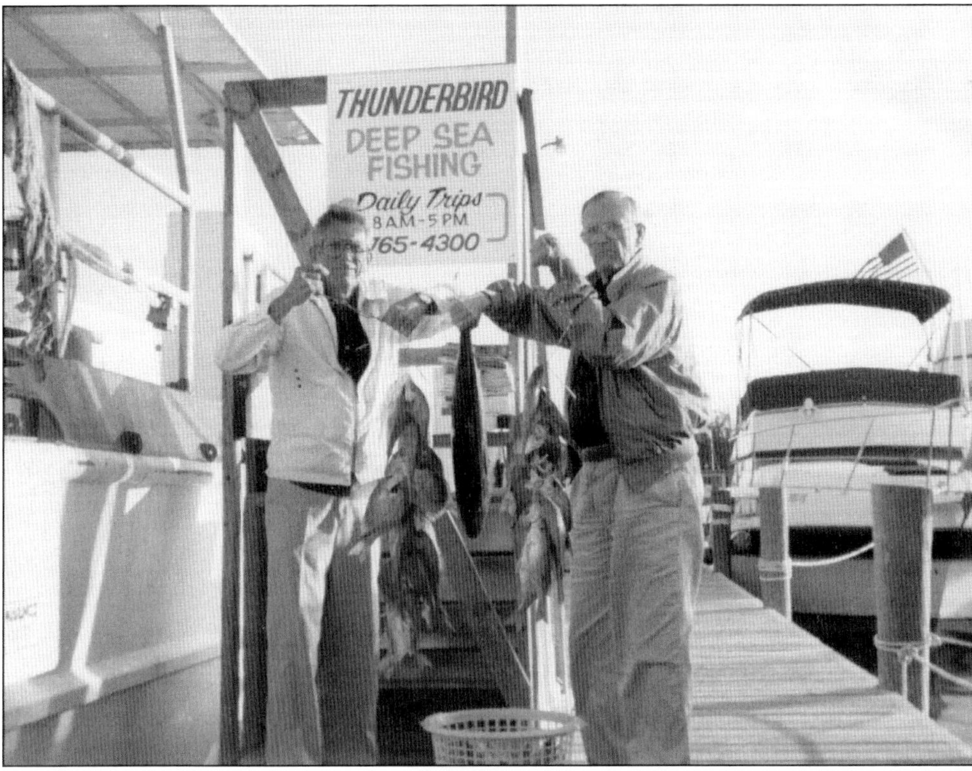

Al Strickland Sr. (left) and his brother Charlie Strickland Jr. were fishing with Capt. Bobby Strickland (Charlie's son) on the *Thunderbird* around 1982 and caught a good mess of bottom fish to take home. (Courtesy of the Strickland family.)

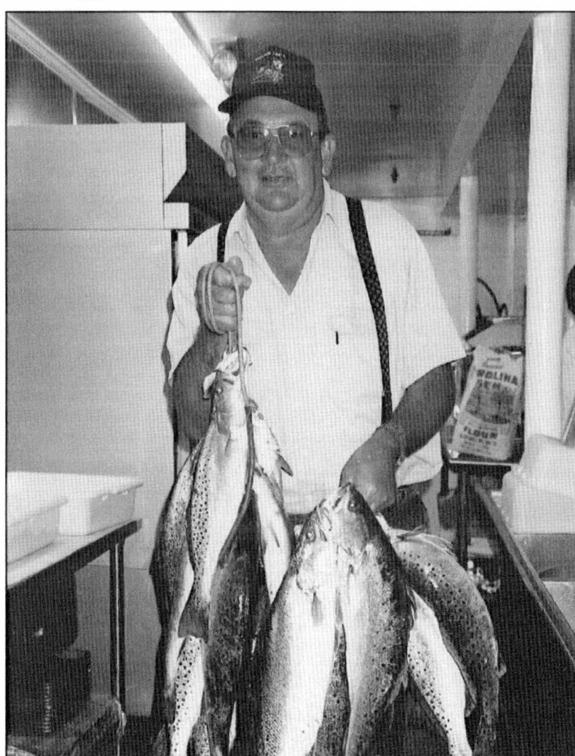

Wallace Lee was a famous seafood cook with several restaurants but was also a great fisherman and would take people on guided fishing trips in the creek. He is shown here in the kitchen of the Ship's Log restaurant showing off a catch of trout. (Courtesy of the Lee family.)

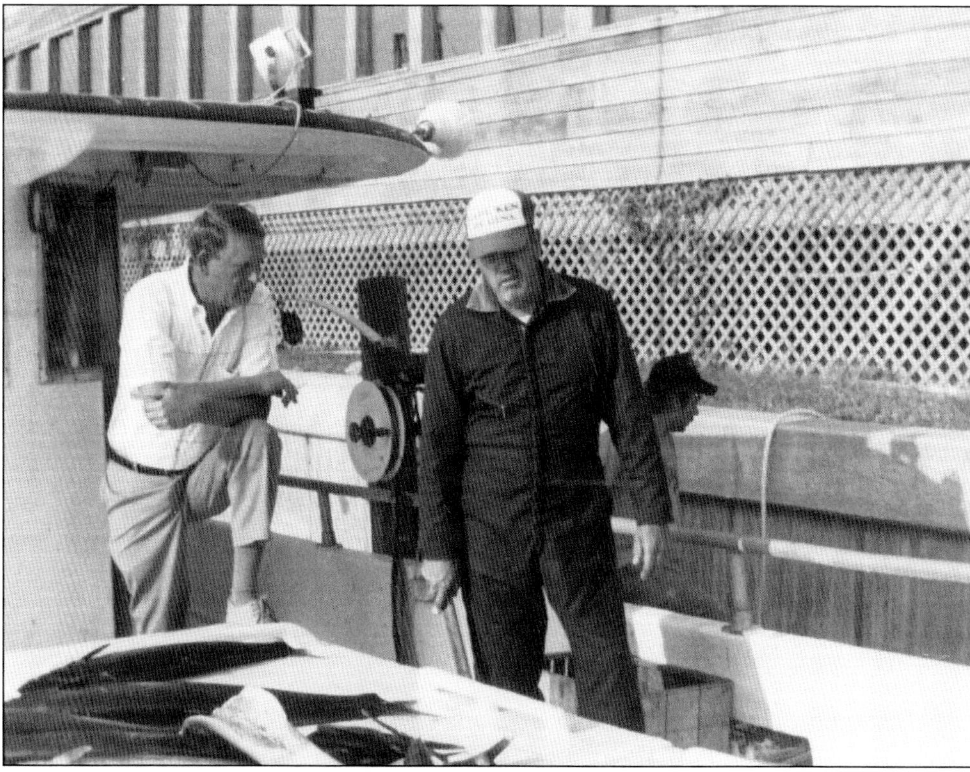

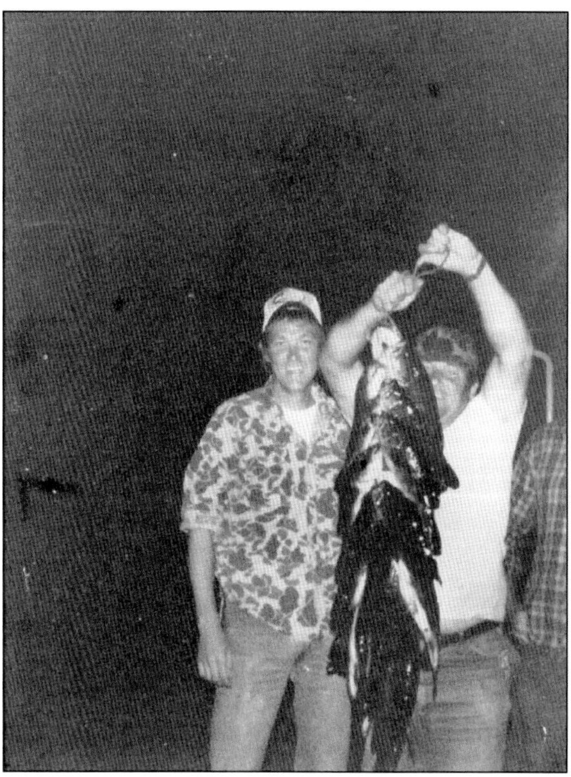

Bobby Milligan (left) and Capt. Ken Hair are looking at the catch of king mackerel on the back deck of the *Miss Gina* around 1985. The commercial fishing fleet in Murrells Inlet docked between Anchor Marina (now Devine Fish House) and H&C Fisheries, shipping fresh fish out to markets along the East Coast. (Courtesy of Dean Hair.)

Mike Ammons (left) and Brownie Brown show off a full stringer of largemouth bass caught in the freshwater creeks that feed into the Waccamaw River. Most of the local fishermen take advantage of the freshwater side of Murrells Inlet to catch a variety of fresh fish. (Courtesy of Pearline Brown.)

Six

People

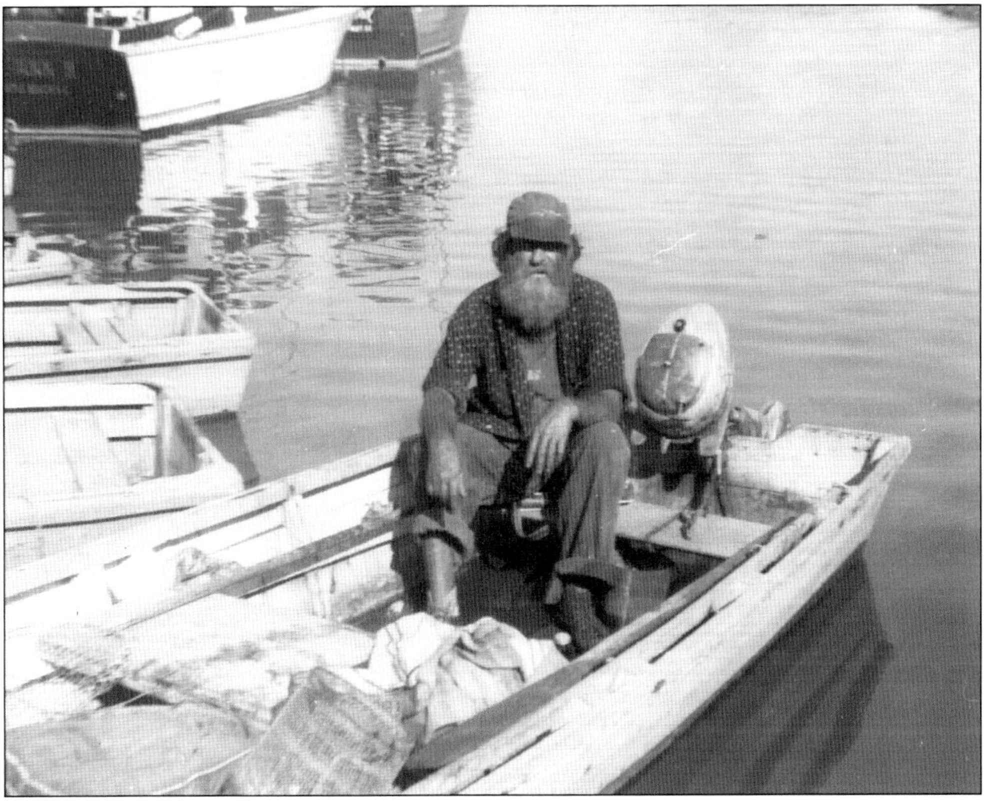

William E. "Bill" Hickman was a well-known Murrells Inlet character who kept a live bait tank on the creek behind Captain Alex's Marina that operated on the honor system, with fishermen leaving the money for the bait in his bucket. Bill was a reclusive fellow originally from Hickmans Crossroads, North Carolina, who spent his days between his one-room shack on the Grant property and the creek between Alex's Bait and Tackle and Sam Barwick's Tackle Shop at Snug Harbor. (Courtesy of Jerry Wells.)

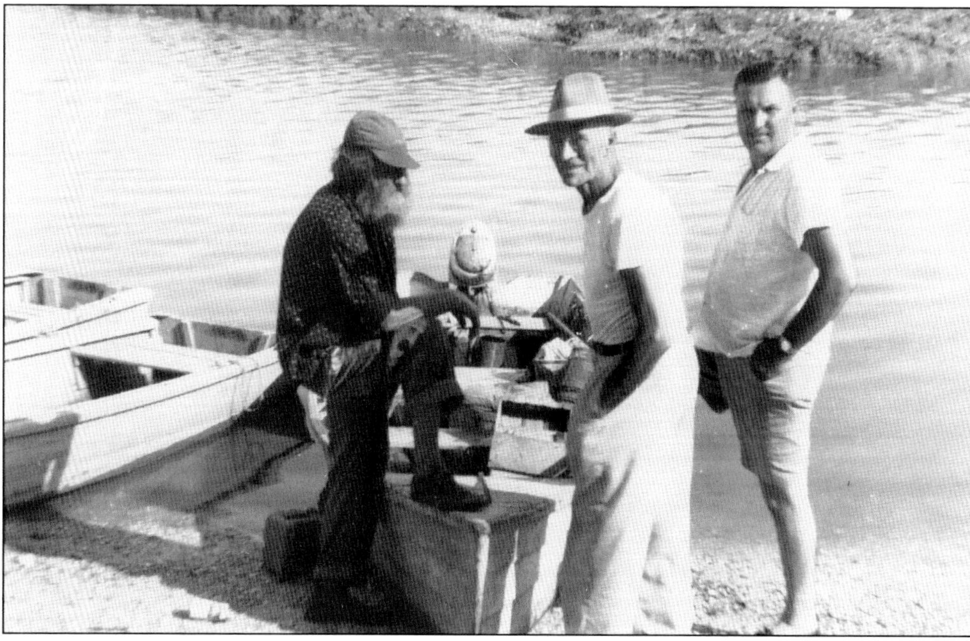

From left to right, Bill Hickman, Homer Wells, and Marvin Wells are standing at Bill's boat beside the rental boats at Captain Alex's Tackle Shop around 1960. Homer Wells was Capt. Sanford Wells's (*Miss Octavia*) brother and was good friends with Bill Hickman. Bill was a local baitman who moved to Murrells Inlet in the 1950s and could usually be found around Alex's or Bay Harbor. (Courtesy of Jerry Wells.)

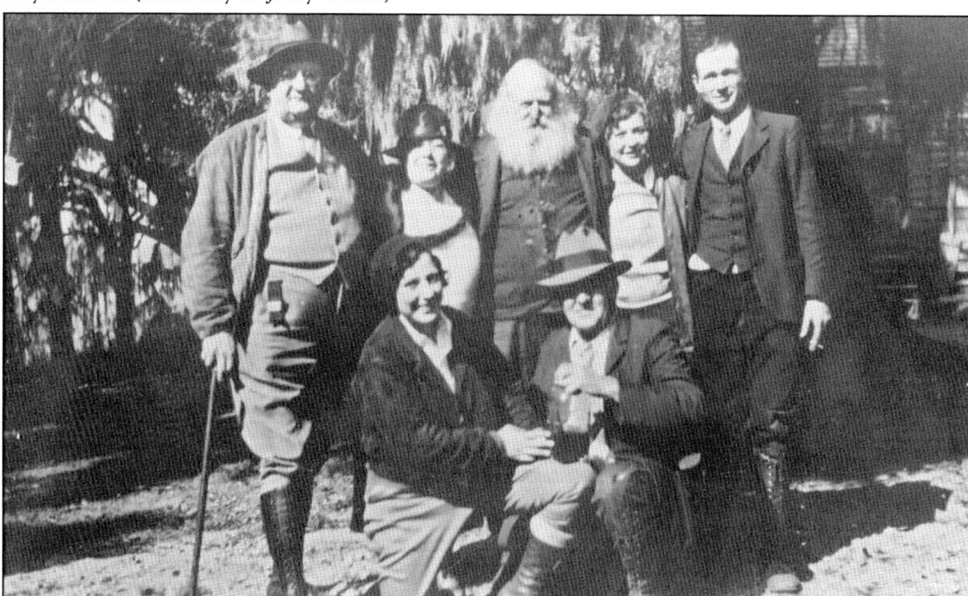

Here, a hunting party at Brookgreen Plantation around 1925 includes Sam Gordon "Sonny" Vereen Sr. (on the right in the second row) and Dr. Ward Flagg (in the center of the second row). Ward Flagg was the only Flagg survivor of the 1893 hurricane, after which he retired to the miller's cottage at Brookgreen. Dr. "Wardie" provided medical treatment to the residents of the Waccamaw Neck for many years. (Courtesy of the Vereen family.)

The First Baptist Church children's class poses on the creek around 1940. Youth in this picture include Dick Vick (left front), Wesley Gordon (center rear), Barbara Howard (right rear) and Ken McDowell (front right). First Baptist Church had been located between Gibson Avenue and William Dal Avenue at the time. Aleene Gordon was the Sunday School teacher for the youth and took them on this outing. (Courtesy of the Gordon family.)

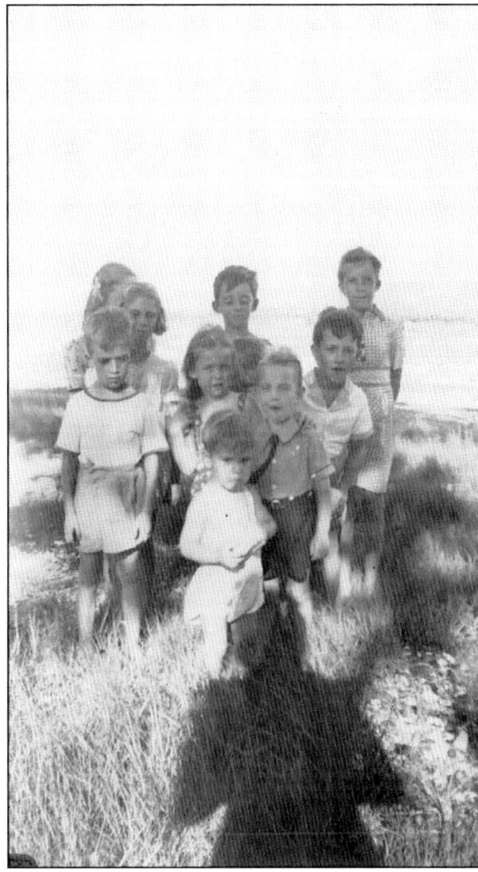

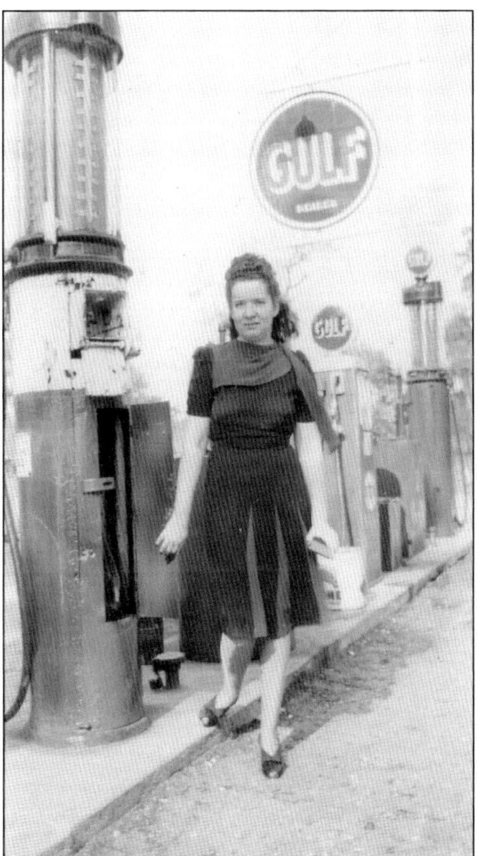

Aleene Gordon was married to Herman Gordon and is shown beside the gas pumps at their grocery store around 1948. This store was located in the building constructed by Joe Parker in the 1940s and owned by the Gordons around 1948. The Gordons later sold this store to R.L. Bone and moved a half-mile north, where they opened another grocery store and later built their Gulf gas station. (Courtesy of the Gordon family.)

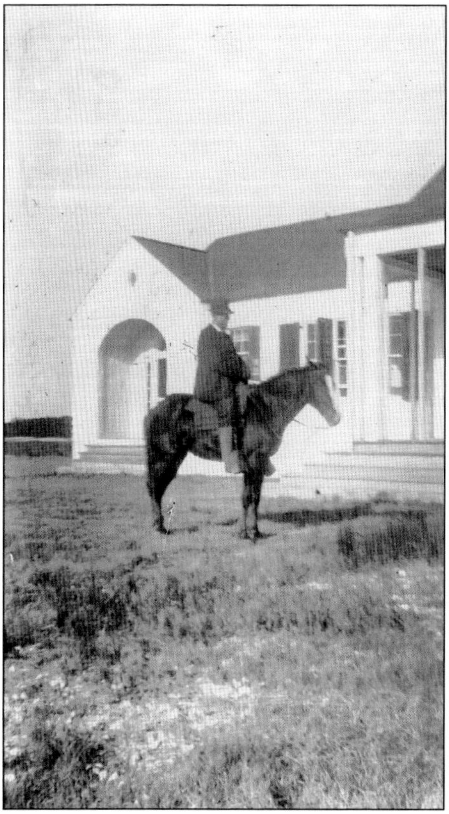

Capt. James Ervin Fulton was the caretaker for Brookgreen Plantation during the 1920s; he is shown here on horseback in front of the beach house at Magnolia Beach (near the site of Atalaya). He married Minnie Belle Moore from Marion, and his son Edwin Fulton was the caretaker at Wachesaw Plantation for the Kimbels in later years. (Courtesy of the Vereen family.)

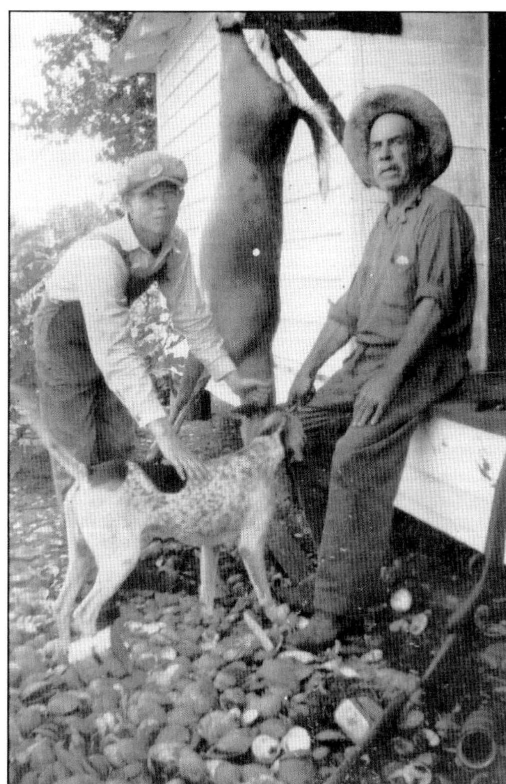

Paul Herbert Wesley (right), Howard Fairfax Wesley, and Old Sport are shown around 1930 at the Wesley home. Paul was the patriarch of the Wesley family, and they were great outdoorsmen, often seen with various wild game, such as deer, wild turkey, ducks, and fish. Paul Wesley moved to Murrells Inlet around 1910 to take advantage of the hunting and fishing. He was a outdoors writer who extolled the opportunities around his home and offered guide services to visiting sportsmen. (Courtesy of the Wesley family.)

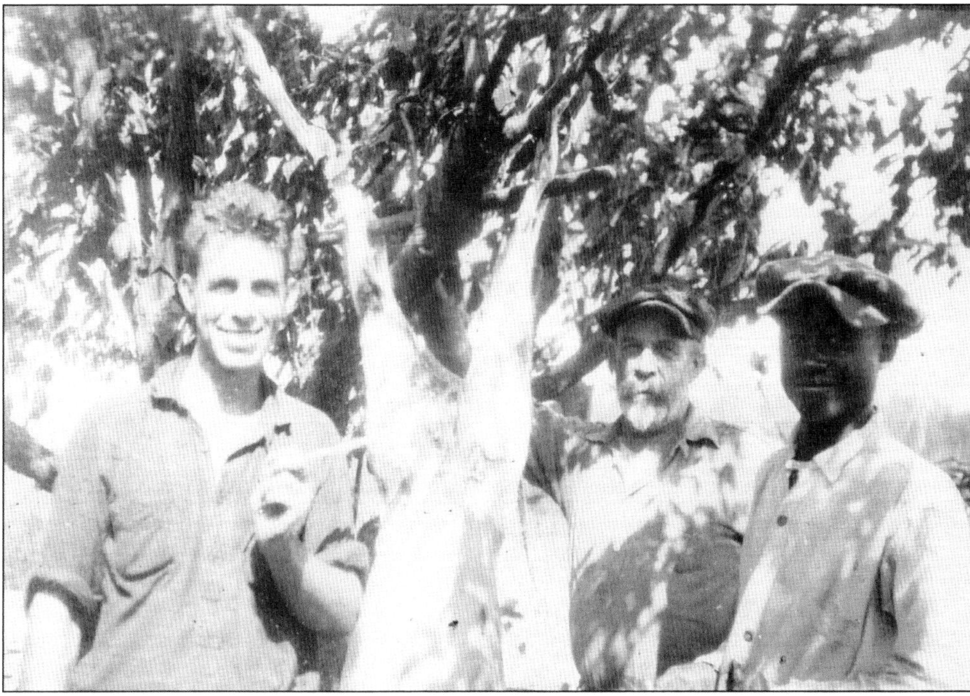

Shown here with a deer being cleaned, from left to right, Howard F. Wesley, Paul H. Wesley, and Franklin "Buster" Alston were frequently pictured with their catch of the day. Paul was a noted author, writing outdoors articles for magazines and newspapers. Howard and Buster were well-known hunting guides for Northern visitors who came to the area to hunt deer, turkey, and waterfowl. (Courtesy of the Wesley family.)

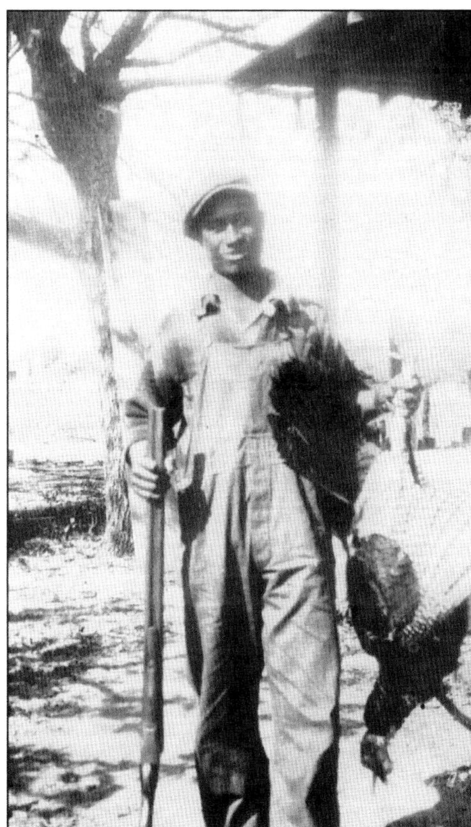

Franklin "Buster" Alston was a hunting companion with Howard F. Wesley, and he was an excellent marksman and game tracker. He worked maintaining the house at Sunnyside, hunting and fishing, and raising 10 children in Murrells Inlet. Several of his children are still living in Murrells Inlet. (Courtesy of the Wesley family.)

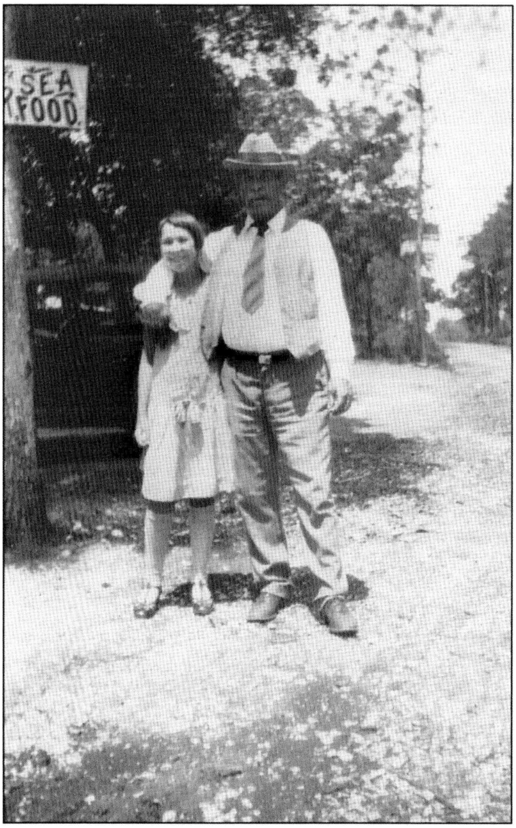

Eula Jean Morse and Paul Herbert Wesley are standing in front of Mae and George "Son" Morse's house, where Mae ran one of the first local restaurants in her dining room. Mae was Paul Wesley's oldest child. This house was located at the same site as the present-day Russell's Seafood Grill and was the Morse family home until they sold it to Dr. Breedlove in the 1950s. Dr. Breedlove used it as a medical office until it was destroyed by a fire in 1957. (Courtesy of the Morse family.)

Here is a crew from the Army Air Force crash boats at the Army dock in Murrells Inlet around 1943. Pictured in the front row at left is Frank Prox, who married Ester Martin and stayed in Murrells Inlet to raise a family, and in the front middle is Howard F. Wesley, a native who was placed into service with the Army crash boats because of his boating skills. Capt. Macfarland "Mac" Oliver (not pictured) was another native who served with the Army crash boats because of his boating capabilities. (Courtesy of the Prox family.)

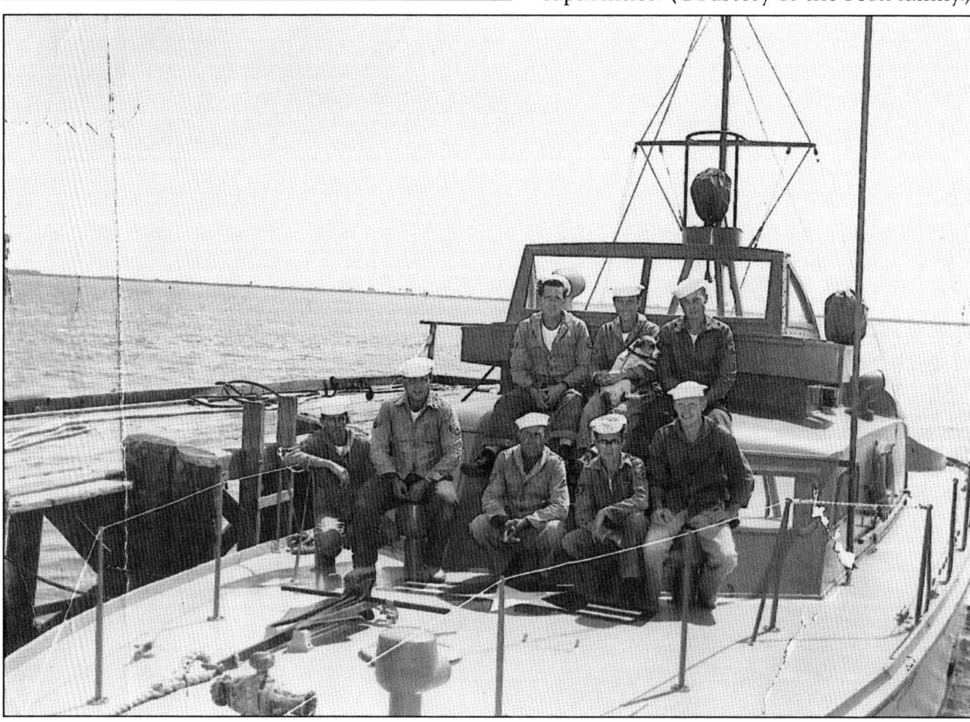

Clarence "Beau" Morse, one of George E. Morse's children, joined the Navy at age 18 in 1942 and served during World War II, then joined the Merchant Marines after the war. He met his wife, Margaret Carter, in 1947 while visiting his aunt Alice Wesley Carter, and they were married shortly afterward and moved back home to Murrells Inlet. (Courtesy of the Morse family.)

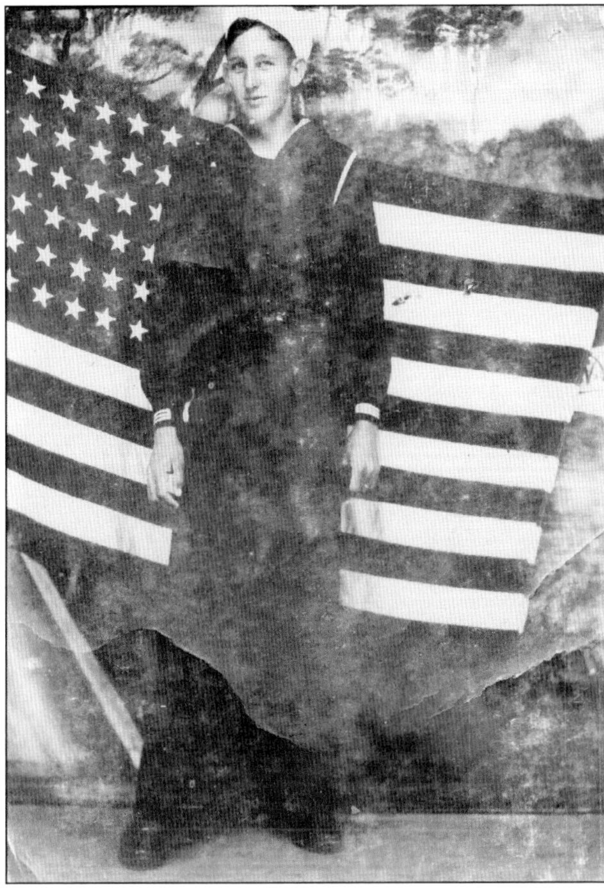

Clarence and Judy Morse are seen in front of the family home around 1952 at the site of Morse Park. His mother, Mae Wesley Morse, signed one of the first shellfish leases for 9.1 acres of shellfish bottoms with the South Carolina Board of Fisheries in 1932 for a fee of $2 per acre for the first year and escalating to $5 per acre in the fourth and subsequent years. (Courtesy of the Morse family.)

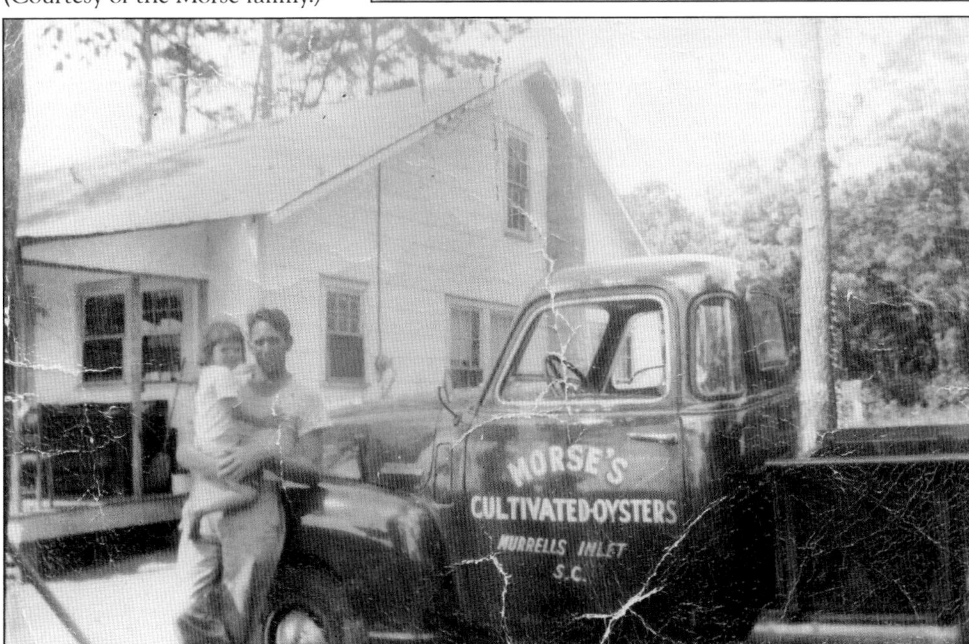

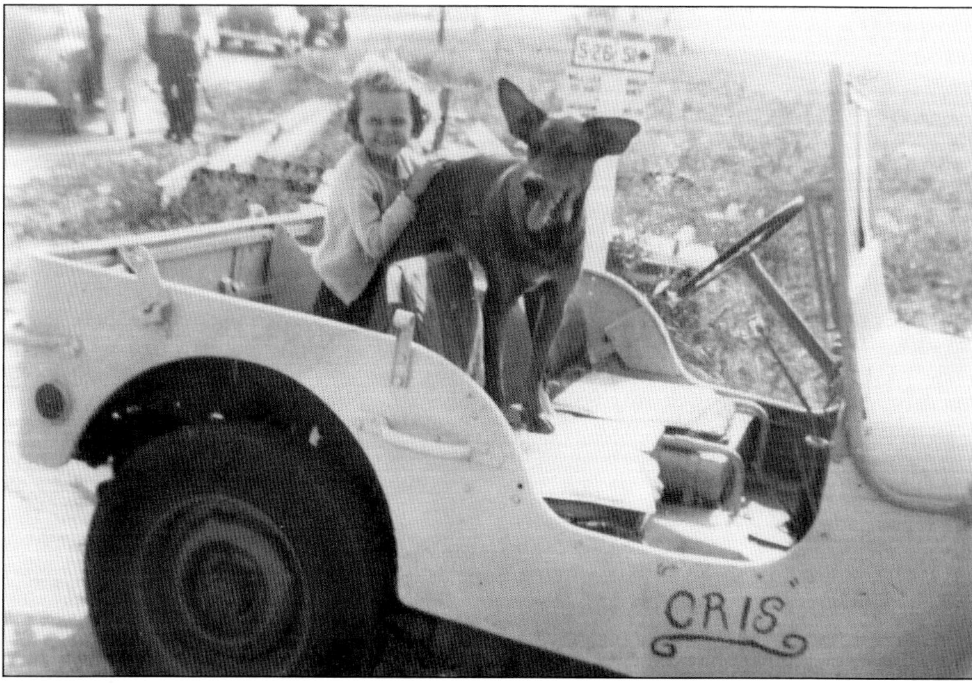

Brenda Eason and Pal are sitting in Maxine Oliver's jeep near the causeway to Garden City Beach around 1950. Maxine was the daughter of Capt. Mac Oliver and Teeny Vereen Oliver. At this time, the road to Garden City was still a dirt road leading to the causeway that crossed the marsh. (Courtesy of the Eason family.)

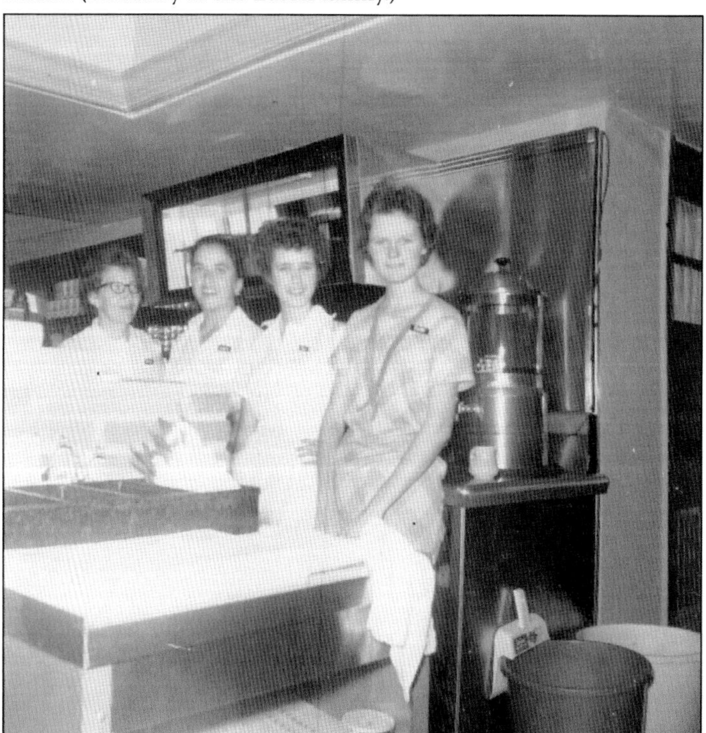

From left to right, Betty Patrick, Jeanette Sing, Mary Miller, and Brenda Eason are posing at the Bay Harbor Restaurant in the early 1960s. Bay Harbor Restaurant was built around 1953 just north of the Bay Harbor Motel. The Bay Harbor Grill had been on the north side of the larger building and moved into this location, making way for the bait and tackle shop. (Courtesy of the Eason family.)

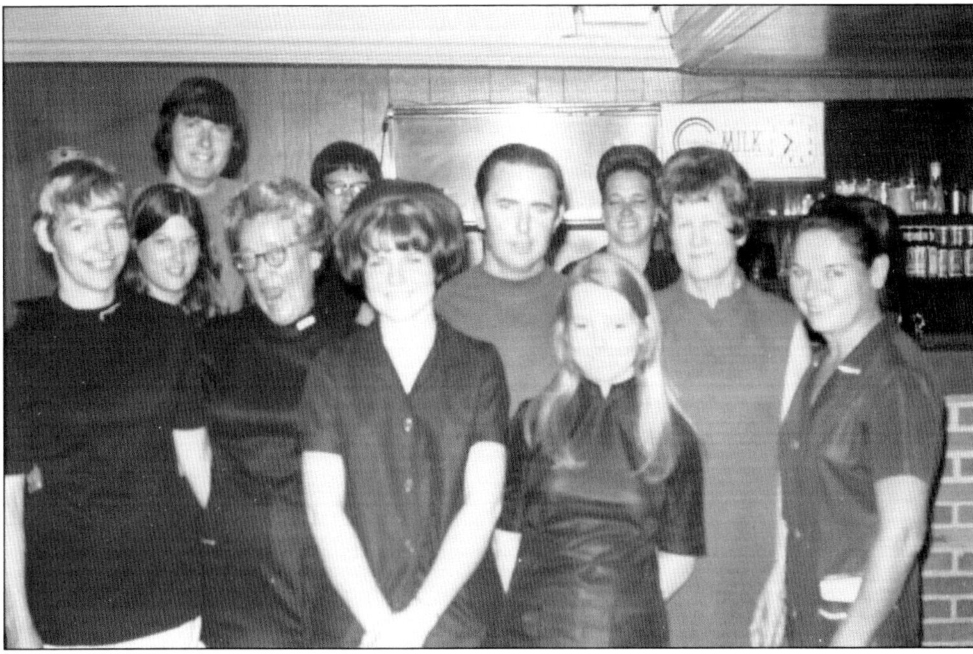

Shown around 1978, the staff of Bay Harbor Restaurant includes, from left to right, unidentified, Ramona "Monie" Wells, Wayne Ammons, Cubie White, unidentified (at rear), Karen McDowell, Ronnie Eason, Denise Eaddy, unidentified (in rear), Dot Eason, and unidentified; restaurant workers often spent more time with each other than their own family. (Courtesy of the Eason family.)

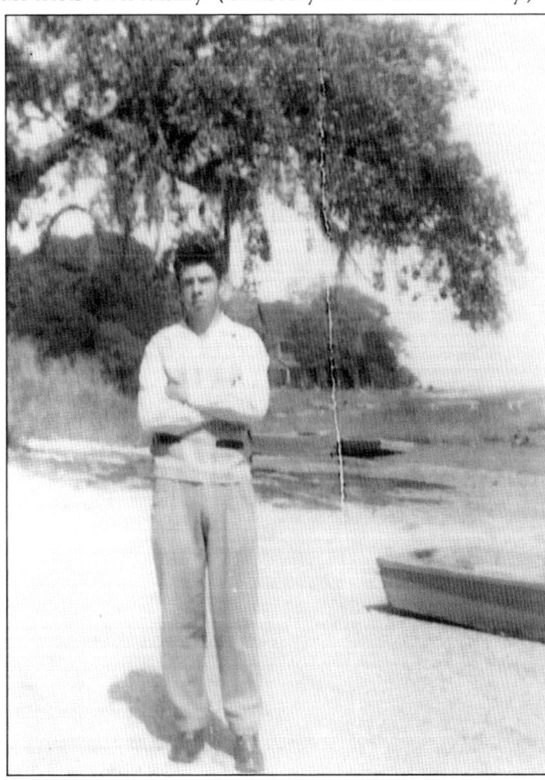

Jimmy Vick is standing at Buck Landing around 1955. Buck Landing was a popular swimming and gathering place for residents. Vaux Hall, home of Dal and Lizzie Johnson, is shown in the background over his shoulder. Jimmy was one of Capt. Ira Vick's five children and had just completed a tour of duty with the Navy. (Courtesy of Dick Vick.)

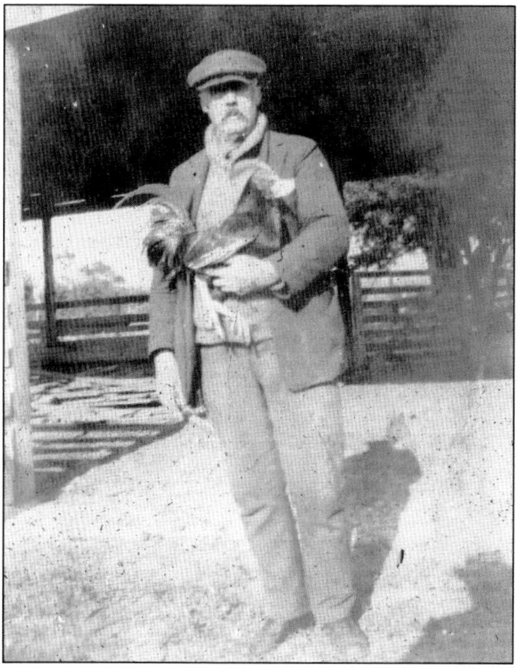

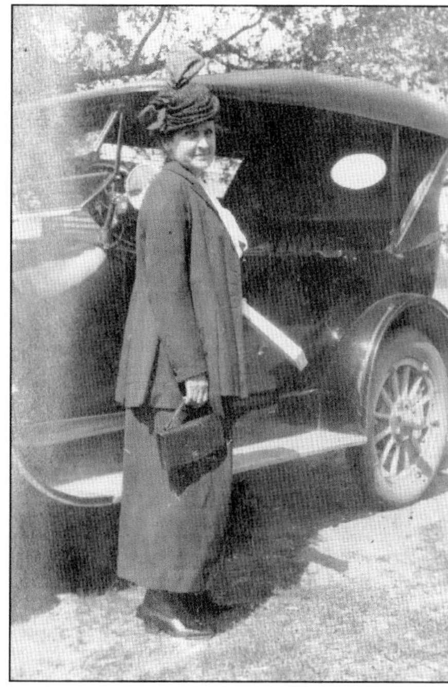

William Dalrymple "Dal" Johnson and Elizabeth "Lizzie" Johnson lived at Vaux Hall from around 1910 to their deaths and were instrumental in the establishment of the Murrells Inlet Presbyterian Church. He was also a noted hunter and sports writer, advertising Vaux Hall as a hunting and fishing lodge during the 1920s. She operated the post office at Vaux Hall for several years as well as a public library. (Both, courtesy of Dorothy Chappell.)

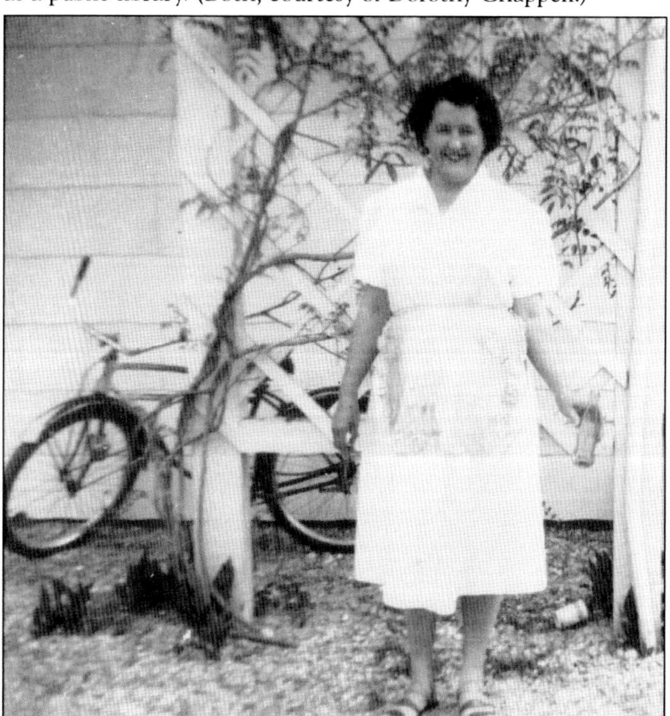

Jessie Johnson was a waitress and restaurant manager in the 1950s, shown here beside the Bay Harbor Grill around 1953. Hoss Johnson was one of her children who later became a well-know creek rat, fisherman, and boat captain. Jessie also worked at several other restaurants, including Lokey's Café. (Courtesy of the Eason family.)

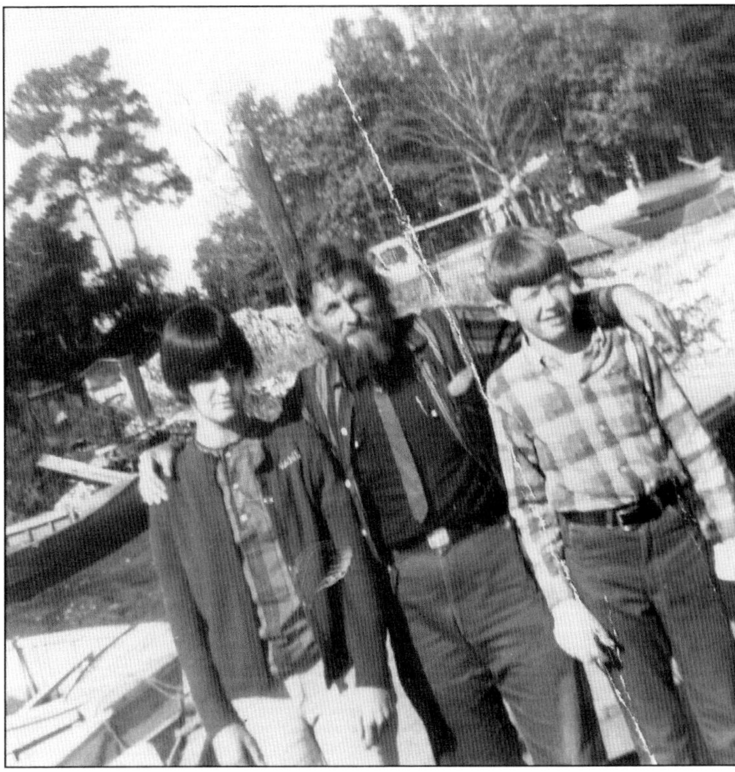

Jodell Hughes (left) and Gerald Benton (right) are pictured with a unidentified traveler at the landing behind Nance's around 1966. Jodell was one of the early volunteers with the Murrells Inlet–Garden City Rescue Squad and was well known for her work with them. Gerald became a licensed captain and worked on the construction of the Murrells Inlet jetties in the late 1970s. (Courtesy of Jodell Johnson-Bridges.)

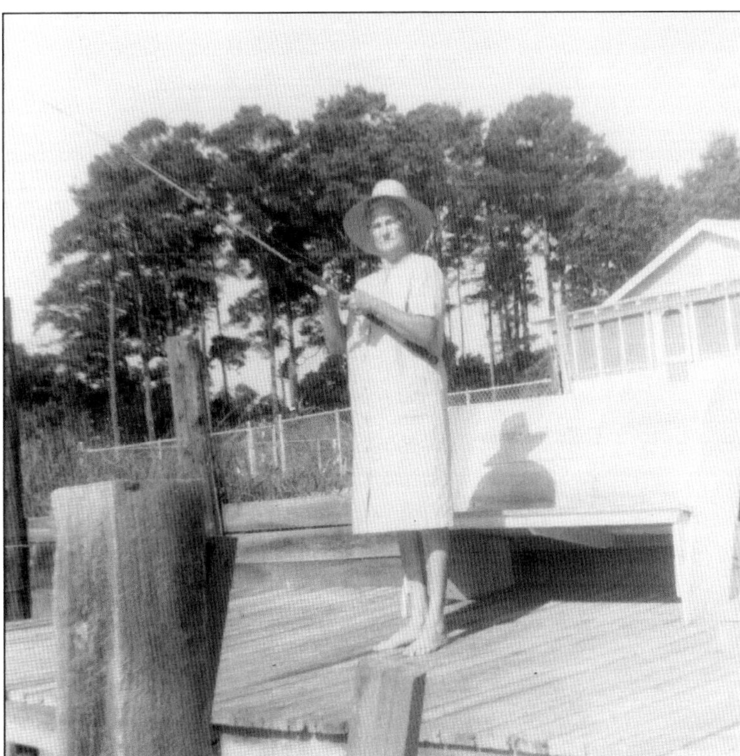

Ozette Hughes is shown fishing off of the dock behind the Nance house just north of the present-day Nance's restaurant. The Hughes family was renting a house on the south side of the property from the Nances at this time. Ozette ran the small dining room at Hughes Landing for breakfast and lunch during the early 1960s. (Courtesy of Jodell Johnson-Bridges.)

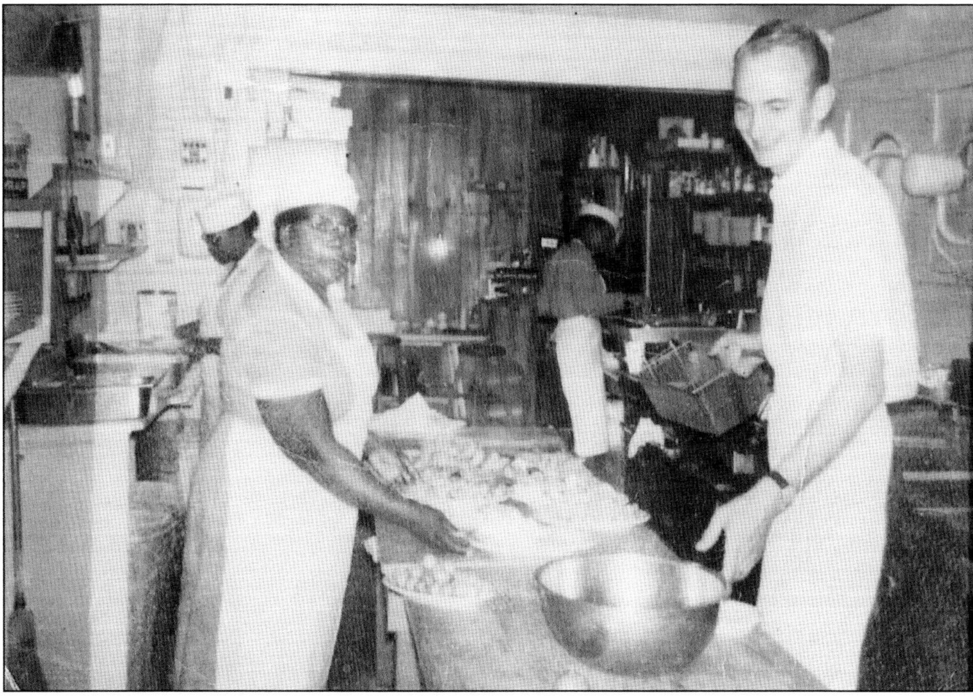

From left to right, Rebecca Green, Dora Neil, Earl Lee Robinson, and Wallace Lee are working at Lee's Inlet Kitchen in the early 1960s. Dora was from Plantersville, and Rebecca was from Marion, and they both lived on-site during the season. Wallace was one of the children of Pearl and Eford Lee and went on to open several of his own restaurants in Murrells Inlet. (Courtesy of the Lee family.)

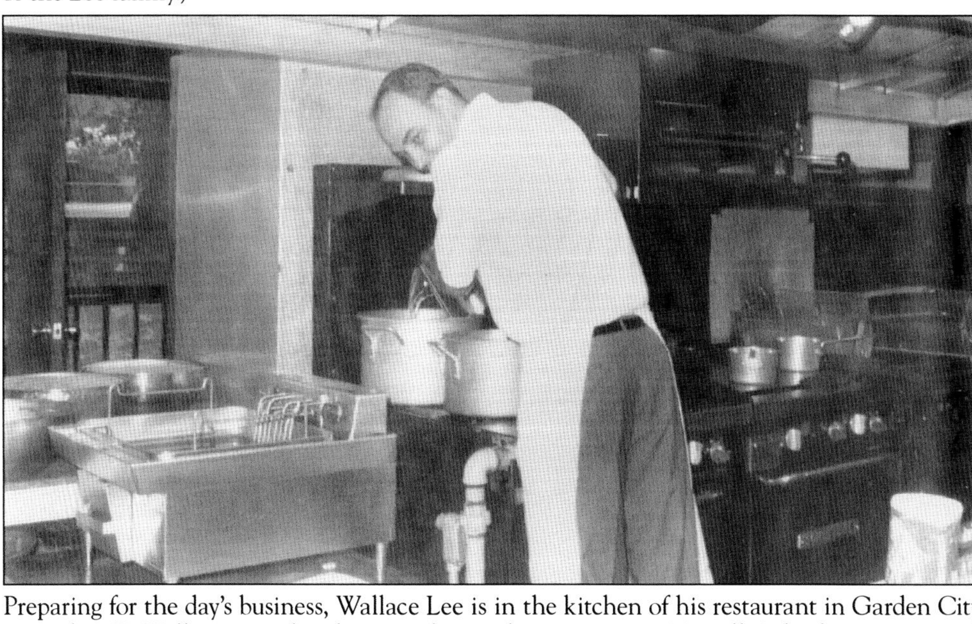

Preparing for the day's business, Wallace Lee is in the kitchen of his restaurant in Garden City around 1967. Wallace owned and operated several restaurants in Murrells Inlet for over 40 years and was an accomplished fisherman as well, running a fishing guide service in his later years. (Courtesy of the McKenzie family.)

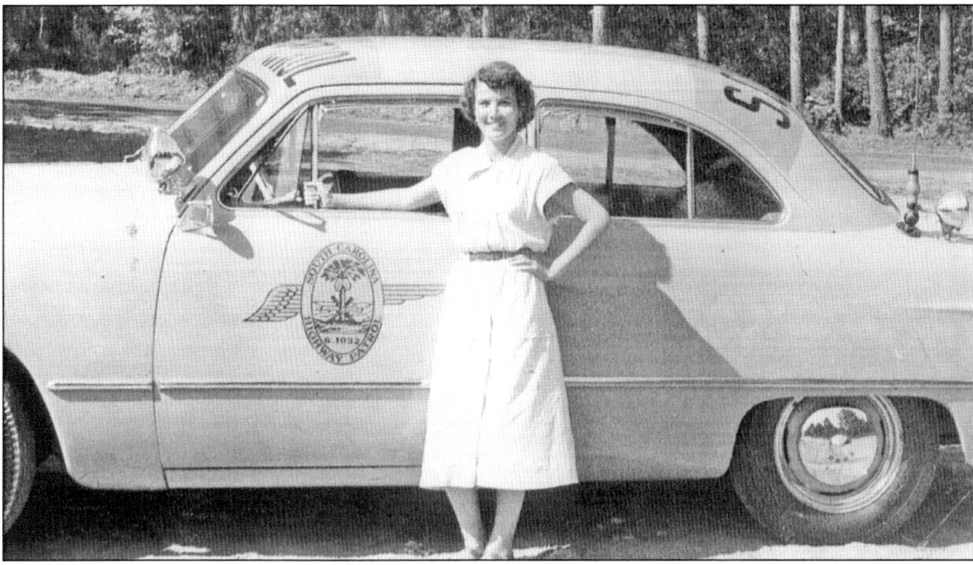

Shortly after Lee's Inlet Kitchen opened, Alzata Lee stands in front of one of the local highway patrol cars in 1948. Alzata has been a fixture at this restaurant for over 60 years and was crowned Miss Myrtle Beach High in 1946. (Courtesy of the Lee family.)

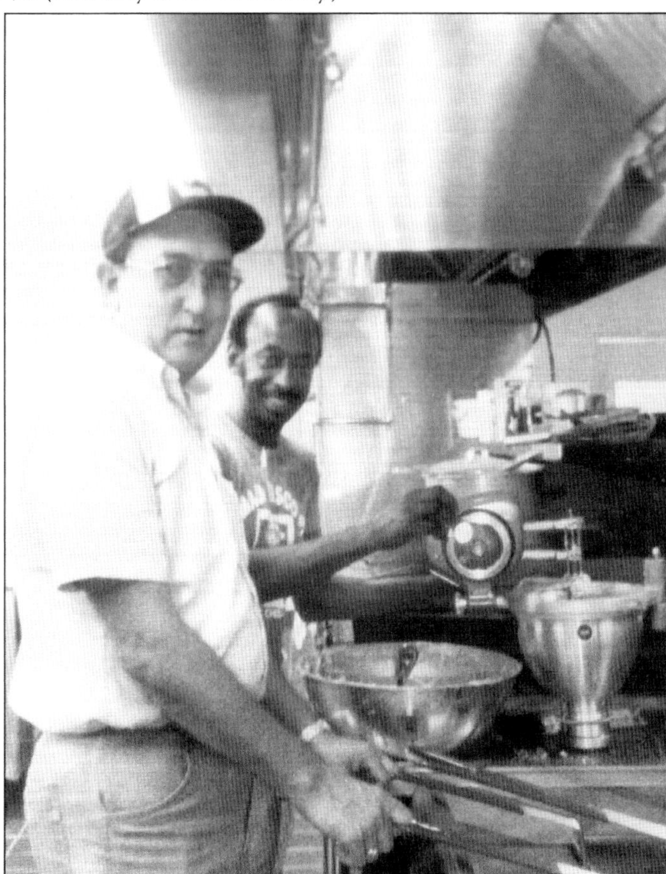

Billy Lee (left) and Earl Lee Robinson are at work in Lee's Inlet Kitchen around 1982. Billy and Wallace were the children of Pearl and Eford Lee and grew up in the restaurant. They went on to run seafood restaurants in Murrells Inlet and Garden City. (Courtesy of the Lee family.)

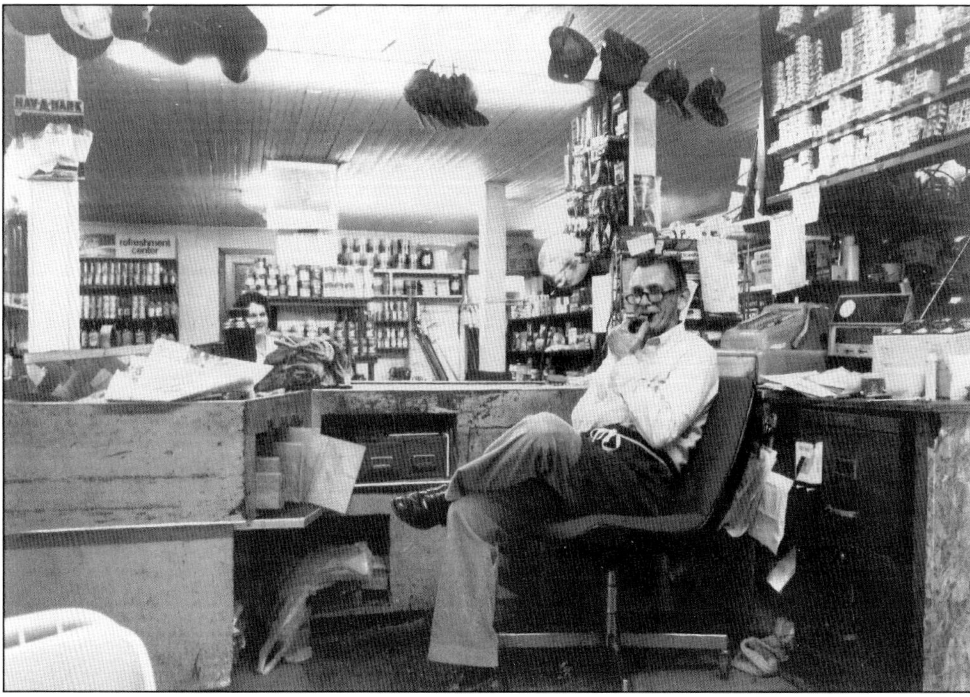

Al Strickland is shown relaxing behind the counter around 1985 at Strickland's Grocery. Al was one of Capt. Charlie Strickland's sons who returned to Murrells Inlet in 1971 to help operate the store. Al ran the store from 1975 to 1989, carrying on the same tradition of service expected from a country store, with a line of fresh-cut meats and produce, local fish, and other necessities. (Courtesy of the Strickland family.)

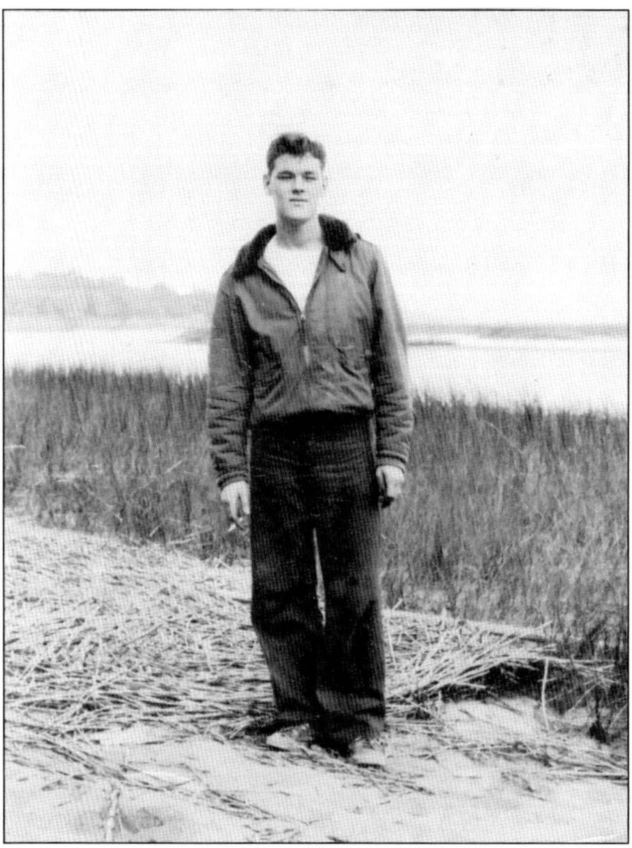

Tommy Chandler Jr. is standing at the edge of the marsh behind the Hermitage after he got out of the Navy around 1952. Tommy and Alex Sing joined the Navy under the buddy program, which allowed friends to serve in the same unit, in 1948. Luther Smith's Landing is the white building in the background. (Courtesy of Tookie Chandler Jones.)

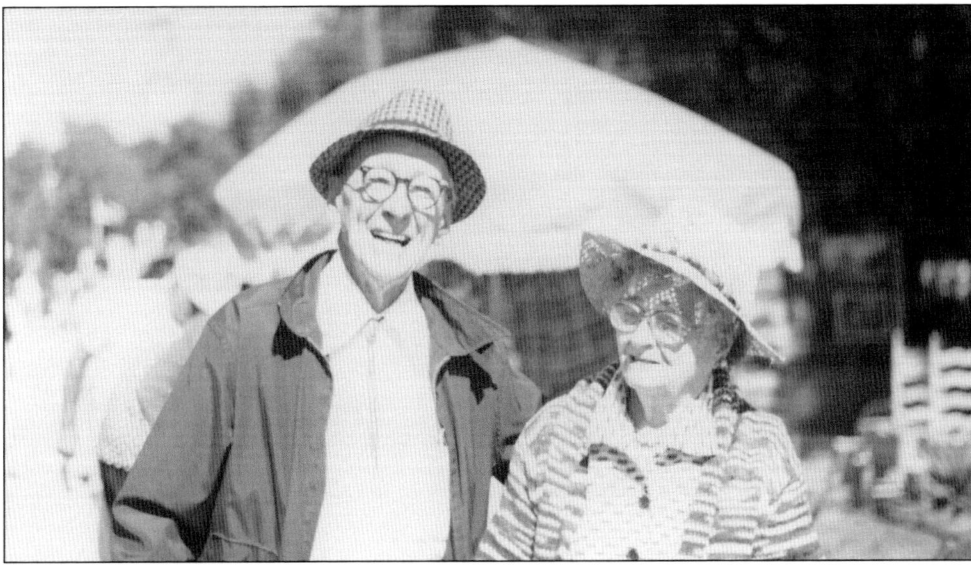

Clarke A. Willcox Jr. and his wife, Lillian Rose Willcox, are pictured at the Murrells Inlet Outdoor Arts and Crafts Festival in 1973. Clarke was local author and nurseryman who lived at the Hermitage from 1956 until his passing in 1989. He was well known for his book *Musings of a Hermit* and his storytelling. His father, Clarke A. Willcox Sr., purchased the Hermitage and Wachesaw Plantation in 1910 to retire in Murrells Inlet. (Courtesy of Tookie Chandler Jones.)

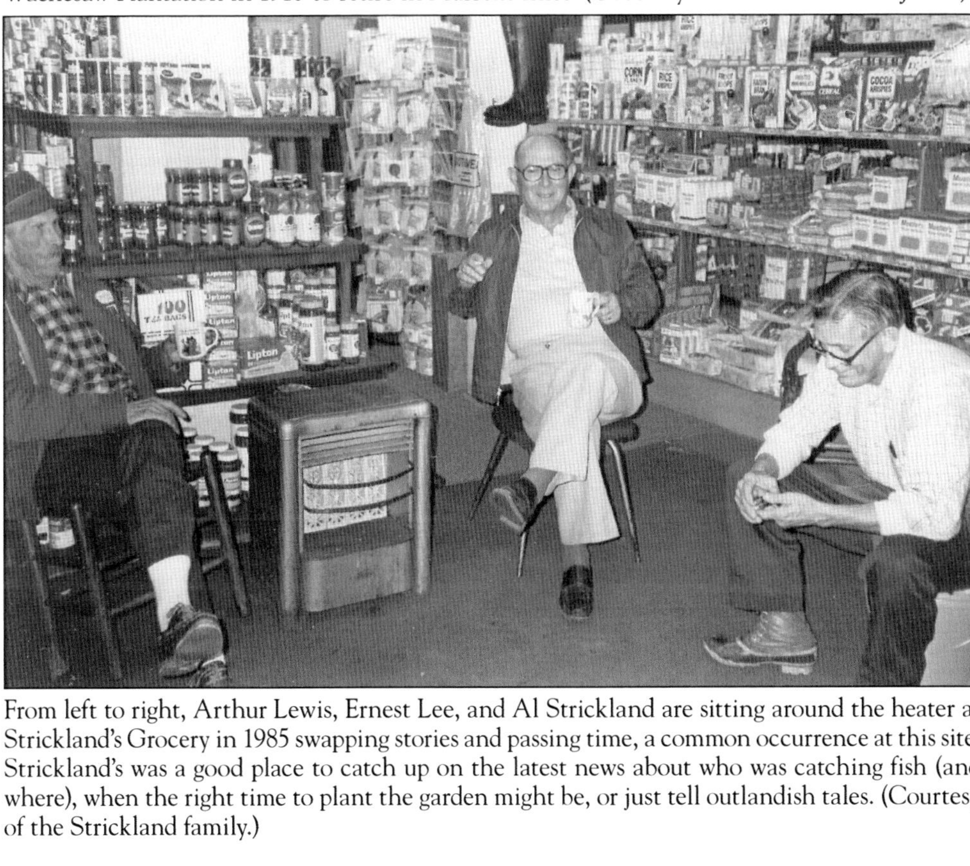

From left to right, Arthur Lewis, Ernest Lee, and Al Strickland are sitting around the heater at Strickland's Grocery in 1985 swapping stories and passing time, a common occurrence at this site. Strickland's was a good place to catch up on the latest news about who was catching fish (and where), when the right time to plant the garden might be, or just tell outlandish tales. (Courtesy of the Strickland family.)

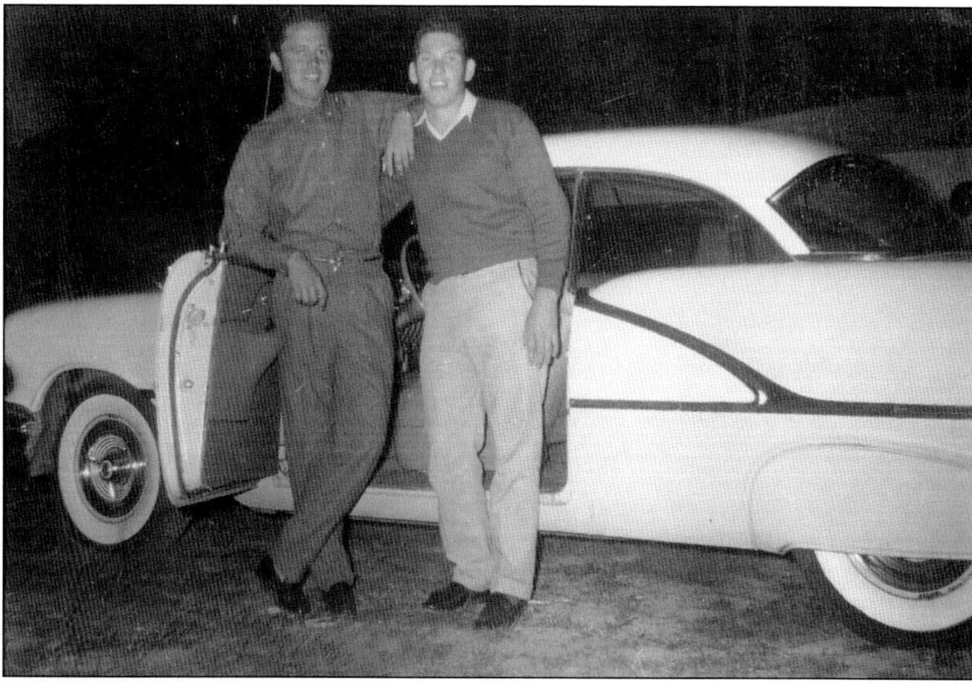

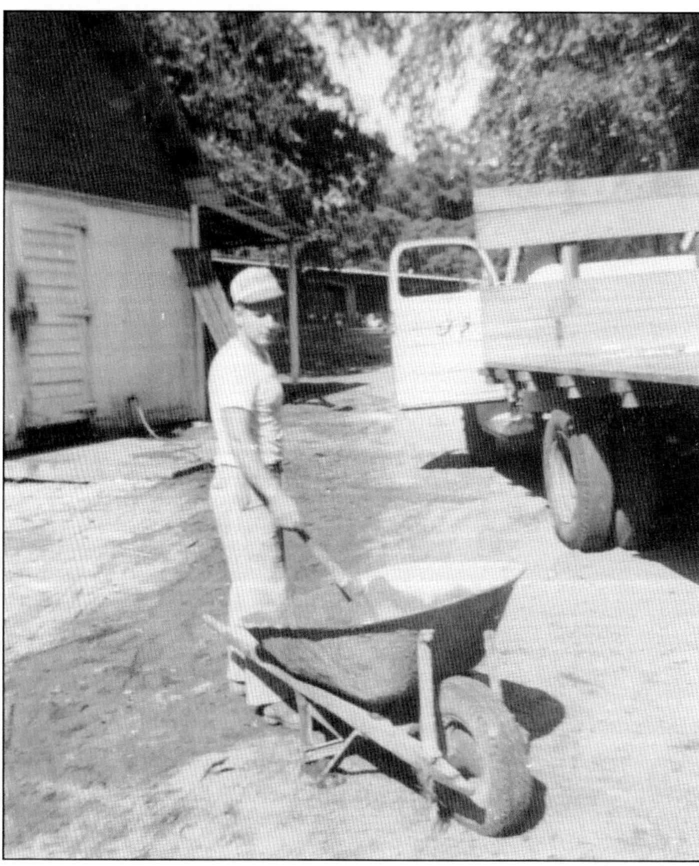

Winston Perry (left) and Douglas "Brownie" Brown, shown 1952, stand with Brownie's 1952 car. Winston was a local baitman and ran Perry's Bait and Tackle for many years on the creek next to Anchor Marina (now Bovines). (Courtesy Pearline Brown.)

Charles Welch is working in front of the chicken cooler at Wagon Wheel Farms about 1960. Wagon Wheel Farms had originally been operated as a turkey farming operation and was later used to raise chickens for slaughter. In the 1960s and 1970s, Wagon Wheel Farms raised laying hens for egg production. (Courtesy of the Welch family.)

Andrew Keith lived near Wachesaw on the Old River Road and had an ox team that he used to move materials and passengers from the landing at Wachesaw into the village. He is pictured here standing at Vaux Hall around 1921. Andrew and George Keith, with the assistance of Buck and Brandy, two stout oxen, moved six massive slabs of red English sandstone from a spot near Wachesaw where they had been buried for a century (they had been part of the old St. John the Evangelist Episcopal Church) to be used for the steps to the Belin Methodist Church sanctuary in 1925. (Courtesy of Dorothy Chappell.)

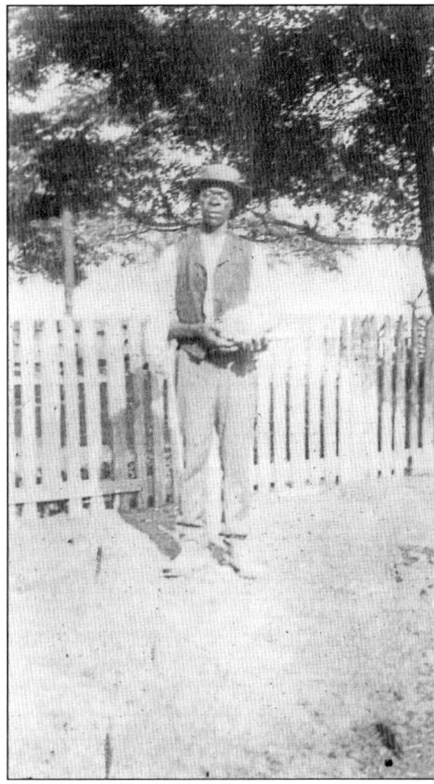

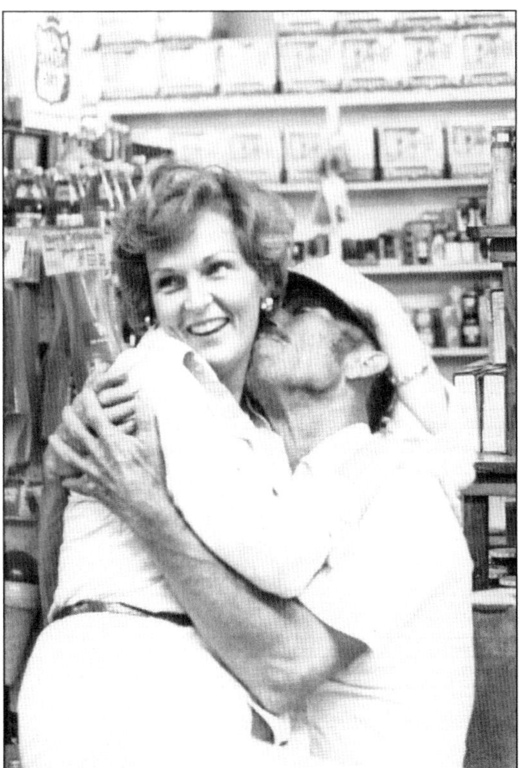

Arthur Lewis was a well-known and well-loved character (and a great fisherman and farmer) who frequently appeared at Strickland's Grocery to tell stories, pass the time, or help fry fish during the 1970s and 1980s. He is shown here cutting up with Kay Winesett, a Marion native who moved to Murrells Inlet in the 1970s. (Courtesy of Garrett Winesett.)

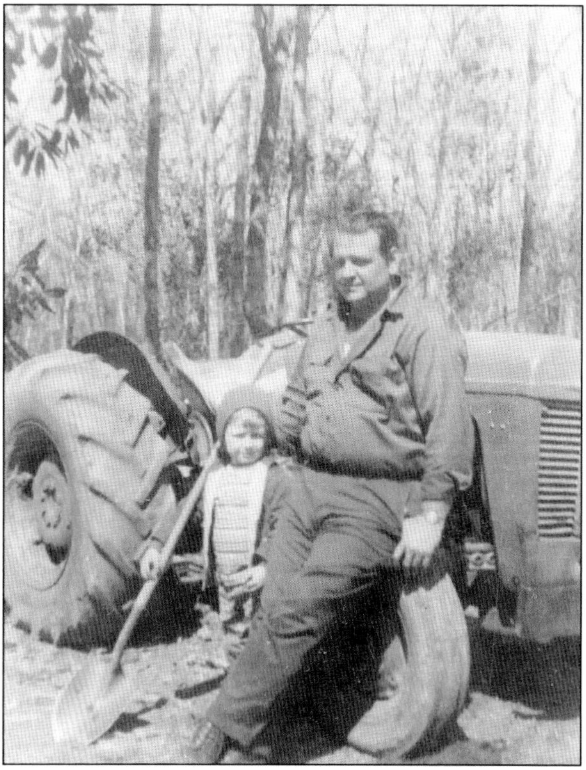

Leon McKenzie and his son Jeff are standing beside his Massey Ferguson tractor around 1970. Leon's father, Simeon McKenzie, was a farmer who lived on McDowell Shortcut, and Leon was known for farming and tractor work; he would plow people's gardens and use his bushhog to cut brush. He also made a red pepper vinegar barbecue sauce that was a local favorite. (Courtesy of the McKenzie family.)

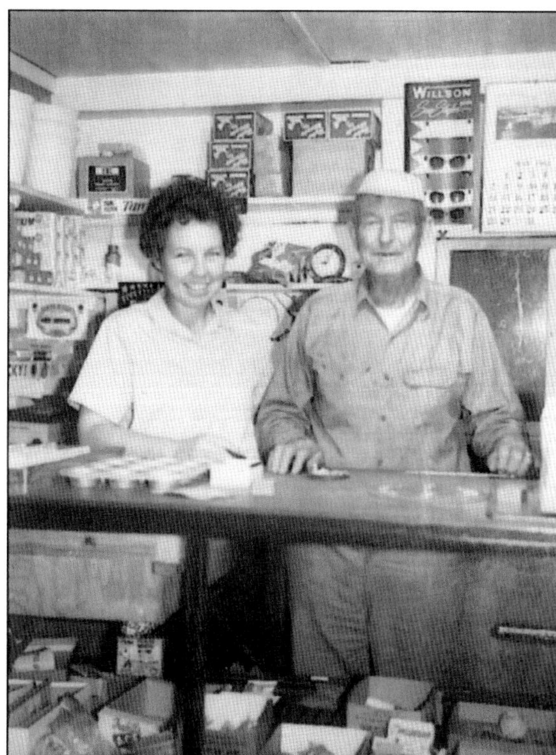

Jessie and Annie Hughes are shown behind the counter at Hughes Landing in 1964. Hughes Landing was the southern focus of creek fishing in Murrells Inlet, with a small channel that led to Oaks Creek, and was a gathering place for locals and visitors alike. Hughes Landing also had sites for camping and a small dining room that served breakfast and lunch. (Courtesy of the Hughes family.)

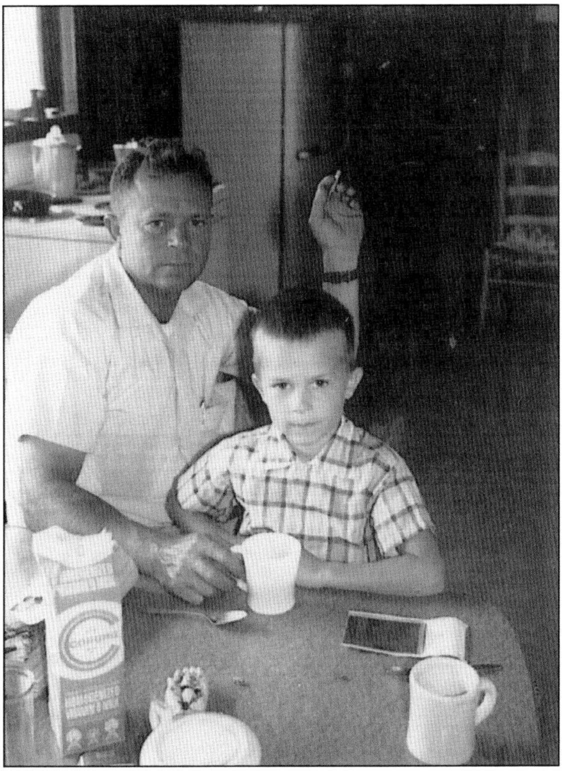

Wesley Hughes Sr. and Wesley Hughes Jr. are shown sitting at the kitchen table around 1960. Wesley Sr. was the son of Jessie Hughes and worked in the construction of roads and excavation of channels around Murrells Inlet. Many of the channels connected into Murrells Inlet contained shallow deposits of coquina, a local limestone material used to construct roads. Wesley Hughes Sr. and Jessie Murdock operated a construction company to help in the growth of the area in the 1950s and 1960s. (Courtesy of the Hughes family.)

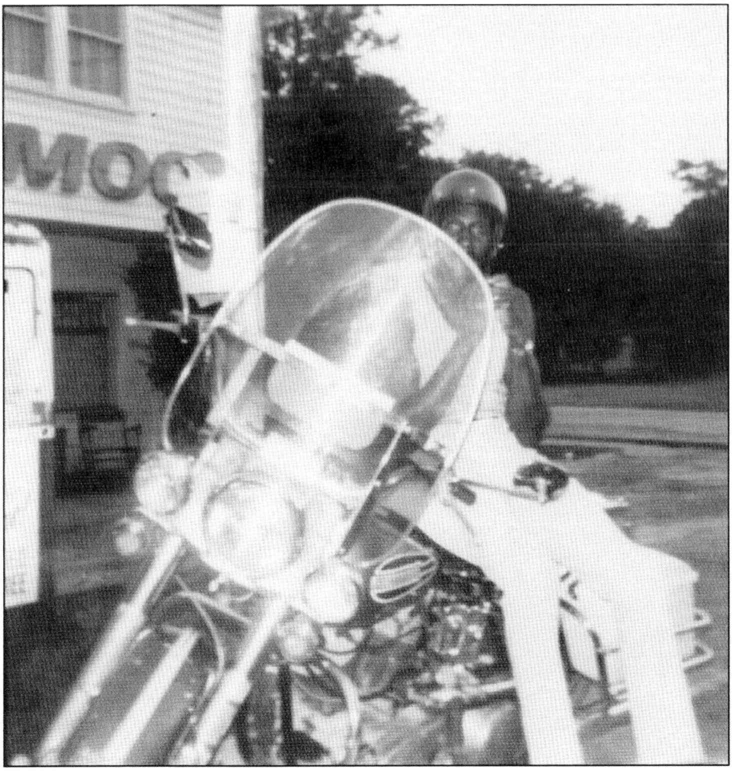

John Singleton is pictured on his Harley Davidson motorcycle in 1973 at the gas pumps of Strickland's Grocery. John was a heavy equipment operator who was involved with the construction of numerous roads and drainage projects and worked with the State Highway Department, the City of Myrtle Beach, and Brookgreen Gardens. John can always be found working with community events, including the Gordon Tabernacle Choir. (Courtesy of the Strickland family.)

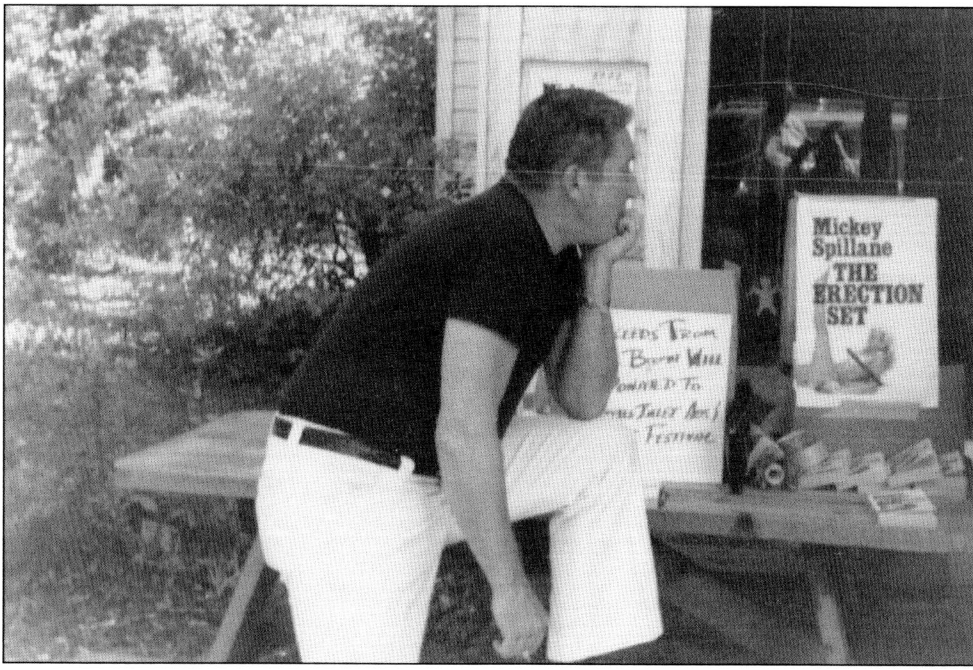

Mickey Spillane was a Murrells Inlet resident who visited in the 1950s and fell in love with the area. He moved to Jordan Landing and raised a family there and was a well-known author made famous by the Mike Hammer crime mystery series. He was a fixture at the local hangouts and participated in numerous community events, including the Murrells Inlet Outdoor Arts and Crafts Festival. (Courtesy of the Gordon family.)

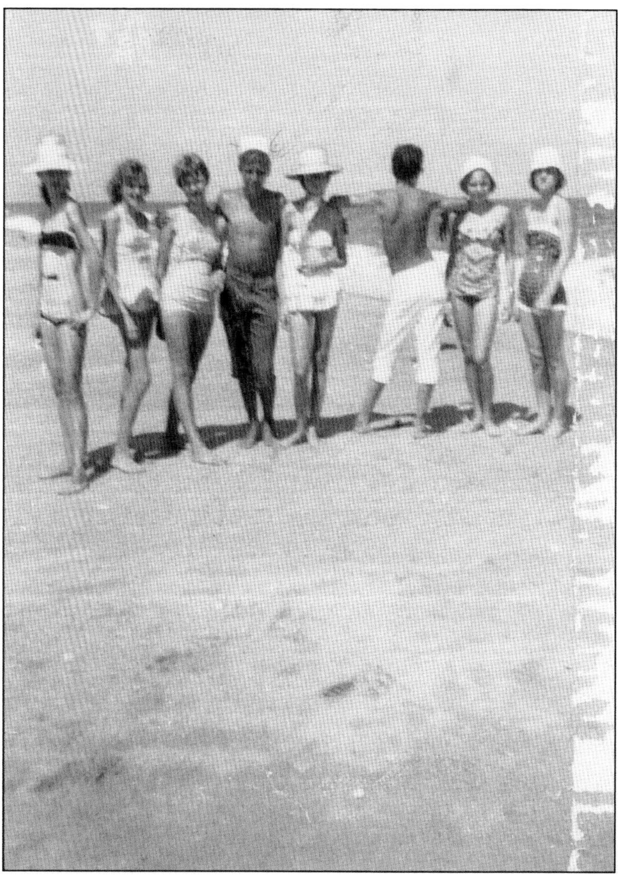

From left to right, Carolyn Eason, Sandra Ammons, Patricia Joyner, Leroy Altman, Brenda Eason, Jack Patrick, Nancy Altman, and Frances Joyner are hanging out at the Garden City Beach around 1960. Garden City was scarcely developed at this time, with scattered beach houses near the causeway from Murrells Inlet. (Courtesy of the Eason family.)

Seven

PLACES

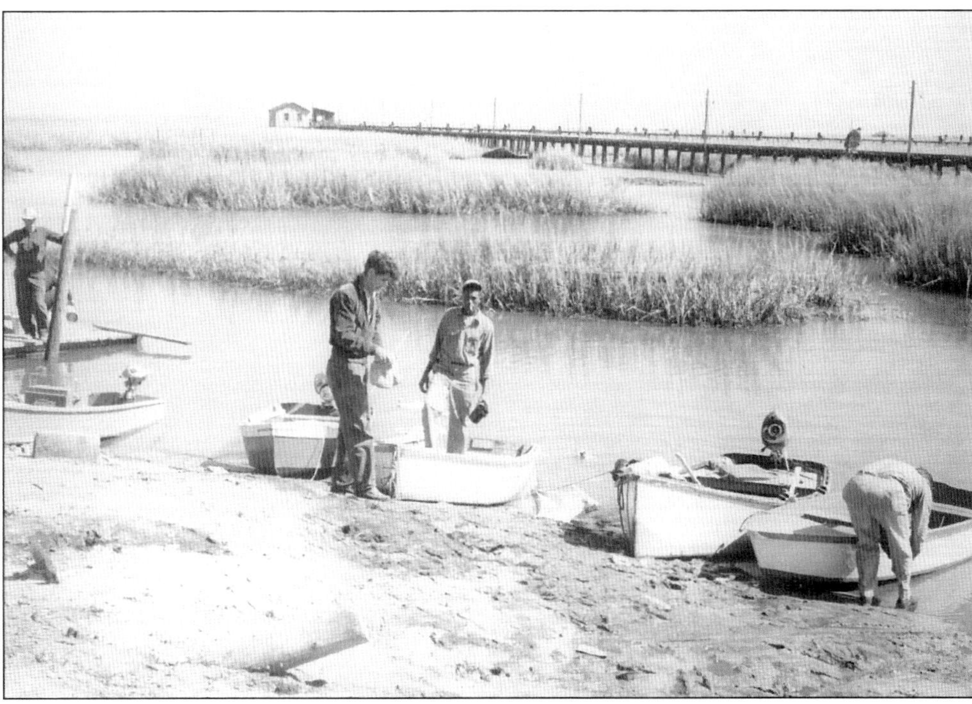

Alex Sing (second from left) and Marchie Smalls (center, standing in boat) are shown at the landing behind Alex's Bait and Tackle around 1955, which was after the channel adjacent to the high ground had been excavated with a dragline but before the marina basin had been dredged. At this time, fishermen could rent small wooden fishing boats to go out into the creek. (Courtesy of the Sing family.)

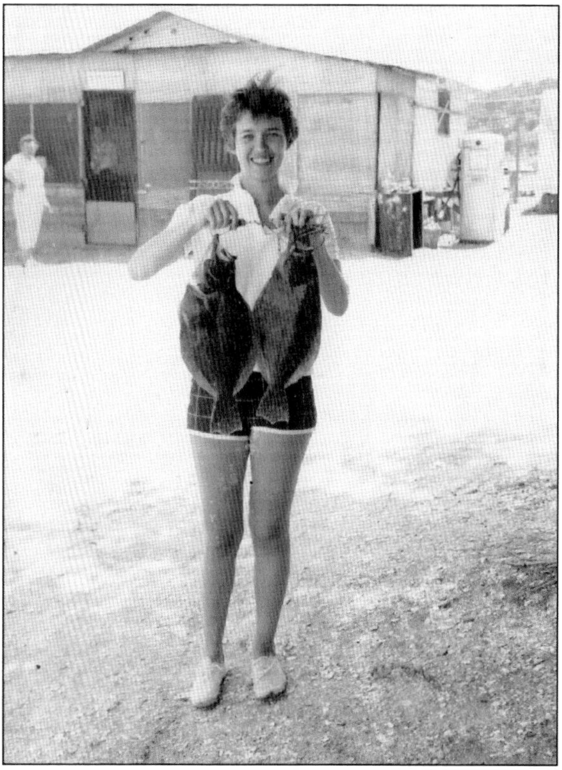

Joyce Hughes is showing off two nice flounders at Hughes Landing in about 1962. Her parents, Jessie and Annie Hughes, operated Hughes Landing at the south end of Murrells Inlet during the 1960s and 1970s and provided fishermen a place to launch boats and get fishing supplies and gas; it also had spaces for camping for visiting fishermen. (Courtesy of the Hughes family.)

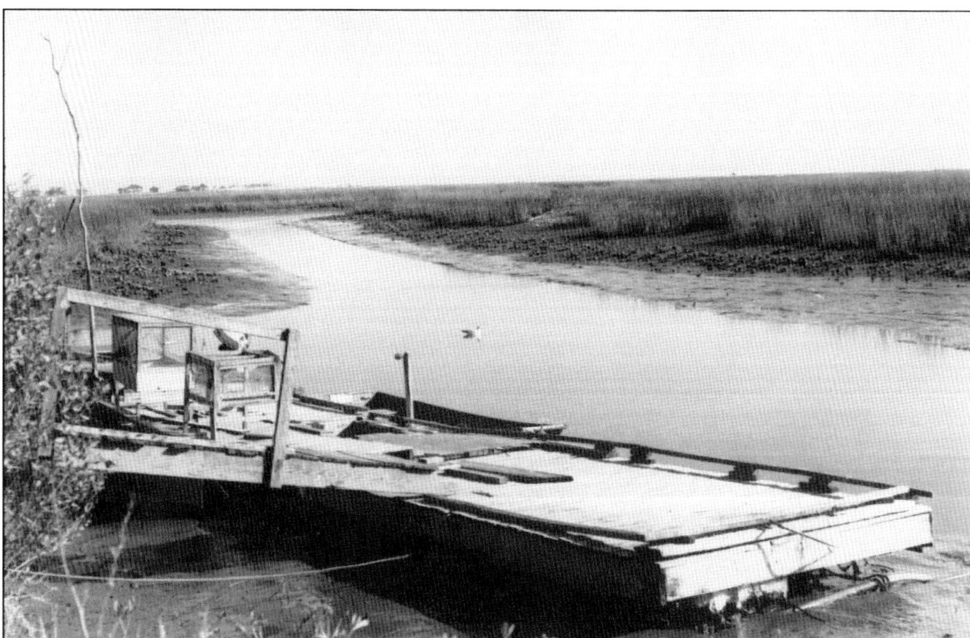

The oyster dock at Morse's Landing is pictured in 1979 at low tide while all the creek men are out gathering oysters and clams. The Morse family had shellfish leases in Murrells Inlet since the state started the leasing program in 1932 and operated an oyster roast during the season from the 1940s until the oyster roast closed in 1979. (Courtesy of the Strickland family.)

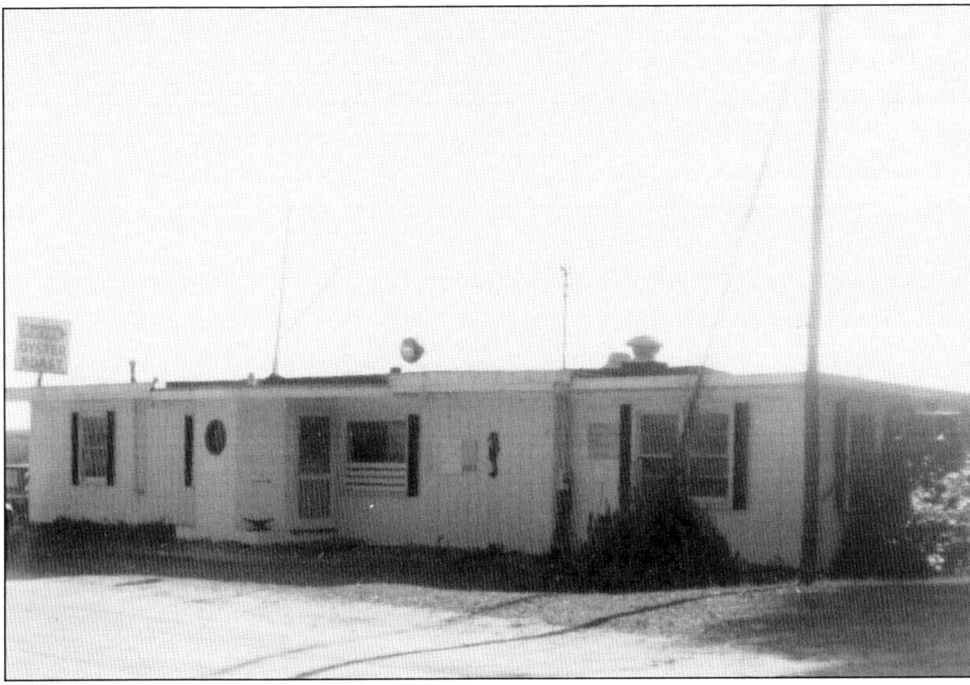

Morse's Oyster Roast was a wood-framed restaurant that specialized in roasted oysters and clams from the 1940s to 1978. Clarence "Beau" Morse and his family operated this restaurant and drew large crowds every weekend during oyster season. The first oyster roast was originally up close to Highway 17, but it was moved to the creek in 1959. The Morse family moved into the oyster roast building for a short time during the 1950s after the family house caught fire and had to be rebuilt. (Courtesy of the Morse family.)

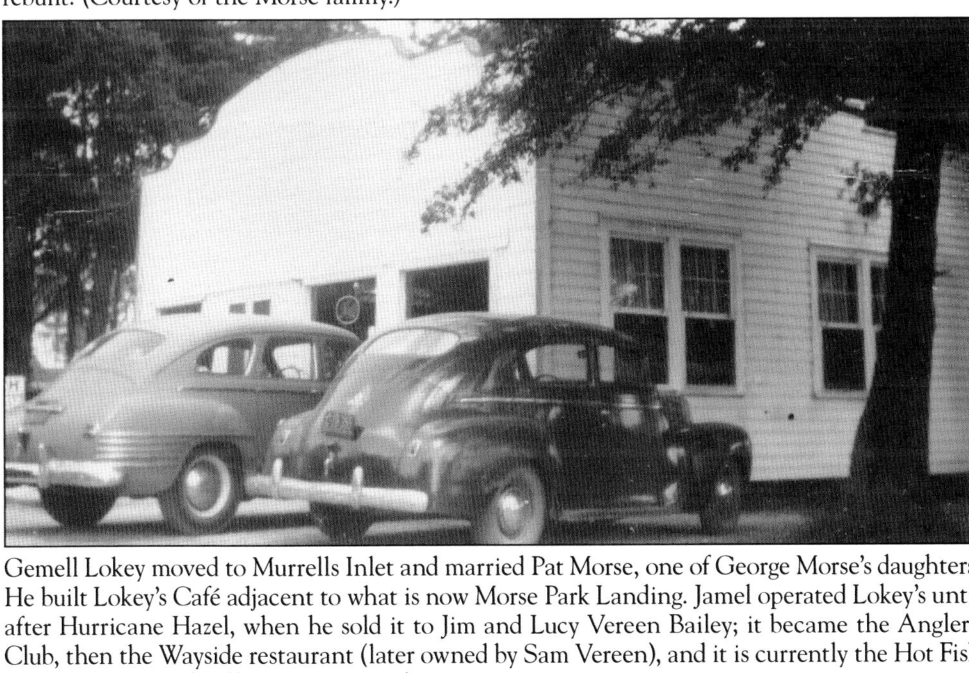

Gemell Lokey moved to Murrells Inlet and married Pat Morse, one of George Morse's daughters. He built Lokey's Café adjacent to what is now Morse Park Landing. Jamel operated Lokey's until after Hurricane Hazel, when he sold it to Jim and Lucy Vereen Bailey; it became the Angler's Club, then the Wayside restaurant (later owned by Sam Vereen), and it is currently the Hot Fish Club. (Courtesy of Kelley Lee-Dorman.)

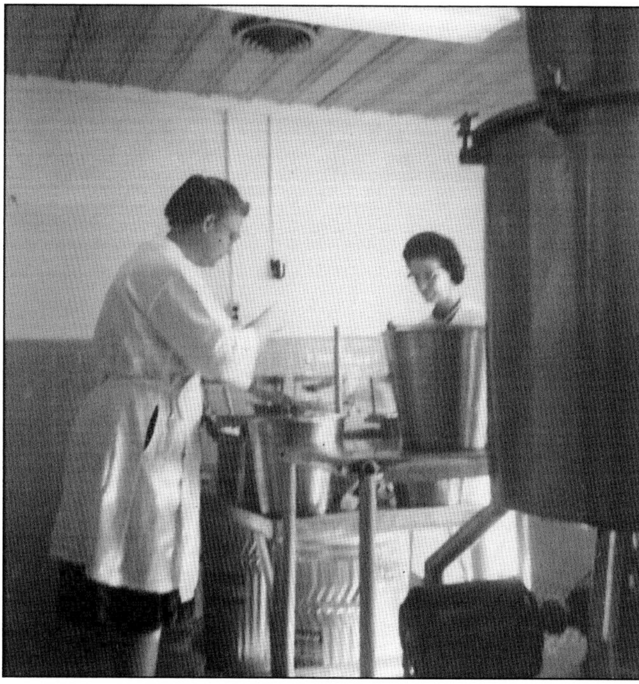

Wagon Wheel Farms was started in the 1940s as a turkey farm; it operated as a chicken-processing facility, raising live chickens and cleaning them, and later as an egg production facility. In 1965, Elsie Alford (left) and Lee Gause are shown working in the egg house, cracking eggs for blending. (Courtesy of the Welch family.)

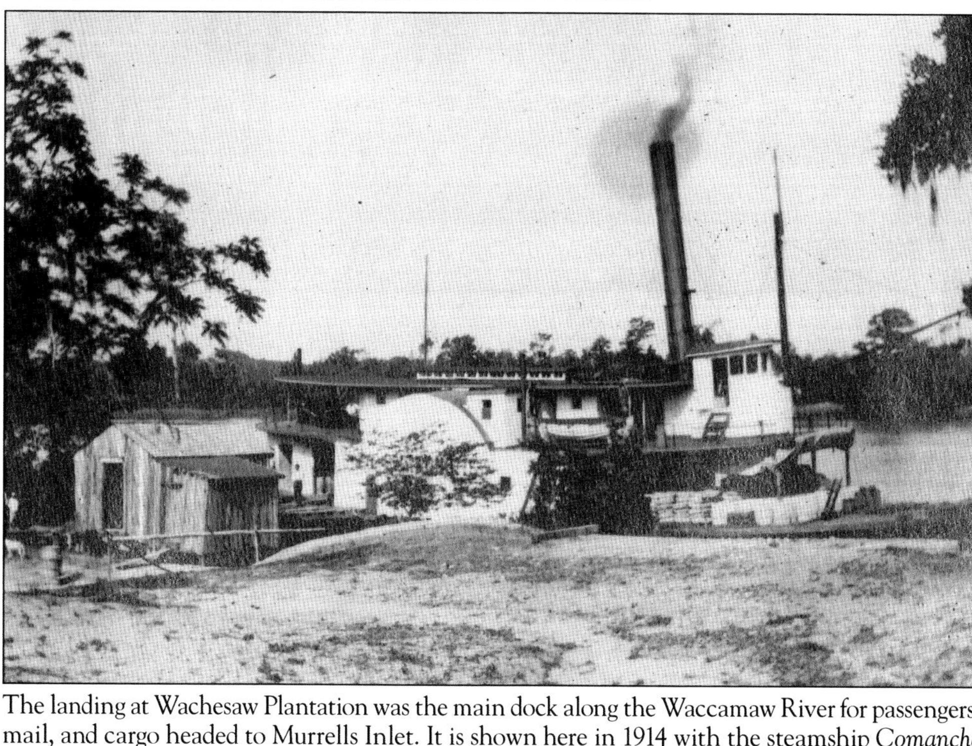

The landing at Wachesaw Plantation was the main dock along the Waccamaw River for passengers, mail, and cargo headed to Murrells Inlet. It is shown here in 1914 with the steamship *Comanche* leaving the dock, headed back to Conway. The site of the present-day marina had been rice fields and a dirt landing up until around the 1950s, when Danny Pendergrass developed the WaccaWache Marina by dredging the old rice fields into a marina basin and building the docks and marina store. (Courtesy of Dorothy Chappell.)

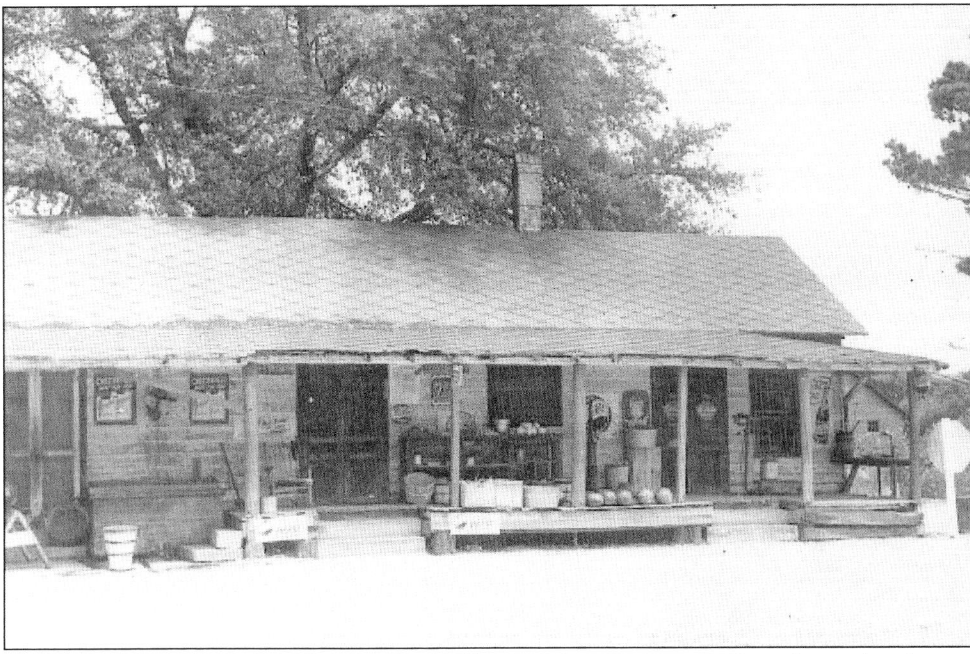

Eason's Store was operated by Edwin Eason and his sons for over 60 years where the road to the river and Wesley Road intersected. It was removed in the mid-1960s to make way for the construction of the Highway 17 Bypass. For many years, this store was a gathering place where one could purchase everything needed, including fresh fish and vegetables in season, and a pot-bellied stove was a good place to hear the latest tales and gossip. (Courtesy of Dorothy Chappell.)

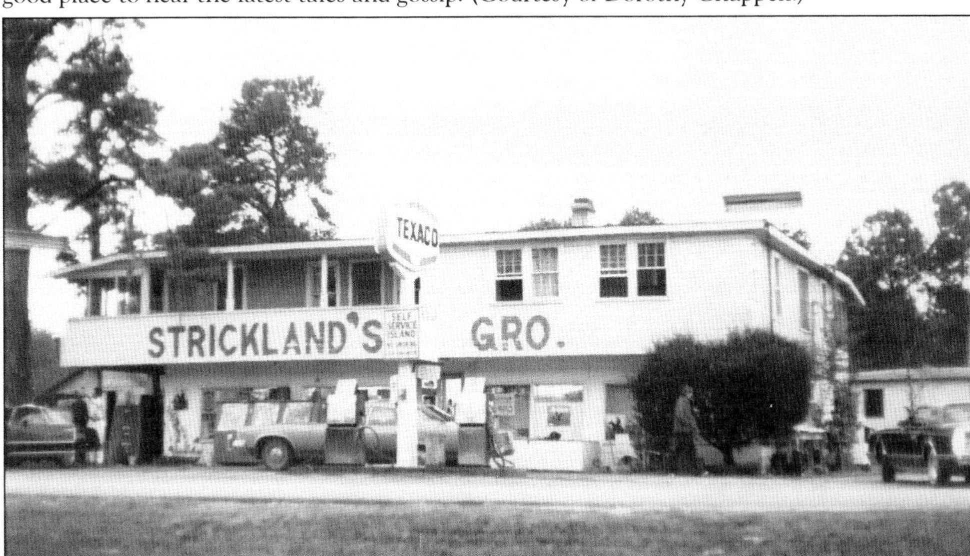

Strickland's Grocery, shown in 1979, was a community gathering place for locals and visitors alike. Joe Parker built the store in 1940, and it was owned and operated by John Ed and Marion Byrd, Herman Gordon, and R.T. Bone before Charlie Strickland purchased it in 1952. The upstairs had two apartments and a wraparound porch on the side and rear, which served as the setting for family dinners every Sunday provided by Grace Lawrimore Strickland for children and grandchildren. (Courtesy of the Strickland family.)

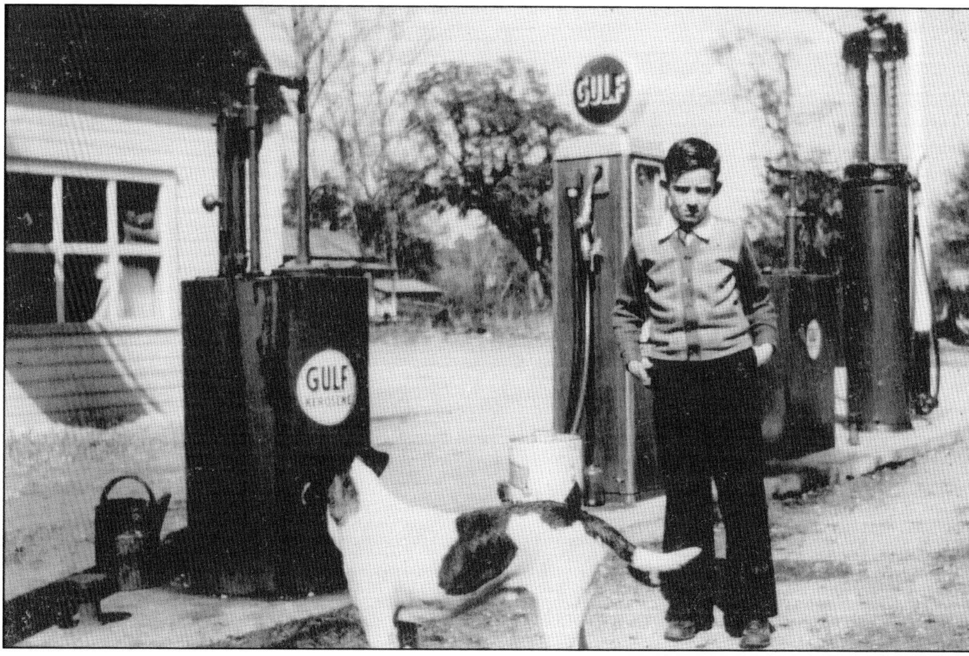

Wesley Gordon and Spot are in front of the gas pumps at the store Herman Gordon bought from John Ed and Marion Byrd around 1948. It was built by Joe Parker. Herman Gordon sold this store to R.T. Bone; Capt. Charlie Strickland later owned it. Creel Oil from Conway was the Gulf Oil distributor at that time. (Courtesy of the Gordon family.)

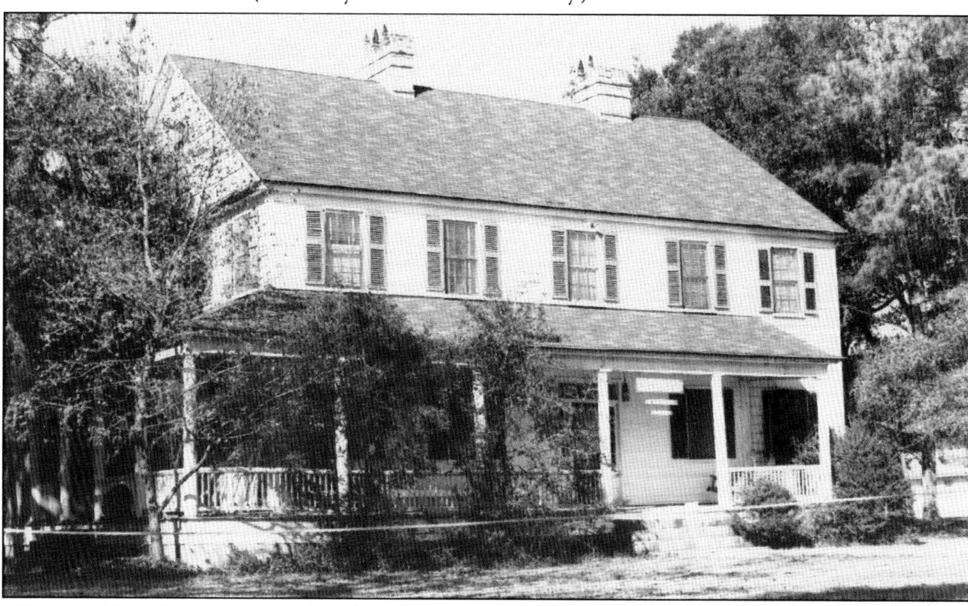

Woodland Landing was one of the boat landings where locals launched small boats and gathered for fish fries and oyster roasts. Many local children learned to swim at the shell landing in front of the house. The Woodland house (shown from 1979) was destroyed by fire in 1980. In the late 1800s, it had been the Vick homeplace where Capt. Ira Vick was born, and it was purchased by Mary Ingram Pate in 1932 as part of the Woodland tract for a hunting and fishing lodge. (Courtesy of the Strickland family.)

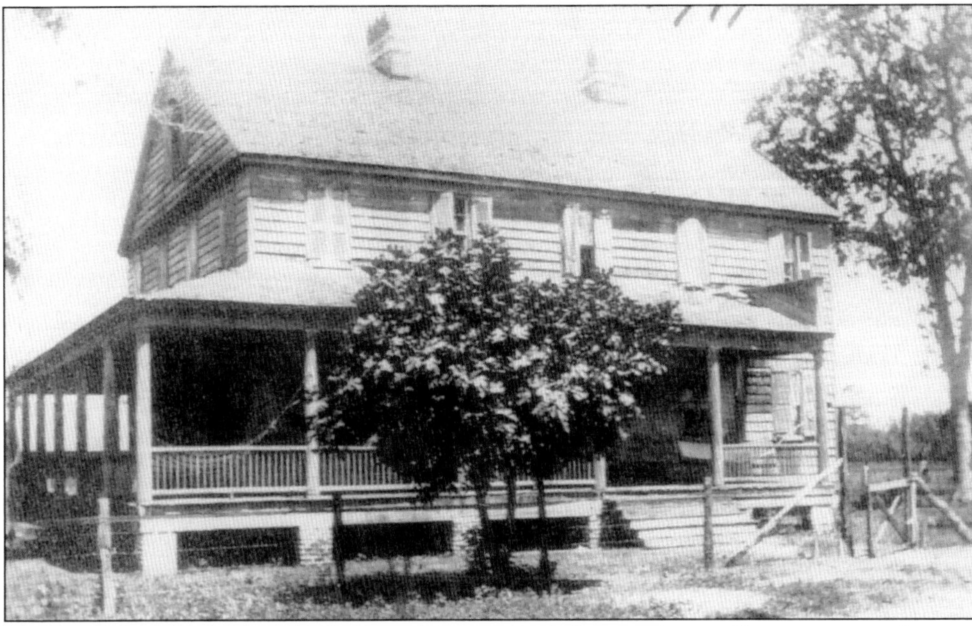

The Woodland house was the summer home of Dr. Edward Thomas Heriot, owner of several plantations in Georgetown County, who lived on Sandy Island at Mount Arena Plantation. The house was reported to have been built by the Belin family in the early 1700s. There was an artesian well in the front yard that was used by the community for drinking water up until the 1940s, and the main north-south road through the inlet ran along the creek in front of the house. (Courtesy of the Lee family.)

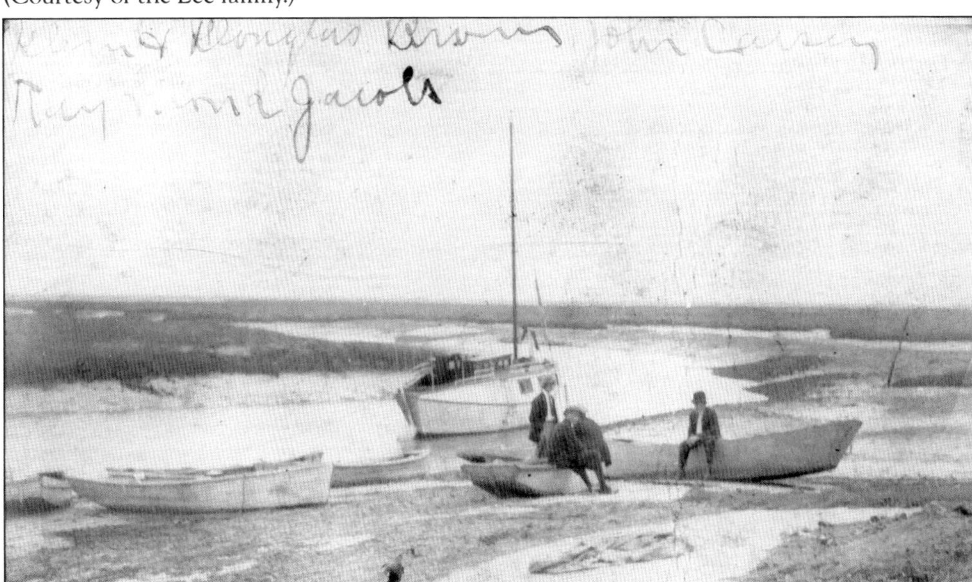

The shell landing at Woodland Landing is pictured in July 1947, after the funeral of George "Son" Morse. From left to right, Glenn and Douglas Brown, John Causey, and Raymond Jacobs are shown sitting on wood boats at the landing. Son's sailboat *Pollywog* is shown floating in the creek behind them. The channel from Woodland Landing to Nance's was excavated with a dragline in the 1950s to connect Woodland Creek to Oaks Creek. (Courtesy of the Morse family.)

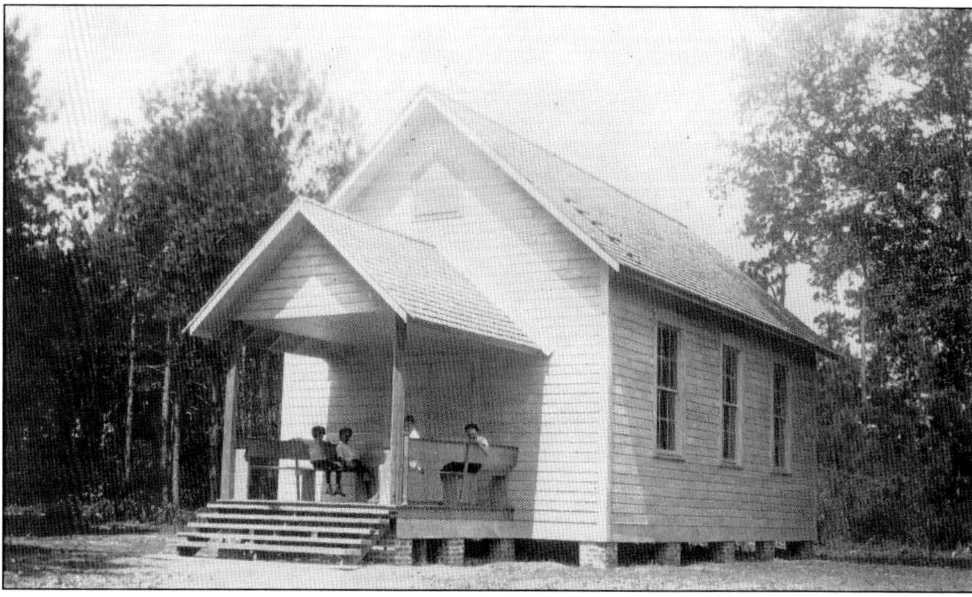

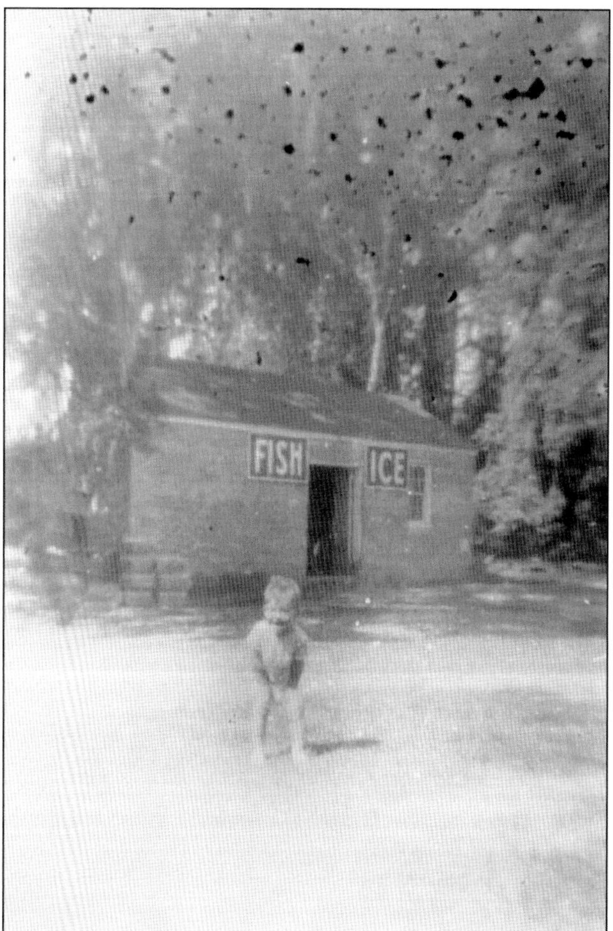

The Little Chapel for Murrells Inlet Presbyterian Church was built around 1925 and named for the Little family, who donated the lumber used to build the church. Dal Johnson (owner of Vaux Hall) donated the land for the church, and Van Turbeville was the builder. The church building is still located on Murrells Inlet and used by a community clothes closet for donations. (Courtesy of the Vereen family.)

Herman Gordon constructed a brick building for a fish market and icehouse in the early 1940s. The fish market purchased spots and mullet from net fishermen like Capt. Andrew "Hobby" Nance and Capt. Ira Vick, shad from fishermen on Sandy Island, and flounder from local creekmen. Excess fish were sometimes shipped to Marion and Mullins by Robbie Vick to sell. (Courtesy of the Gordon family.)

Wayne Gordon is wearing his Hopalong Cassidy outfit at Gordon's Grocery about 1951. This store sold grocery items, seafood, and gas. For a short time, it had a soda fountain that Margie Bellamy worked at along with Ester Martin, who later married Frank Prox (a frequent patron of the soda fountain). Herman Gordon sold this store to Gene Cannon around 1959. (Courtesy of the Gordon family.)

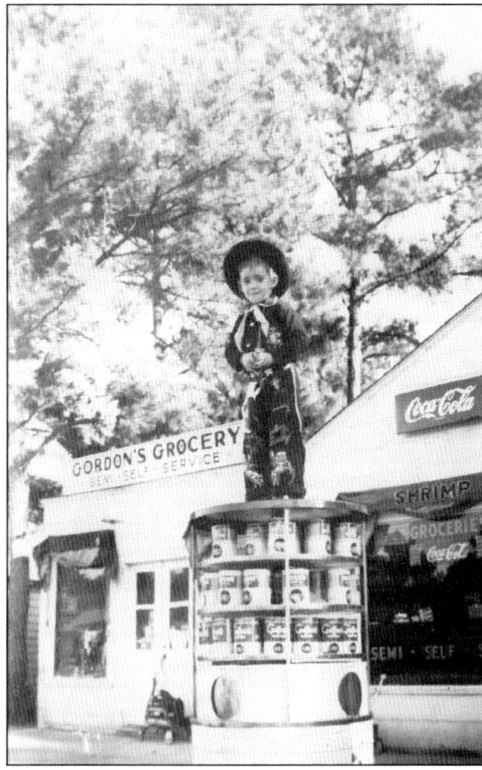

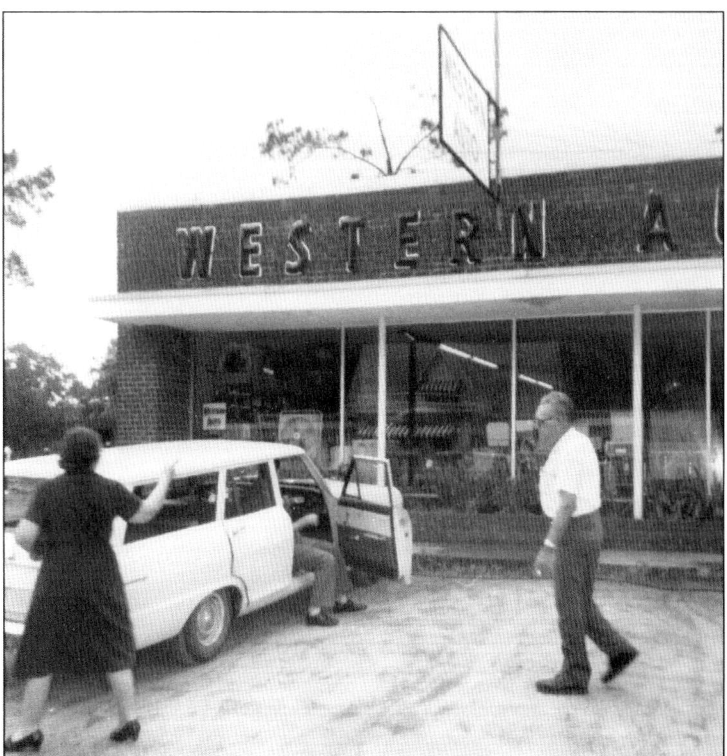

Herman Gordon is shown outside of the Western Auto building around 1962. He built the Western Auto building on the north side of his Gulf Oil station after he sold the grocery store to Gene Cannon around 1959. He closed the Western Auto franchise in Murrells Inlet, and later Booty Shelley was involved with opening a Western Auto franchise to the south in a building that Gene Cannon built between the grocery store and the gas station. (Courtesy of the Gordon family.)

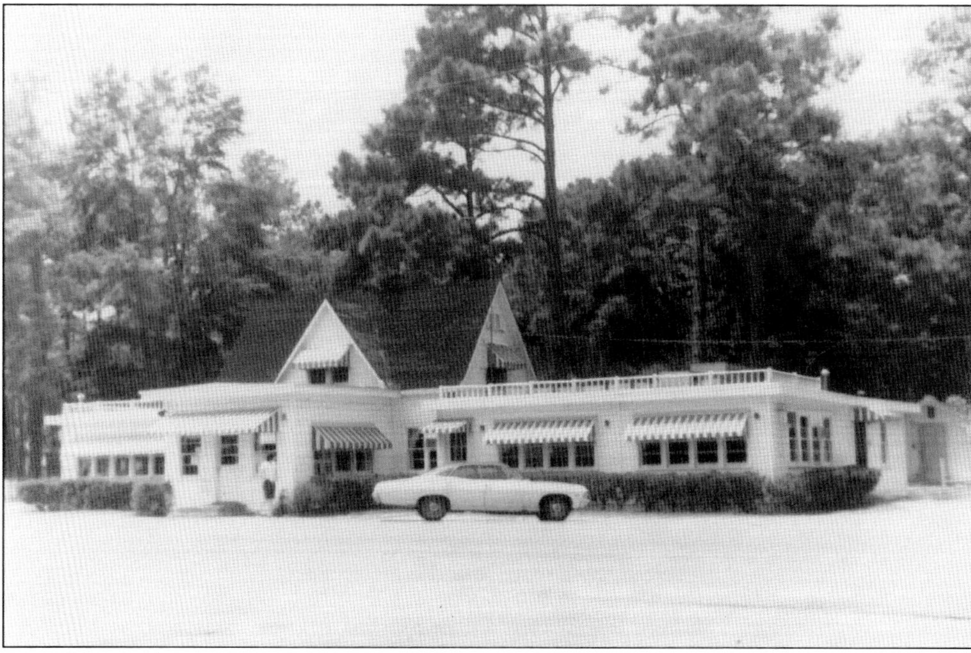

Lee's Inlet Kitchen, pictured in the 1970s, shows the current look that is familiar to Inlet visitors today. Pearl and Eford Lee opened Lee's Inlet Kitchen in October 1948 at this location, which was previously a gas station and a saloon. Beginning with 10 tables, the restaurant has been enlarged four times. (Courtesy of the Lee family.)

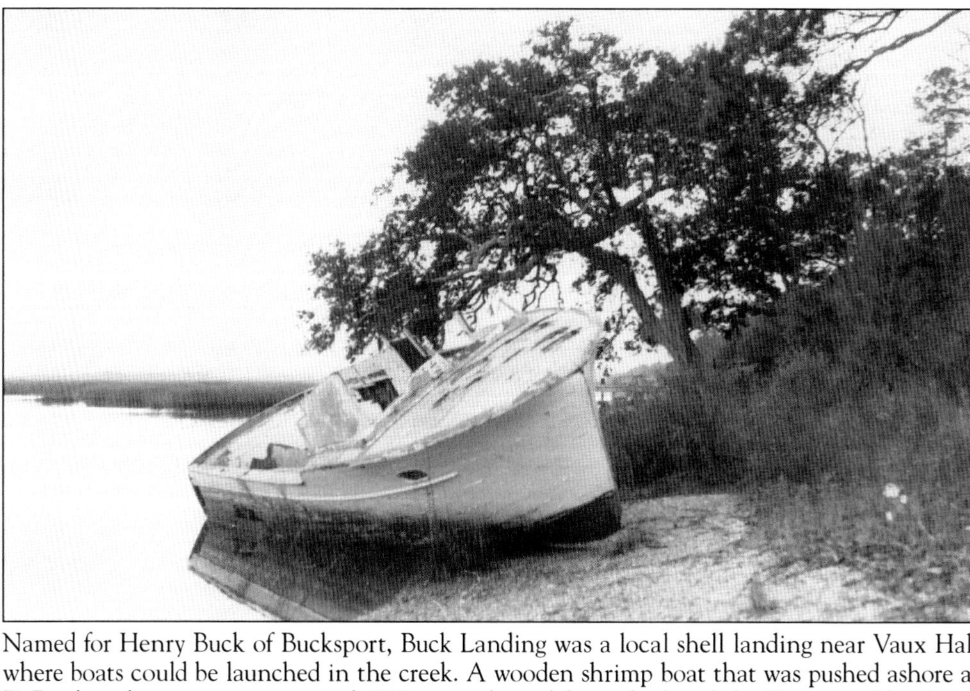

Named for Henry Buck of Bucksport, Buck Landing was a local shell landing near Vaux Hall where boats could be launched in the creek. A wooden shrimp boat that was pushed ashore at DeBordieu during a storm around 1973 was salvaged from the beach by H.C. Strickland and Tommy Gaede, who removed the motors and machinery. The remaining wooden hull was left on the hill at Buck Landing until it fell apart. (Courtesy of the Strickland family.)

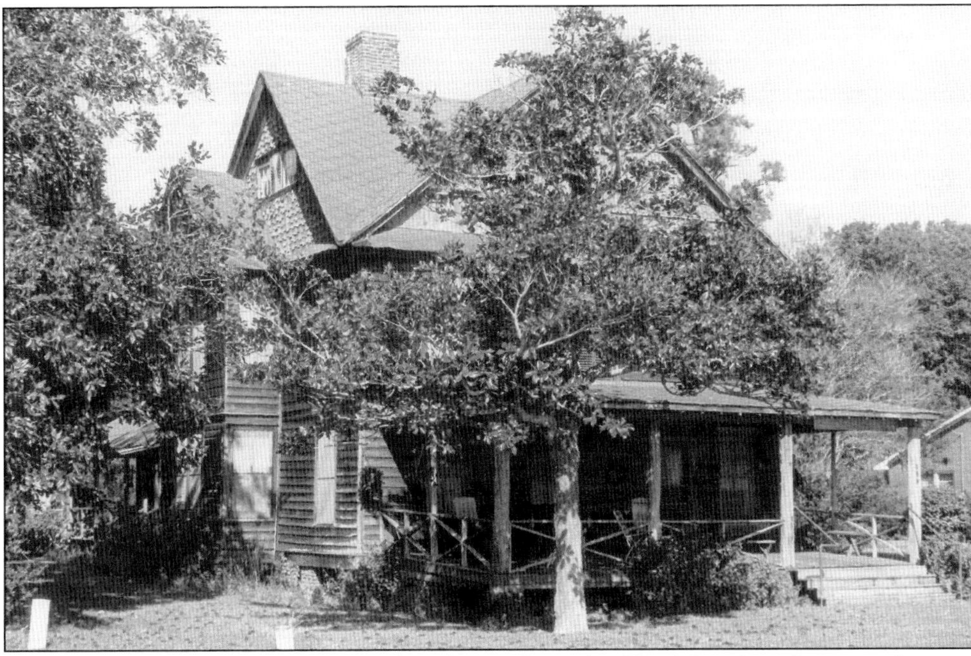

Vaux Hall was a historic home located on the creek north of Buck Landing that was advertised as a hunting lodge by Dal Johnson in the 1910s. It was later used as a post office and as a public library during the 1940s and 1950s. Dal Johnson wrote articles for *Field and Stream* and was a hunting buddy of Paul Herbert Wesley. (Courtesy of Tookie Chandler Jones.)

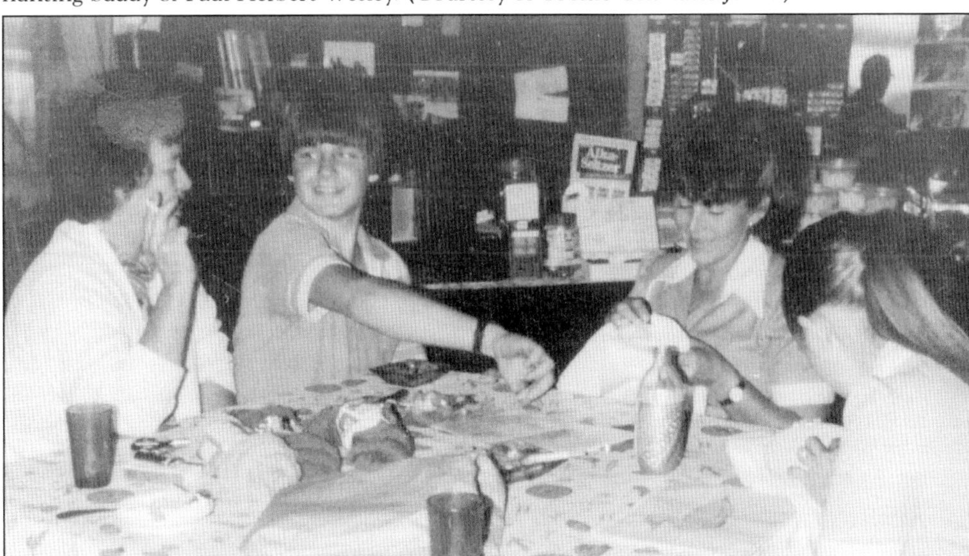

From left to right, Maxine Oliver Hawkins is sitting at her table in Oliver's Lodge around 1983 with Jeff McKenzie, Carolyn Eason, and another waitress. Maxine's grandfather was Capt. William "Bill" Oliver, who opened the lodge in the early 1900s, and her father was Capt. Mack Oliver, who worked with the Army crash boats and later ran the *Ann Howe* from the docks at Oliver's Lodge during the 1950s. Maxine held court at her table in front of the cash register at Oliver's Lodge, playing card games to pass time when it was slow. Her table was only cleaned off for customers when it was busy. (Courtesy of the MacKenzie family.)

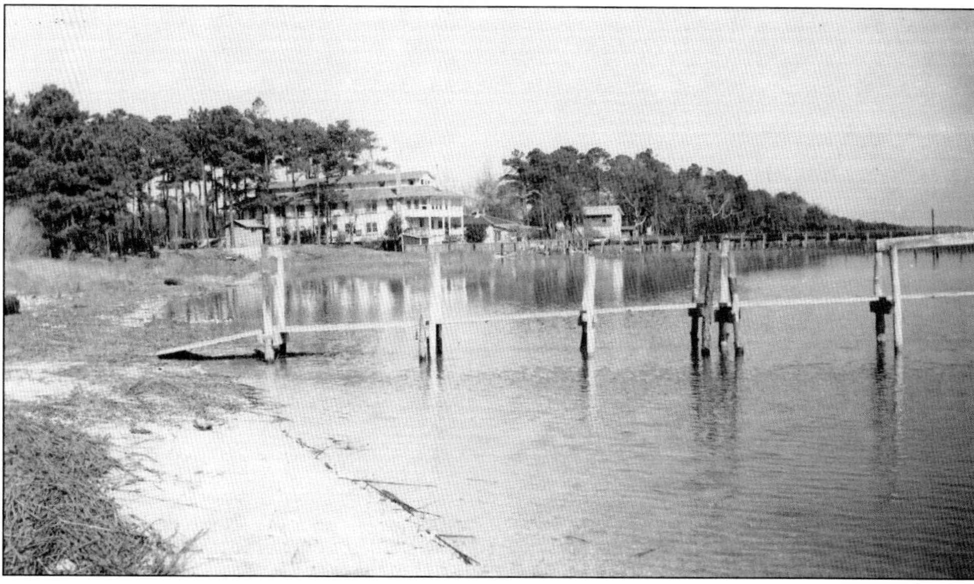

This view of the creek front was taken from Oliver's Lodge in 1944, with Mac Oliver's dock in the foreground and the Army barracks, mess hall, and Army dock in the background. The two-story building on the right was an oyster roast at Sing's Place, which had a small upstairs apartment. (Courtesy of Gwen Watson and Murrells Inlet 2020.)

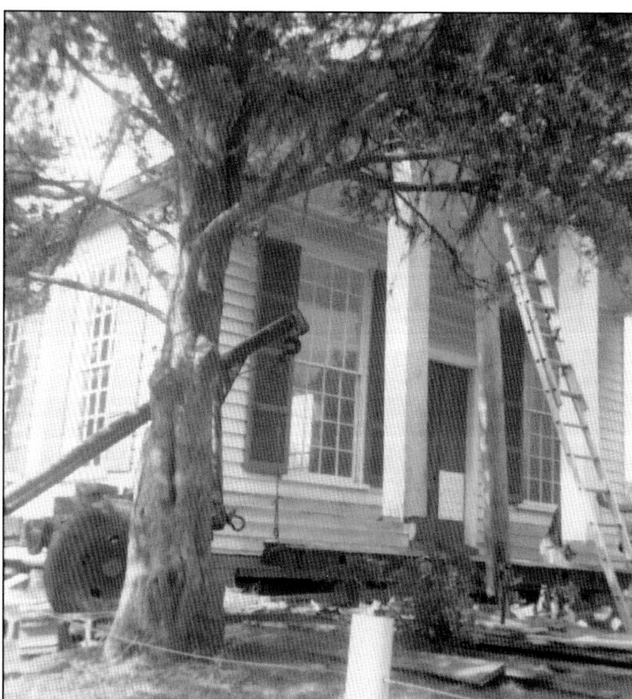

Belin Methodist Church is shown around 1977, when the original sanctuary was relocated to the center of the property and the size of the sanctuary was doubled. Belin Methodist Church, named for the Reverend James L. Belin, was built in 1925 with materials salvaged from the dismantling of the Turkey Hill Methodist Church near Litchfield. Emma Oliver was instrumental in having the building moved piece-by-piece to the present site by Boo Lachicotte and his mule teams. Belin Church was built on the site of Cedar Hill, which was established as the Waccamaw Mission in 1836 by Allard Belin, owner of Wachesaw Plantation. (Courtesy of the Welch family.)

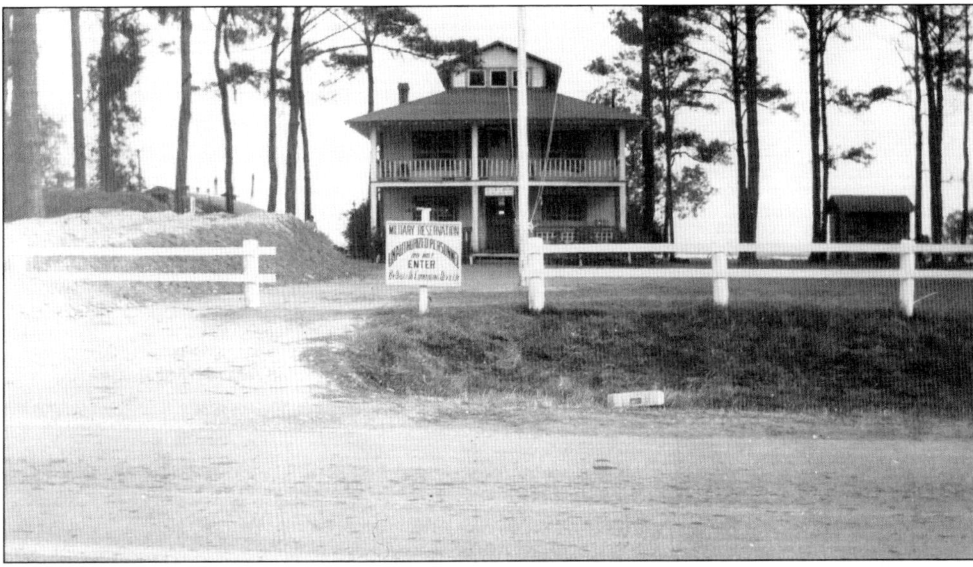

The Army leased the Future Farmers of America Lodge during World War II to establish barracks and construct docking facilities for the crash boats used to rescue downed pilots who trained shooting targets on the beach and towed targets near Murrells Inlet and Garden City. Clarke A. Willcox Sr. constructed the original building as the Flagg Hotel after 1910. (Courtesy of Gwen Watson and Murrells Inlet 2020.)

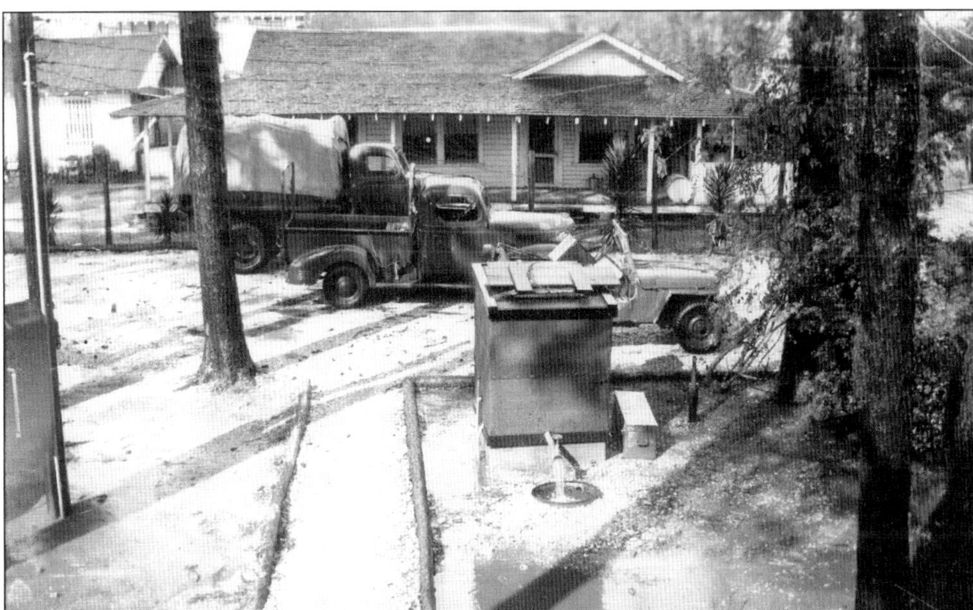

Here is a view of the flowing artesian well in front of the Army barracks and mess hall and the houses owned by Walter Macklen between the barracks and Sing's Place (the roofline of second story visible in background). Oliver's Lodge would fill its water jugs at this well to make the coffee and tea for the restaurant. H.C. Strickland and Esau Lazarowitz lived in these houses during the 1950s. (Courtesy of Gwen Watson and Murrells Inlet 2020.)

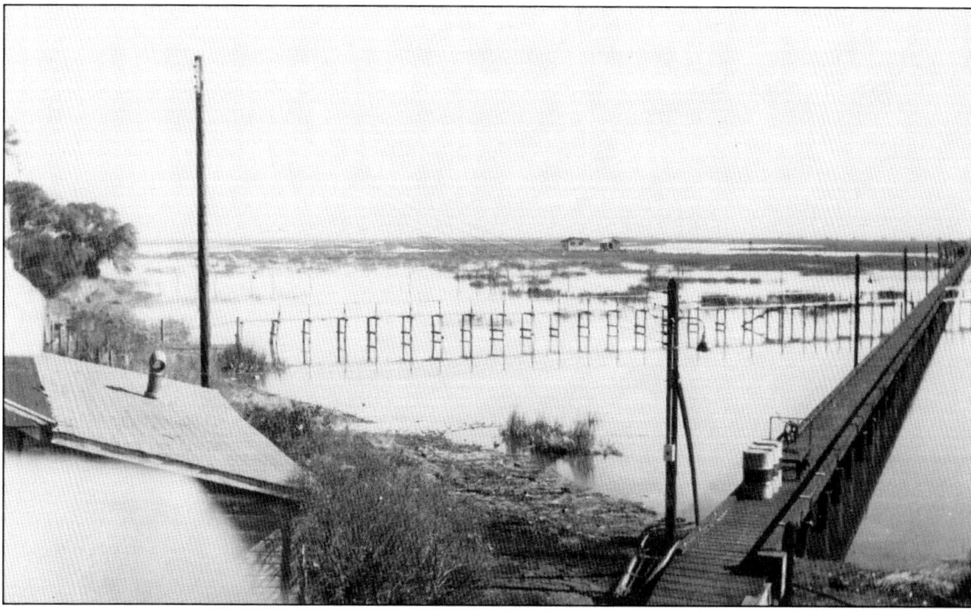

Here is a view of the Army dock and Sing's dock from the Army barracks in 1944. Oil storage and a radio room are on the Army dock, and the two houses on the creek are behind Neimeyer's property in the background. The Army built a house on Neimeyer's dock while the Army dock was under construction in 1942. (Courtesy of Gwen Watson and Murrells Inlet 2020.)

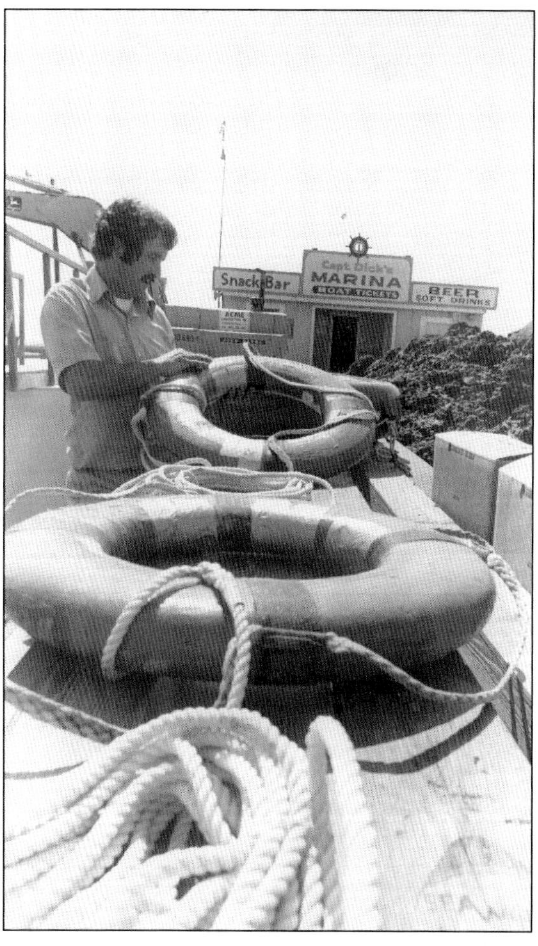

Capt. Johnny Strickland is seen working on the life rings aboard the *Carolina Princess* at Captain Dick's Marina around 1974 while the bulkhead was being installed. Dick Eason bought the marina property from Danny Pendergrass around 1971 and excavated the marina basin in front of the bulkhead. The ticket office was moved from Anchor Marina to this location and remained until Hurricane Hugo in 1989. (Courtesy of the Strickland family.)

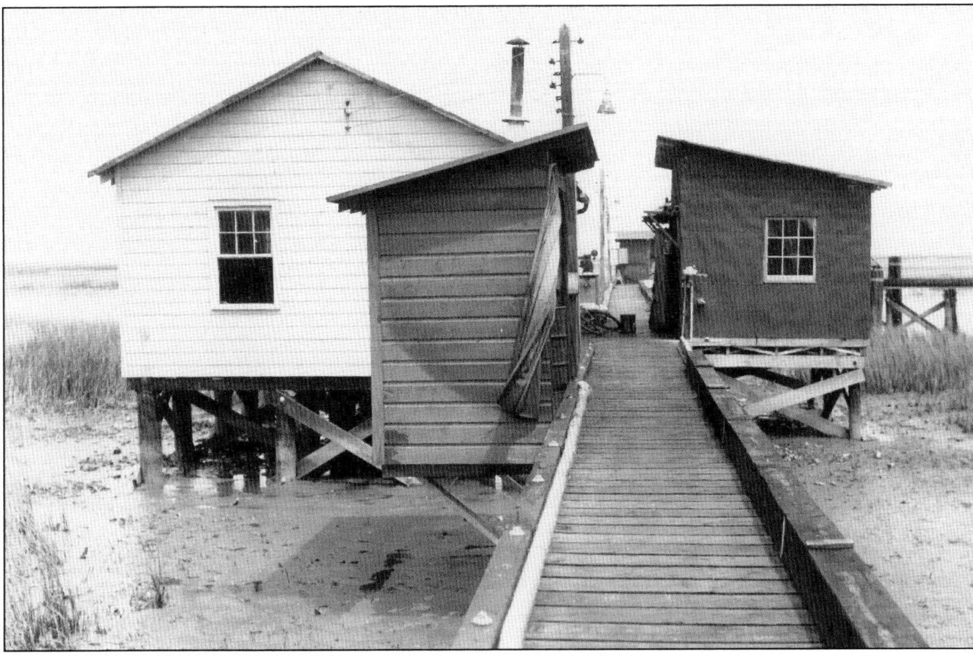

A radio room and an oil storage room were constructed on the Army dock around 1942 to provide space for the crash boat operations. This building was later used as a tackle shop and ticket office and as a growing shed for soft-shelled crabs. The building fell into disrepair and was destroyed by Hurricane Hugo in 1989. (Courtesy of Gwen Watson and Murrells Inlet 2020.)

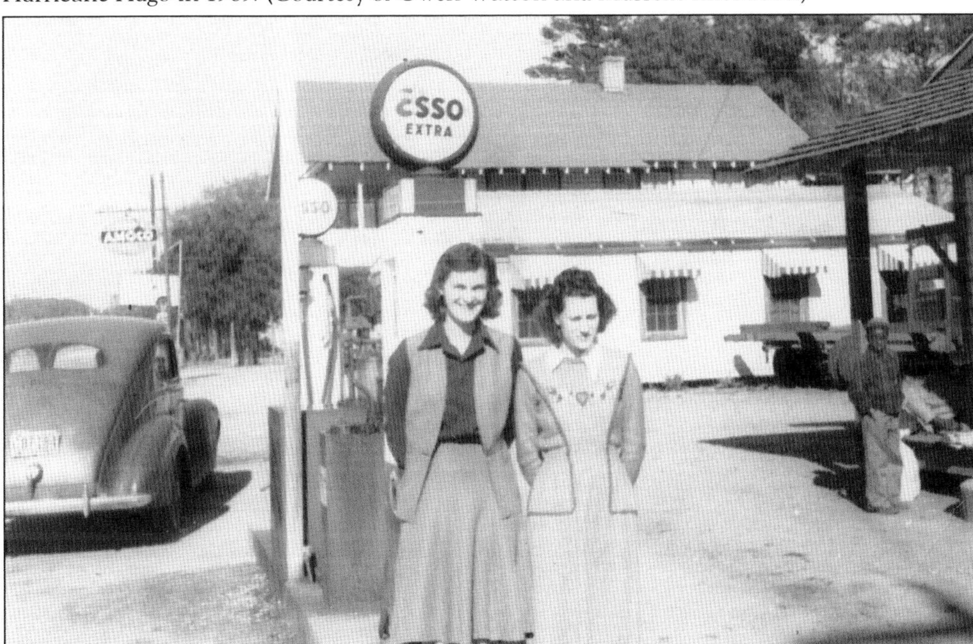

Dot Eason (right) is shown in front of Jimmy Eason's grocery store, which he rented from Walter Macklen around 1944, shortly before he built the Bay Harbor Motel across the street from this location. The two-story Sing's Place is shown in the background. (Courtesy of the Eason family.)

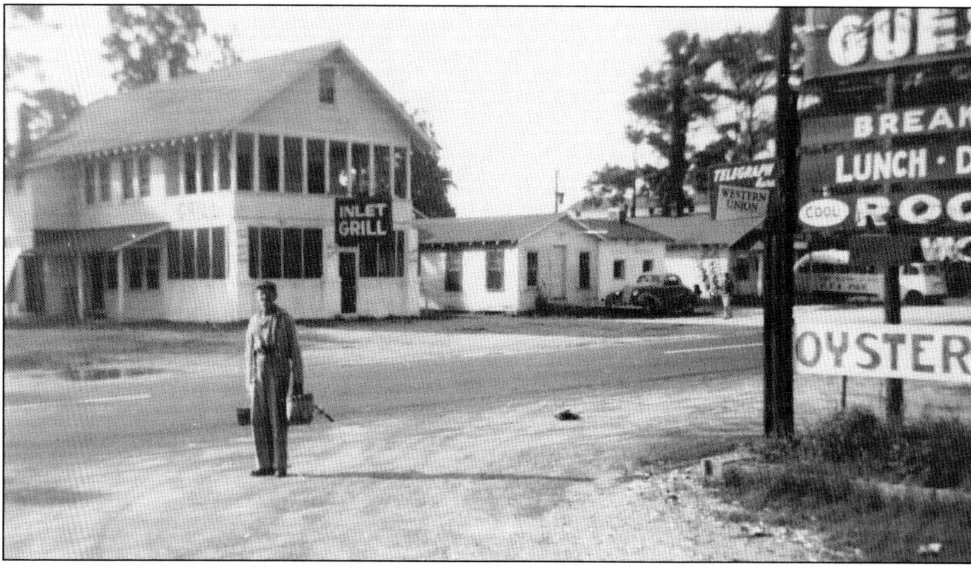

Alvia "Pops" Goodman heads to the creek from Bay Harbor around 1951, with Sing's Inlet Grill shown on the other side of Highway 17. Other buildings in the background include, form left to right, a small wooden building beside Sing's Inlet Grill that later became Bunny Venter's pizza restaurant and the original store that Jimmy Eason operated before he built the Bay Harbor motel and grocery store. (Courtesy of the Eason family.)

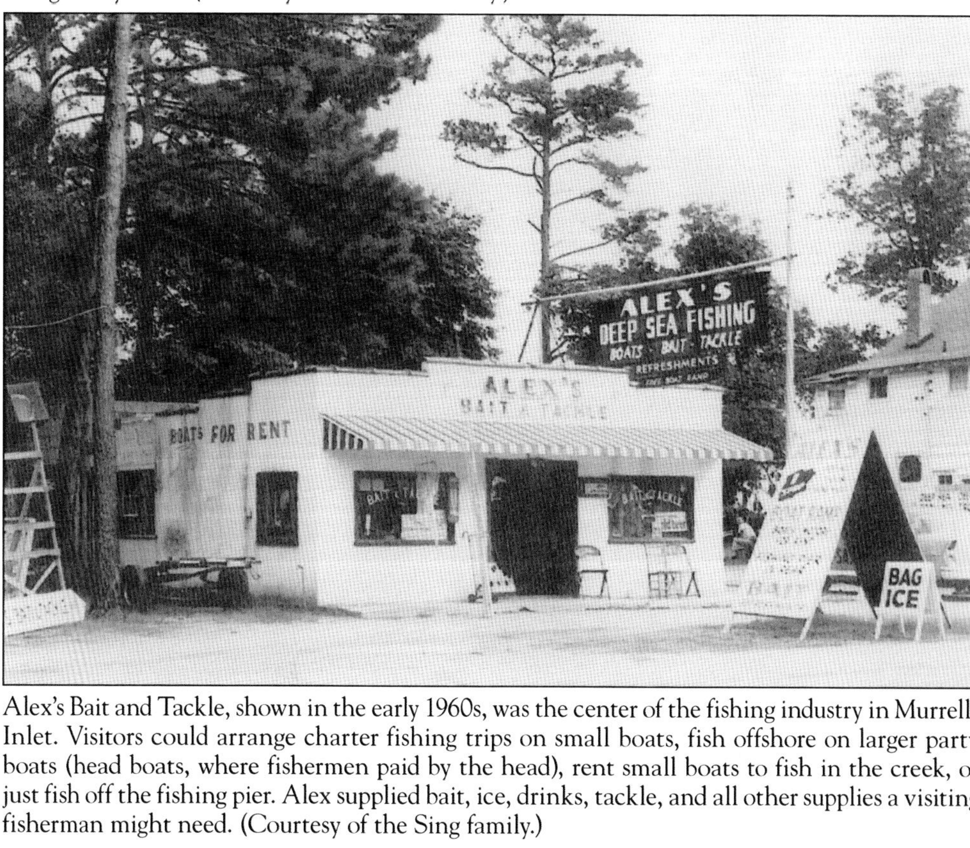

Alex's Bait and Tackle, shown in the early 1960s, was the center of the fishing industry in Murrells Inlet. Visitors could arrange charter fishing trips on small boats, fish offshore on larger party boats (head boats, where fishermen paid by the head), rent small boats to fish in the creek, or just fish off the fishing pier. Alex supplied bait, ice, drinks, tackle, and all other supplies a visiting fisherman might need. (Courtesy of the Sing family.)

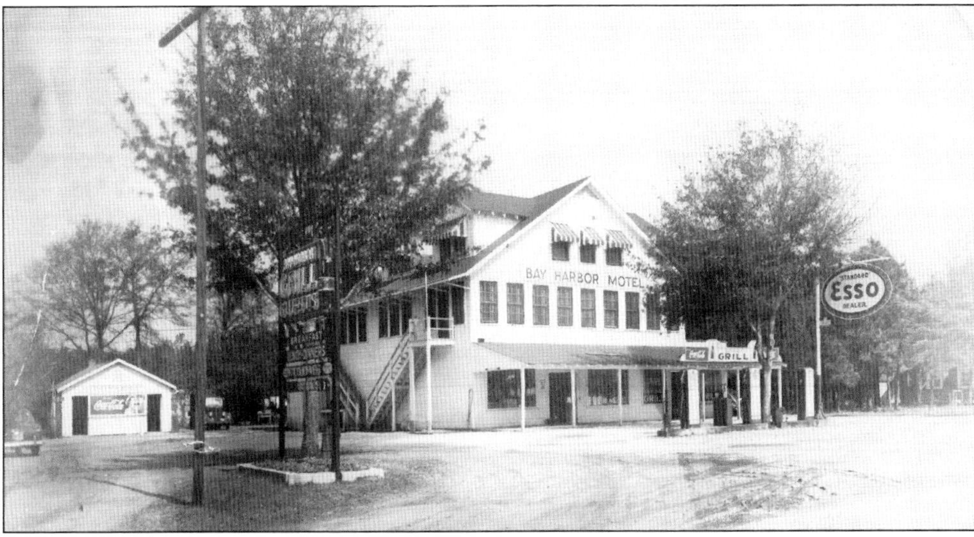

The Bay Harbor Motel was built by Jimmy Eason around 1945 across the street from Sing's Place and had a grocery store, a restaurant, an oyster roast, his family's living quarters, and rental rooms. Mac and Teeny Vereen Oliver ran the Bay Harbor Grill for a short time before opening the restaurant at Oliver's Lodge. The second floor had a sunroom that extended across the front of the building where neighbors would gather to watch television on one of the first television sets in Murrells Inlet. (Courtesy of the Eason family.)

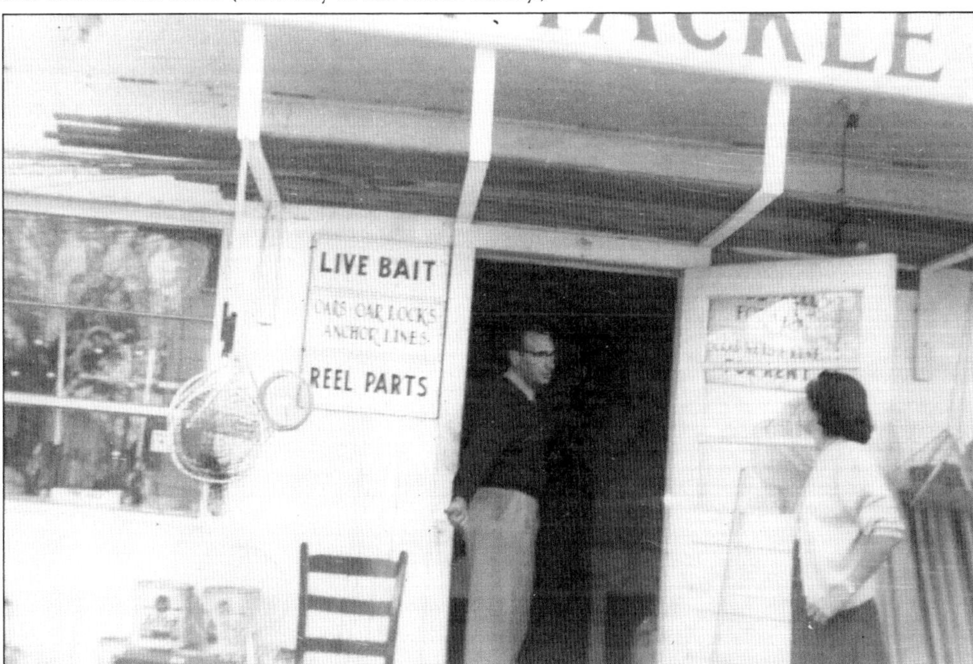

Sam Barwick is seen at his first tackle shop location behind Bay Harbor Motel. Sam Barwick was a mechanic who got his start in the fishing business working for Luther Smith, eventually owning several businesses around the present-day Drunken Jacks area. He would sell tickets for the fishing boats from his tackle shop and help publicize the charter fishing boats to attract business. (Courtesy of the Eason family.)

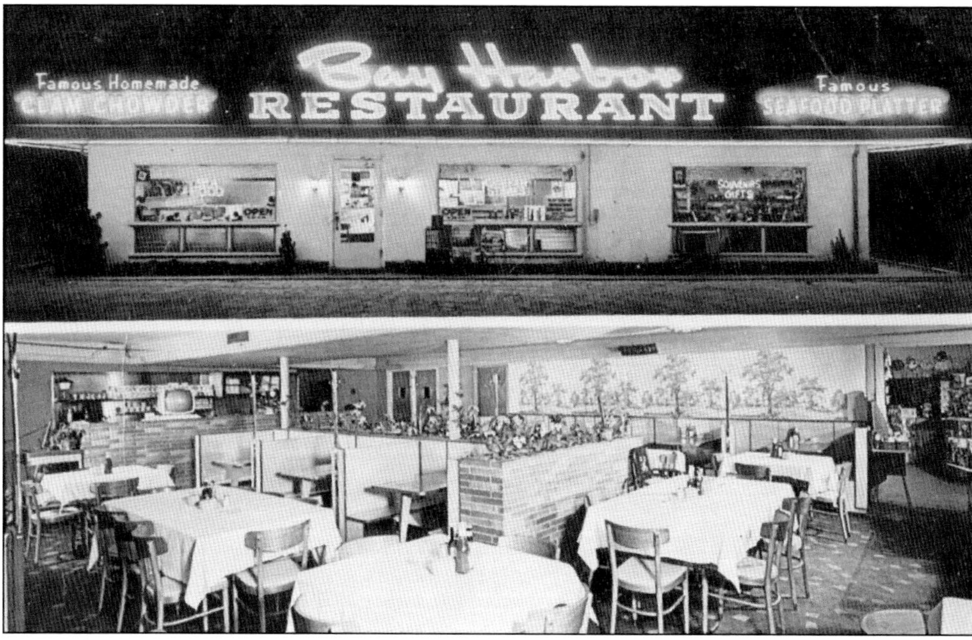

Bay Harbor Restaurant was constructed in 1953 by Jimmy and Dot Eason north of the Bay Harbor Motel. This postcard was printed around the mid-1960s. Bay Harbor restaurant was operated by the Eason family and later by Wayne Ammons until it was destroyed by fire around 1985. (Courtesy of the Strickland family.)

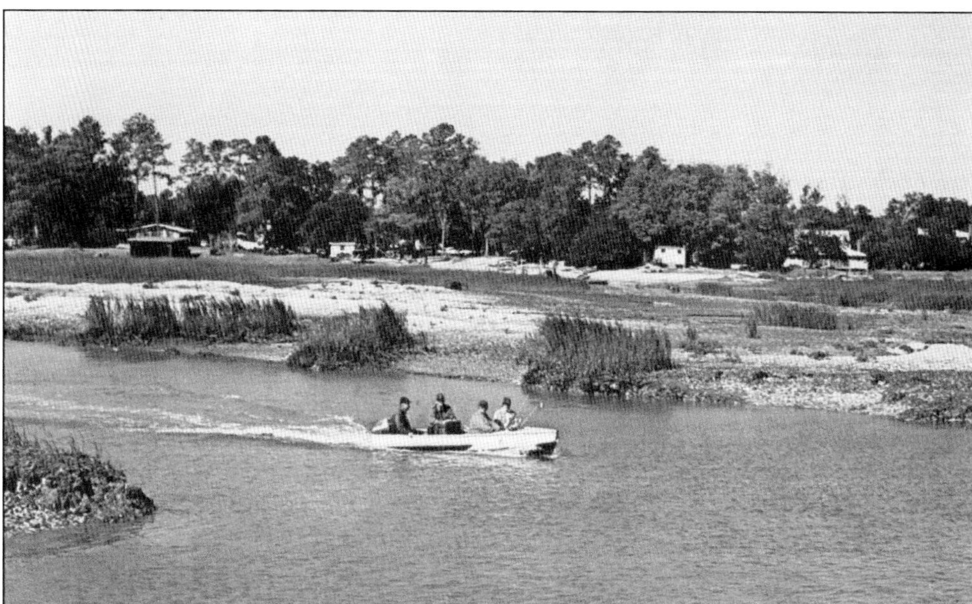

A small fishing skiff is pictured coming out of the channel from Captain Alex's Marina to the main creek, with the Ebb Nell restaurant (far left), Sam Barwick's tackle shop and boat docks (his third location), O.T. Maynard's boat rentals, and Genevieve Willcox Chandler's house pictured on the creek front. (Courtesy of the Strickland family.)

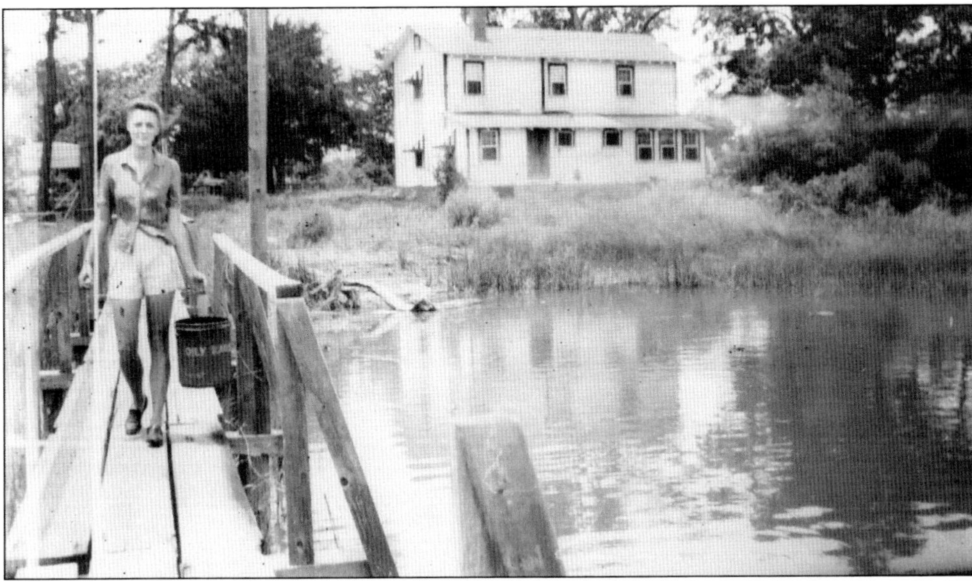

Herbert Neimeyer owned property on the creek where he operated a restaurant and a marina in later years. He rented the downstairs of his house to military personnel during World War II and excavated the channel from the main creek to his property along his dock, which later became Anchor Marina. Shown in this picture is Gwen Watson walking out on the Neimeyer dock around 1944. (Courtesy of Gwen Watson and Murrells Inlet 2020.)

Anchor Inn was a seafood restaurant that was operated by Tommy Chandler and Bill Crosswell in the 1970s and 1980s at the Anchor Marina. The restaurant was originally built by Herbert Neimeyer and later remodeled several times by different owners. (Courtesy of Tookie Chandler Jones.)

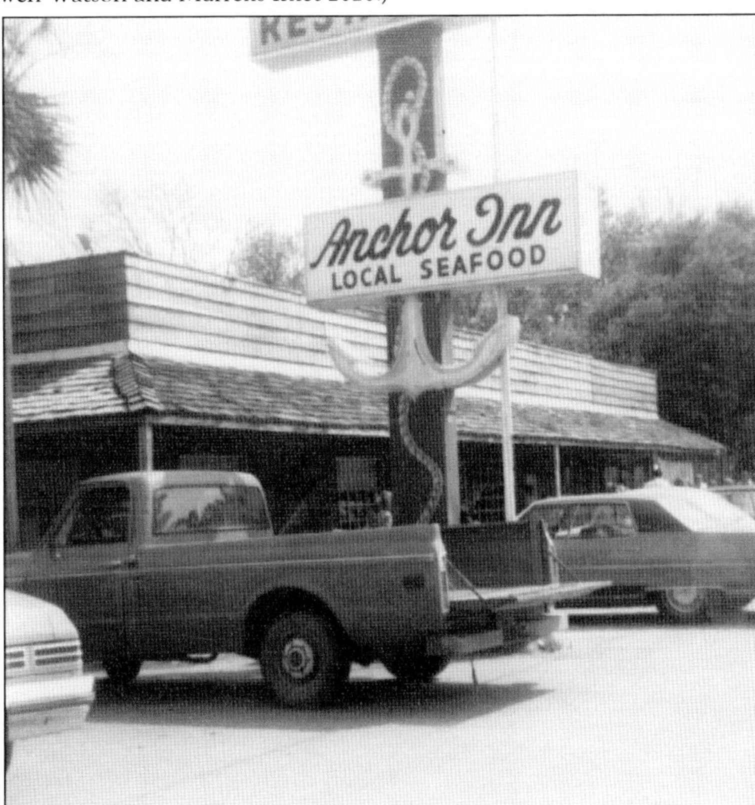

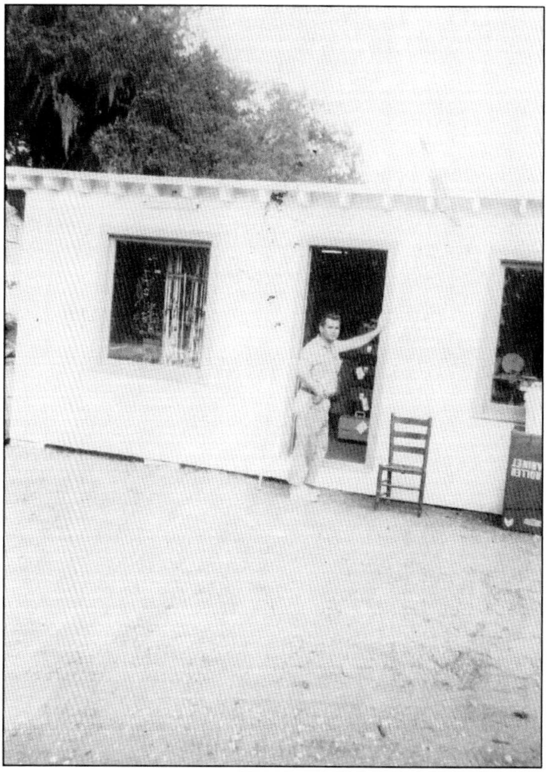

Dick Eason is seen standing in front of the original tackle shop at Anchor Marina in the late 1960s. John Frink bought Anchor Marina from Herbert Neimeyer and sold it to Dick Eason, who sold the marina to Thurmon Bostick and moved to Captain Dick's Marina around 1971. This tackle shop was moved to Captain Dick's at the same time and served as the ticket office until it was destroyed by Hurricane Hugo in 1989. (Courtesy of the Eason family.)

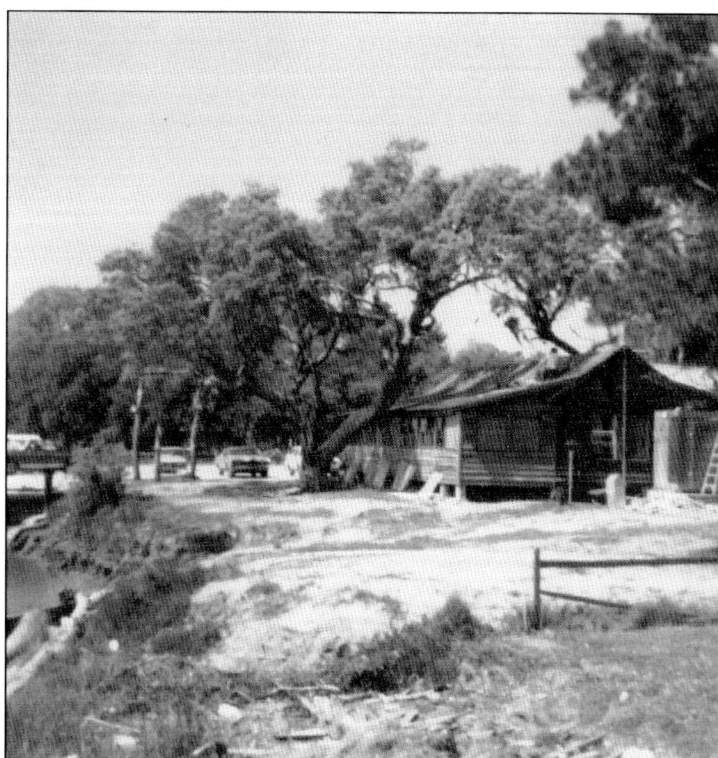

Tommy and Wayne Chandler built the Galley Restaurant in the 1970s north of Anchor Marina (where present-day Bovines is located). The Galley offered traditional fried seafood as well as oyster roasts during the season; the restaurant expanded both ground-floor decks by the creek and the upstairs deck (the Crow's Nest) over the years. (Courtesy of Tookie Chandler Jones.)

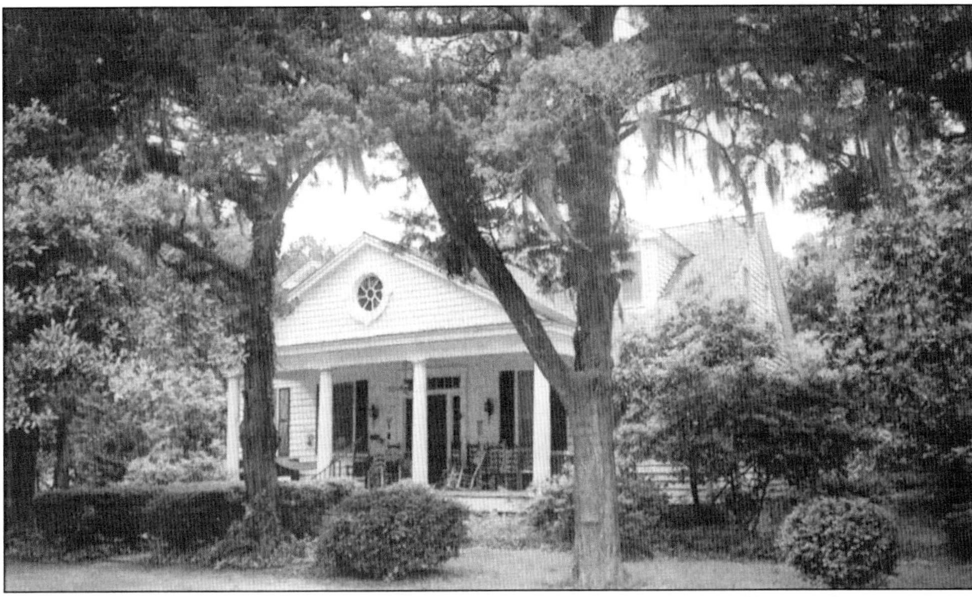

Dr. Allard Flagg constructed a summer home at Wachesaw in 1849, calling it the Hermitage. Clarke A. Willcox Sr. purchased the property, and he moved his family here around 1910, keeping the property around the creek when he sold the larger part of Wachesaw in 1930. Clarke A. Willcox Jr. moved back into the Hermitage around 1956 when he left Marion, South Carolina. He continued to spread the legend of Alice Flagg into popular culture until his passing. Alice was the sister of Dr. Allard, and she fell sick with fever while in Charleston. When her brother found an engagement ring around her neck, he threw it in the creek, and she is said to have haunted the Hermitage for years afterward. The house was relocated in the 1990s and is still in the hands of Willcox and Chandler descendants. (Courtesy of Tookie Chandler Jones.)

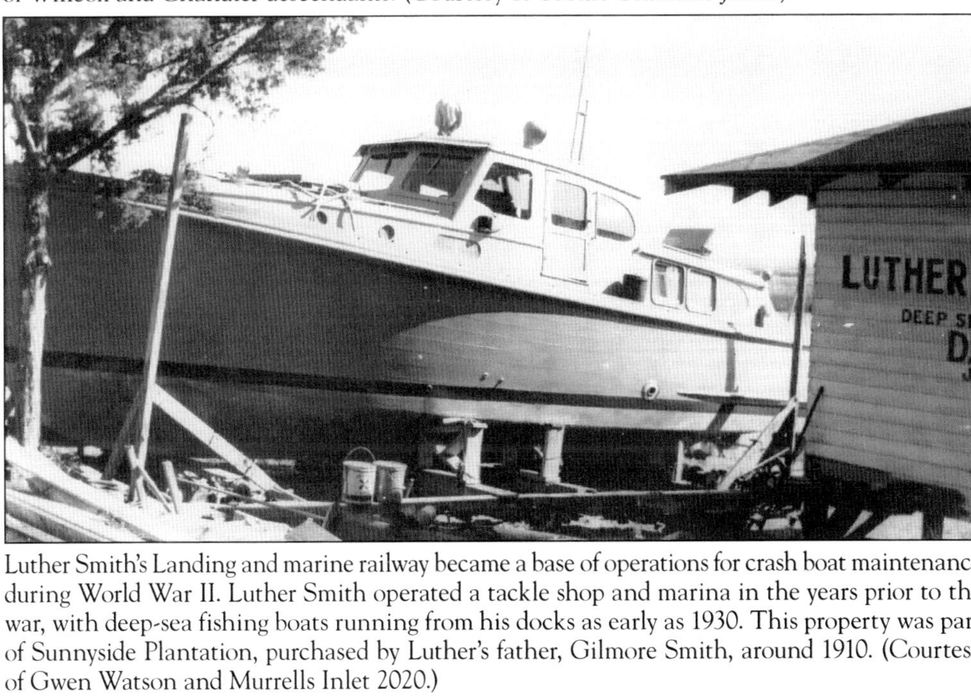

Luther Smith's Landing and marine railway became a base of operations for crash boat maintenance during World War II. Luther Smith operated a tackle shop and marina in the years prior to the war, with deep-sea fishing boats running from his docks as early as 1930. This property was part of Sunnyside Plantation, purchased by Luther's father, Gilmore Smith, around 1910. (Courtesy of Gwen Watson and Murrells Inlet 2020.)

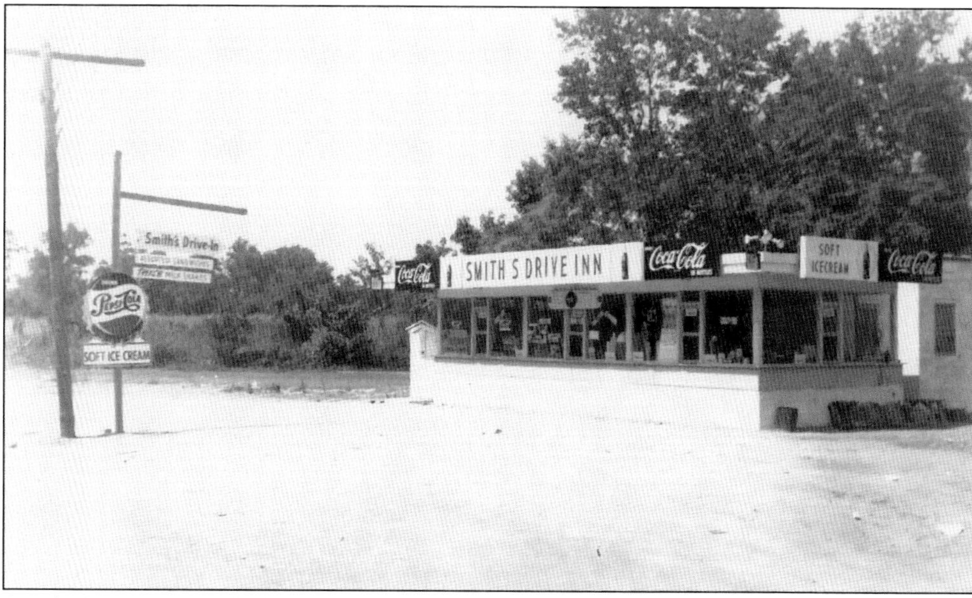

Smith's Drive Inn was built in 1953 by Ashby Smith and operated by his son Ken Smith into the 1960s, when Ken changed it to the Harbor House seafood restaurant. He leased it in the 1970s to Johnny and Bubby Vereen, who operated it as Sunnyside Restaurant until the late 1980s. The roof from the original building was removed by a tornado in 1956 and picked up and set back in place by a crane. (Courtesy of the Smith family.)

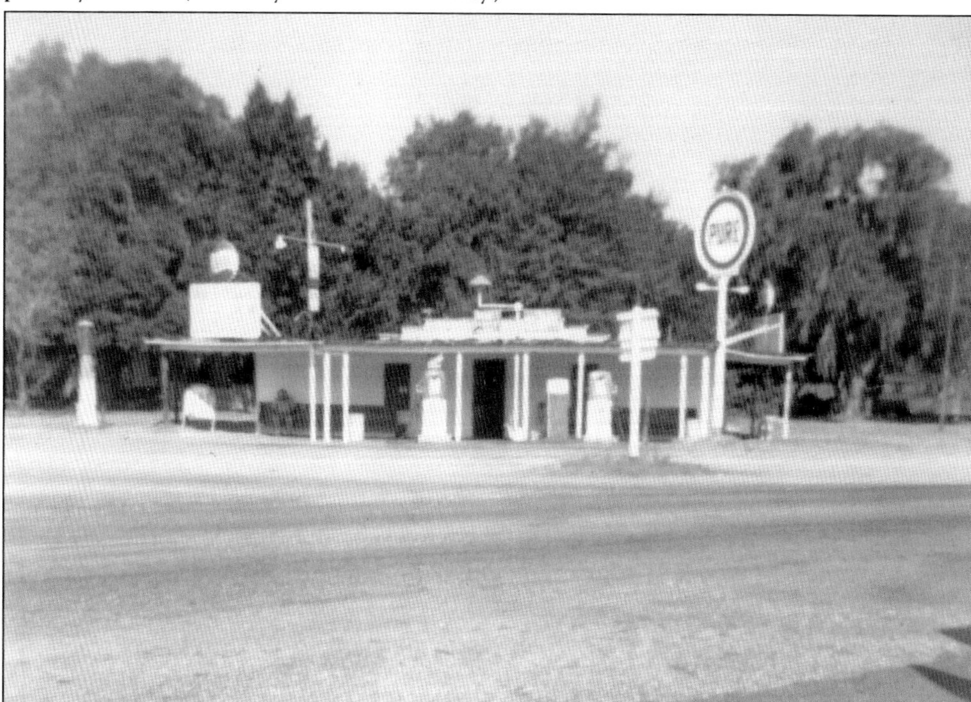

George Watts ran a gas station during the 1950s and 1960s at the intersection of Highway 17 and present-day Highway 707. This station was later converted into a local bar called the Grass Hut, managed by Margie Ferguson. (Courtesy of the Smith family.)

Eight

Special Events

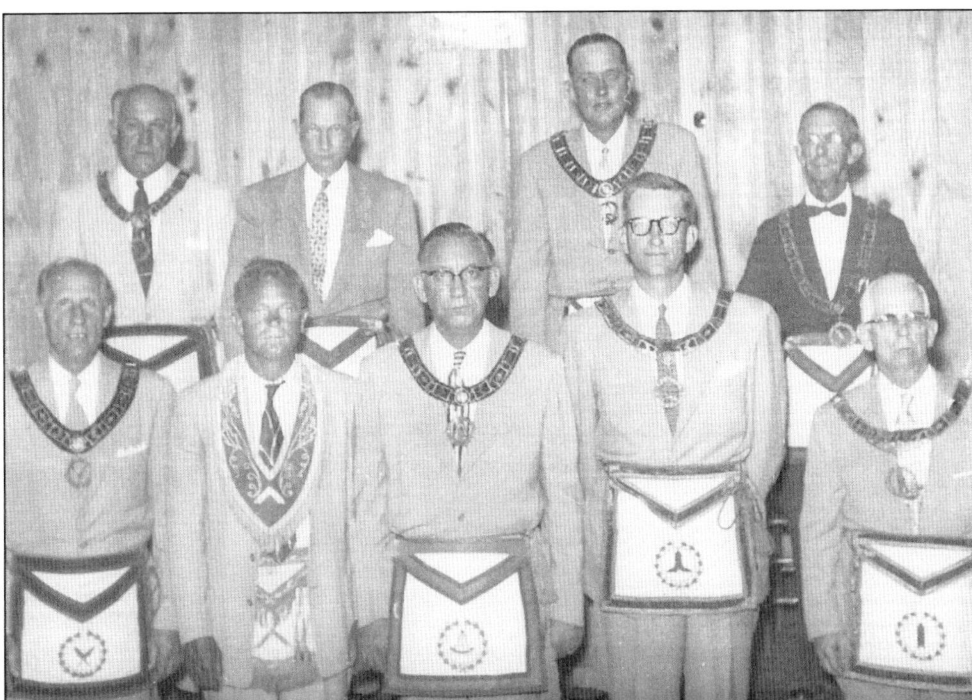

The Murrells Inlet Masonic Lodge No. 368 was chartered in 1947 and constructed a new lodge in 1954, voting to approve the building in February 1954 and holding the dedication ceremony in May 1954. J. Wesley Hughes Sr. was the worshipful master of the lodge that year, pictured with a full complement of South Carolina Grand Lodge officers, including, from left to right, (first row) Henry F. Collins, grand secretary; J. Wesley Hughes; J. Ansel Eaddy, grand master; Thomas H. Pope, senior grand warden; and Hugh N. Layne, junior grand warden; (second row) W. Curtis Sheely, grand treasurer; John I. Smith, grand chaplain pro tem; Herbert Guerry, senior grand deacon; and George C. Nauful, grand pursuivant pro tem. (Courtesy of Murrells Inlet Masonic Lodge.)

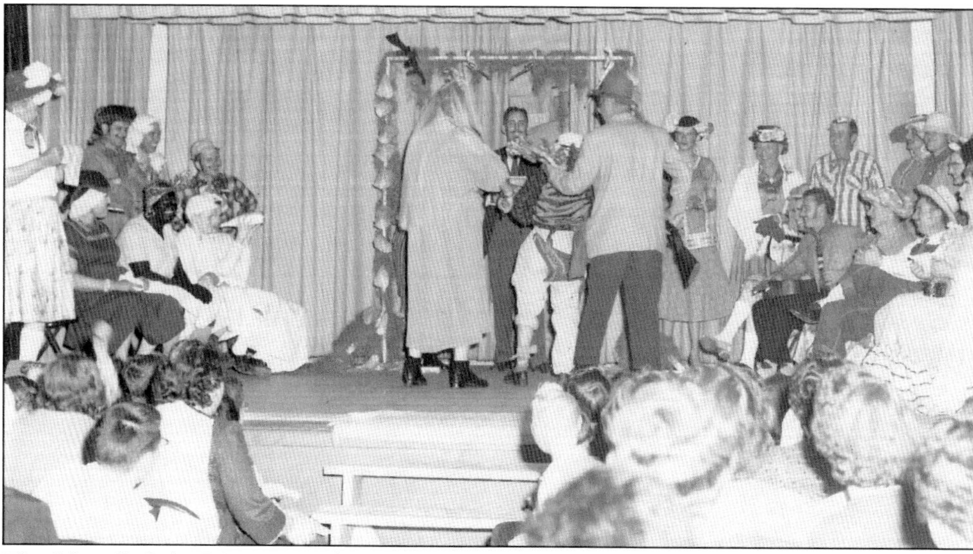

The Murrells Inlet Masonic Lodge staged a play in 1955 entitled *The Womanless Wedding* as a fundraiser. The play was said to have been so funny that the actors could not keep a straight face during the show. Actors in this photograph include, from left to right, Edwin Eason, Ray Joyner, Ken Smith, Charlie Welch, Tommy Jordan, Oliver Pierce, Danny Pendergrass, M. G. Caughman, Alex Sing, and Tommy Chandler. (Courtesy of the Smith family.)

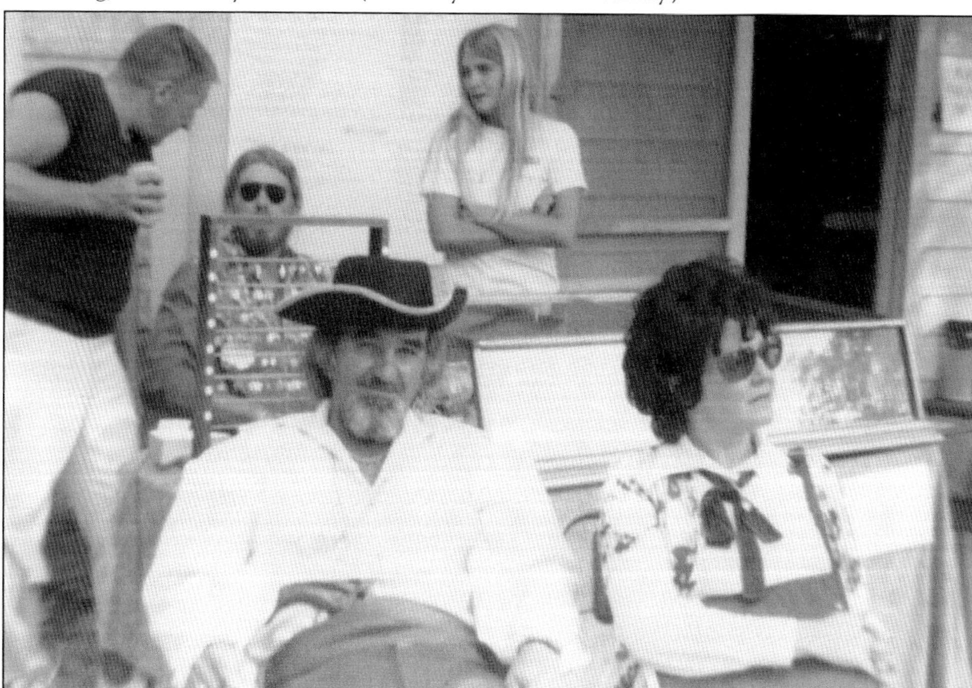

Herb and Wilma Martin (foreground) were organizers of the first Murrells Inlet Outdoor Arts and Crafts Festival in 1973. Wilma Martin was the chairwoman, and Herb Martin was dressed as Captain Murrell for the festival. They are shown sitting in front of the old Murrells Inlet Motor Court, which served as festival headquarters the first year. Mickey Spillane is in the background at left talking with other vendors. (Courtesy of Taryn Gordon Wilson.)

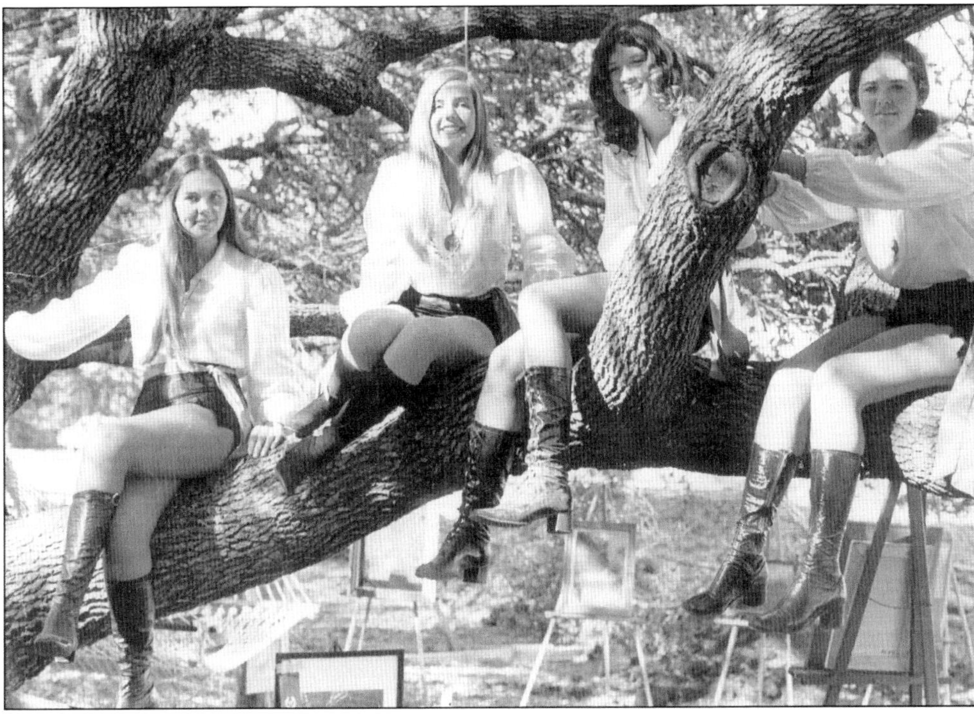

During the first years of the Murrells Inlet Outdoor Arts and Crafts Festival, the Festival Committee had "Pirates" and "Pirettes" dressed up to serve as ambassadors and be the public face of the festival. From left to right, Pirettes Gail Morse, Taryn Gordon, Tookie Chandler, and Ginger Morse (members of the publicity committee) are shown posing in their costumes in the branches of a live oak tree above some of the art displays at the festival in 1973. (Courtesy of Taryn Gordon Wilson.)

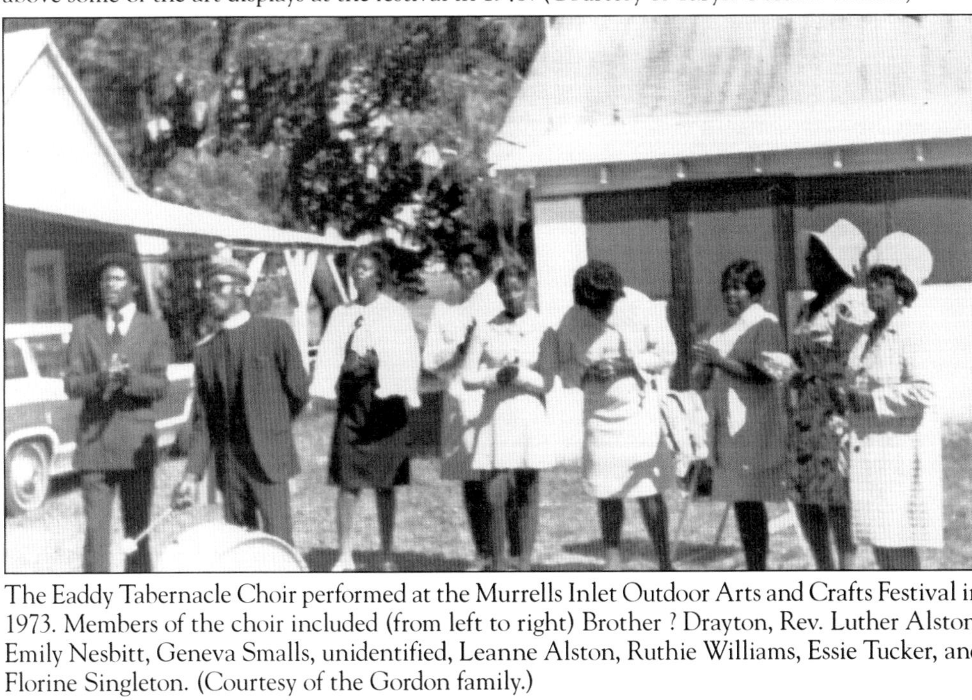

The Eaddy Tabernacle Choir performed at the Murrells Inlet Outdoor Arts and Crafts Festival in 1973. Members of the choir included (from left to right) Brother ? Drayton, Rev. Luther Alston, Emily Nesbitt, Geneva Smalls, unidentified, Leanne Alston, Ruthie Williams, Essie Tucker, and Florine Singleton. (Courtesy of the Gordon family.)

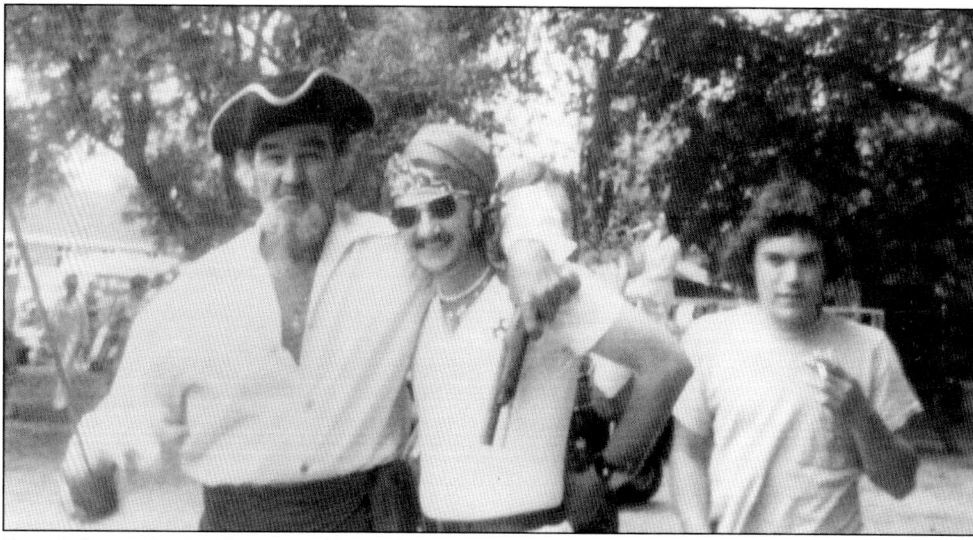

From left to right, Herb Martin (dressed as Captain Murrell), Wendell Powers (dressed as a pirate), and Robin Tyson are at the first Murrells Inlet Arts and Crafts Festival in 1973. The Murrells Inlet Outdoor Arts and Crafts Festival was organized in 1973 by the Murrells Inlet Fishermen & Merchants Association to promote growth and the arts for the community and included several stages for performers and outdoor exhibits from Belin Church to Anchor Inn. (Courtesy of Taryn Gordon Wilson.)

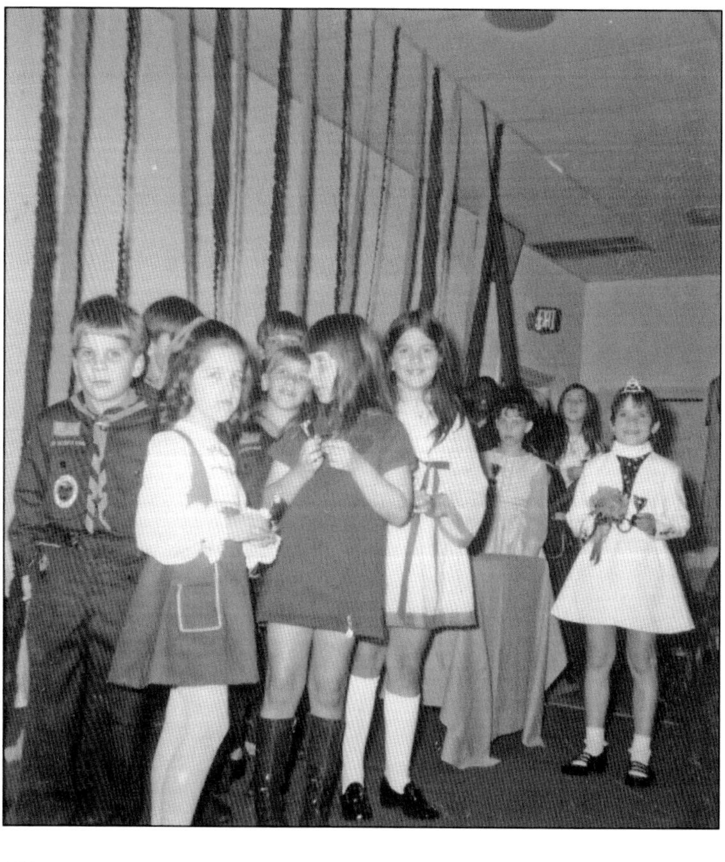

The Blue and Gold Banquet was held in 1972 at Belin Church Education Building for the Cub Scouts. Shown in this picture are, from left to right, Glenn Welch, Monica Eason, Wes Gordon, John Smith, Carol Eskridge, Lynette Ayers, Frankie Scott, and Sandy Gordon. (Courtesy of the Welch family.)

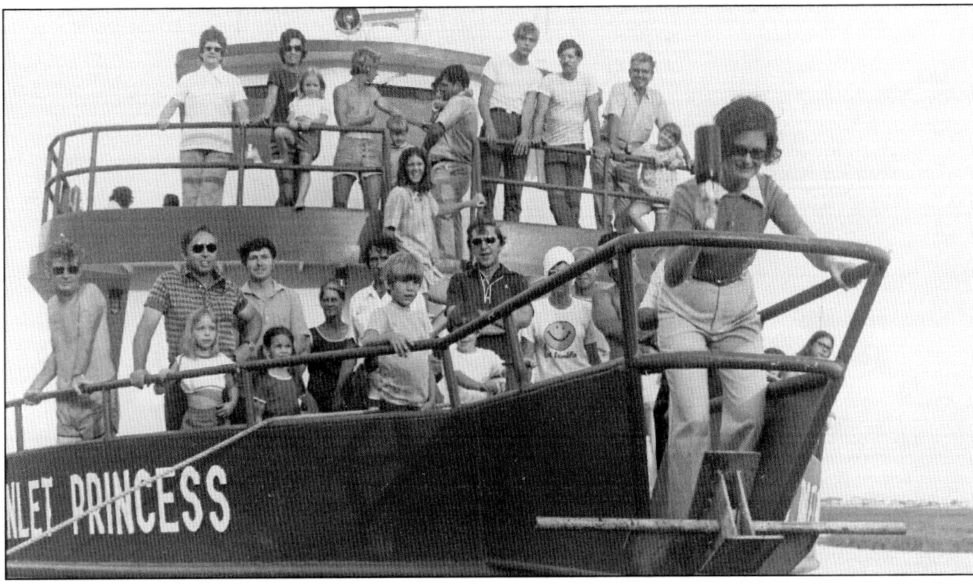

Brenda Eason is shown christening the *New Inlet Princess* in 1973, one of the only times the boat was pulled into its slip at Captain Dick's Marina bow first. Other people shown in the picture include (on the top deck) Dot Eason, Cat and Allison Taylor, Dick Eason, and Debbie Strickland; (on the lower deck, from left to right) Capt. Rusty Draper, Connie Gause, Winnie Belle Strickland, Nick Gause, and Everette Ayers. (Courtesy of the Eason family.)

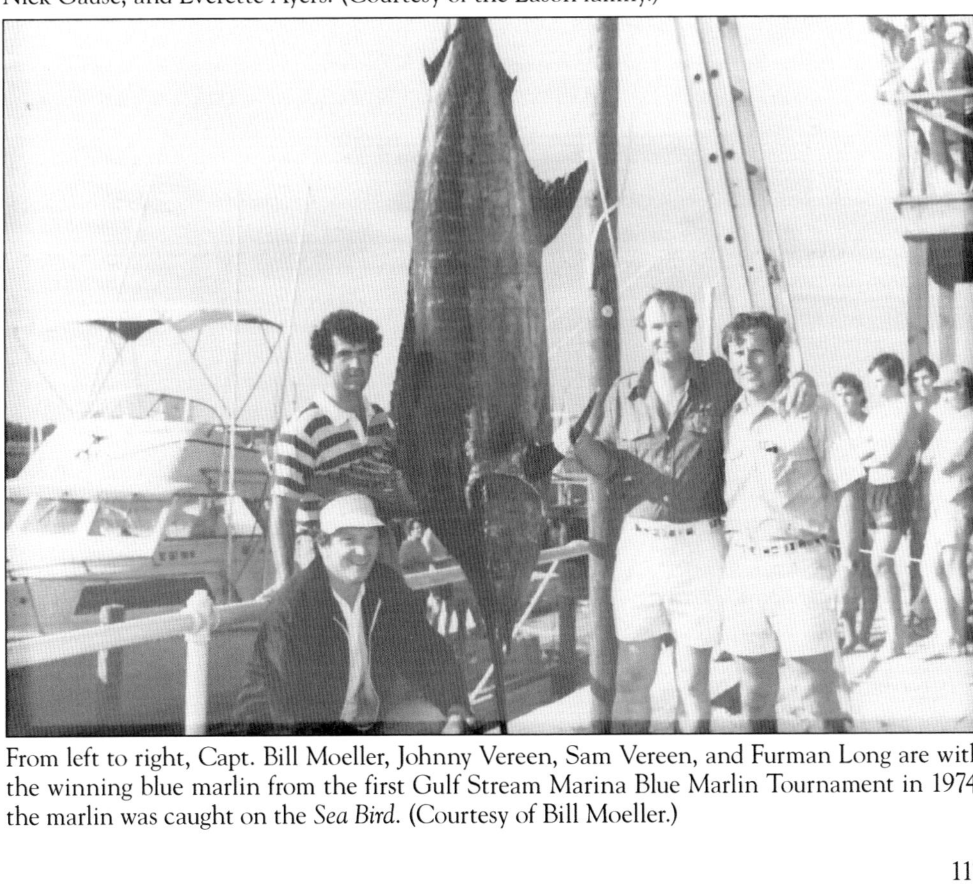

From left to right, Capt. Bill Moeller, Johnny Vereen, Sam Vereen, and Furman Long are with the winning blue marlin from the first Gulf Stream Marina Blue Marlin Tournament in 1974; the marlin was caught on the *Sea Bird*. (Courtesy of Bill Moeller.)

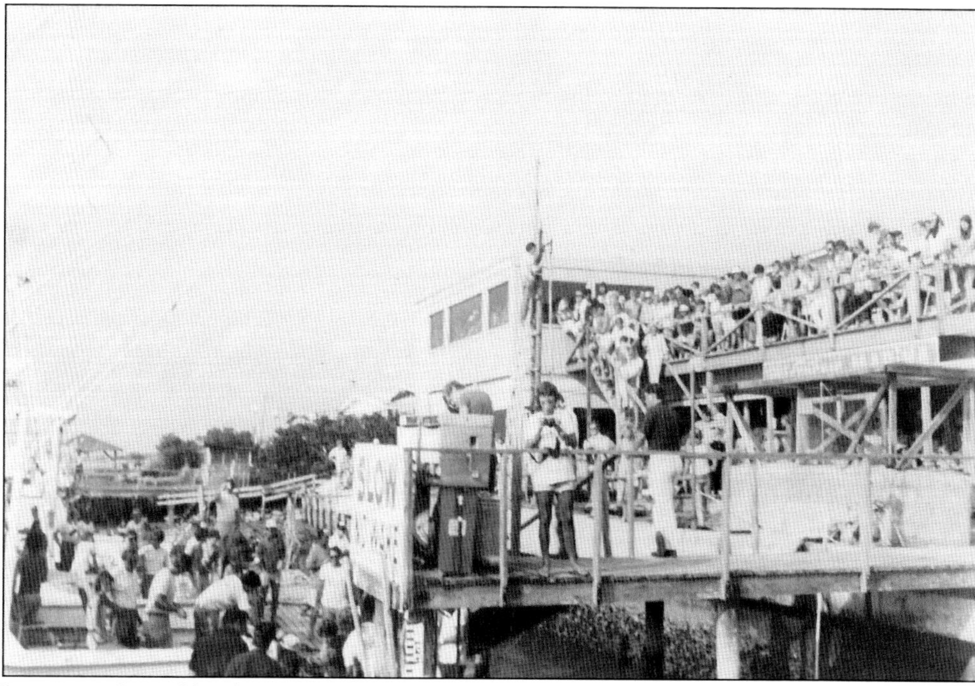

Large crowds would gather at Gulf Stream Marina during the fishing tournaments to see the boats return after a day of offshore fishing. Shown here in 1975, crowds line the upper deck to socialize and see who caught the largest fish during the day's event. (Courtesy of Robin Loud.)

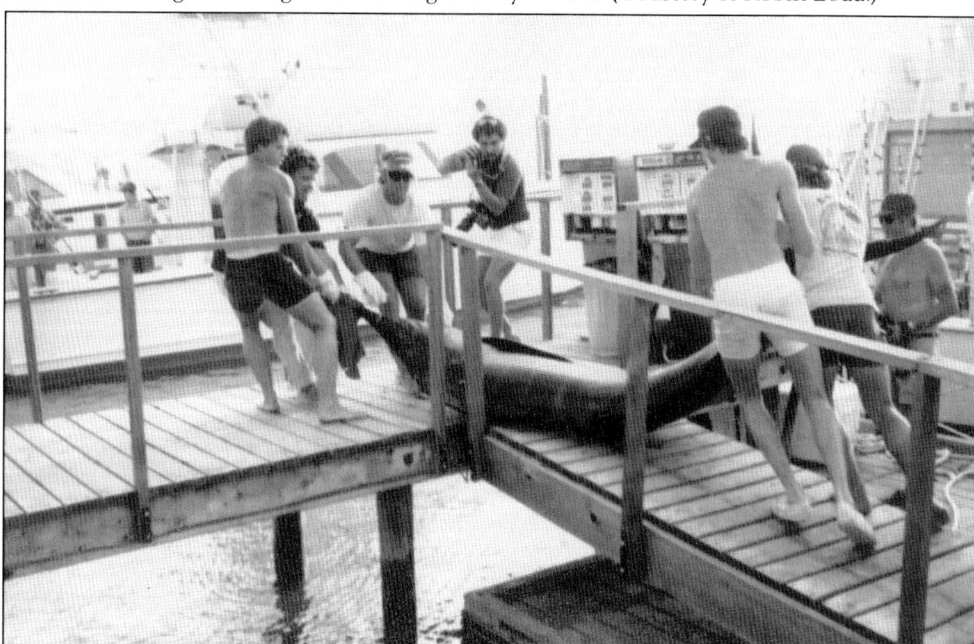

A fishing team is unloading a large blue marlin during the Gulf Stream Marina Blue Marlin Tournament in 1975. Some of the larger fish weighed in over 500 pounds and required a small crowd to unload them off of the boat and carry them up the ramp to the weigh-in station. (Courtesy of Robin Loud.)

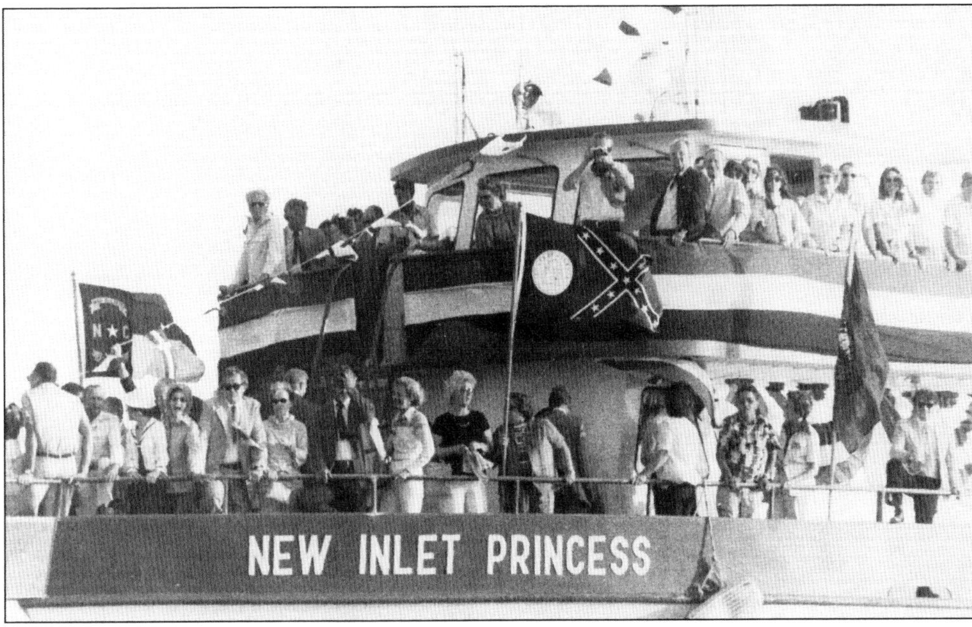

The *New Inlet Princess* was one of the boats that carried dignitaries during the dedication ceremony for the Murrells Inlet jetties in September 1977. The dedication ceremony included political speeches by the legislative delegation and a trip out to the mouth of Murrells Inlet, where the boats circled up near the proposed jetty entrance and then came back in and cut a ceremonial ribbon over the creek. Crossing the bar at low tide prior to the jetties often required that the passengers stand near the bow of the boat to lift the propellers and allow the boat to "hop" across the sandbars with each wave. (Courtesy of the Eason family.)

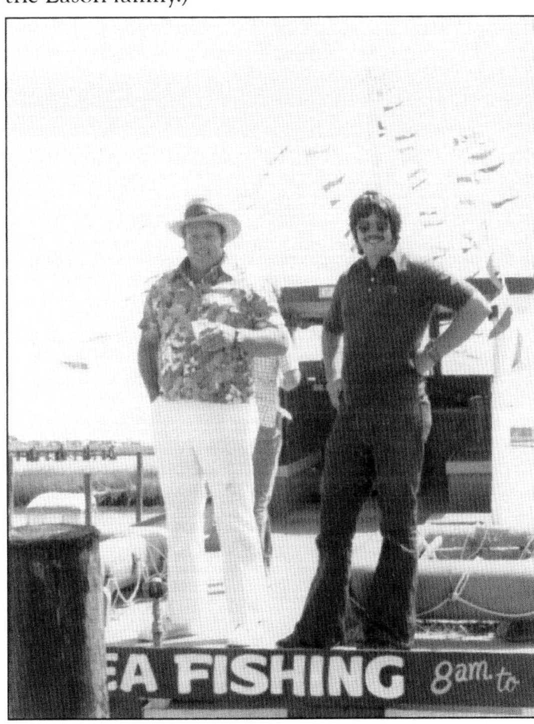

Capt. James Legette "Hoss" Johnson (left) and Buster Newby are standing on the top deck of the *Inlet Princess* during the dedication ceremony for the construction of the Murrells Inlet jetties on September 13, 1977. The natural migration of the Murrells Inlet bar north and south of its present location did not provide a consistent depth at low tide for vessels crossing the bar, and the jetty project was designed to provide access to the ocean for all vessels during all tidal stages. (Courtesy of Taryn Gordon Wilson.)

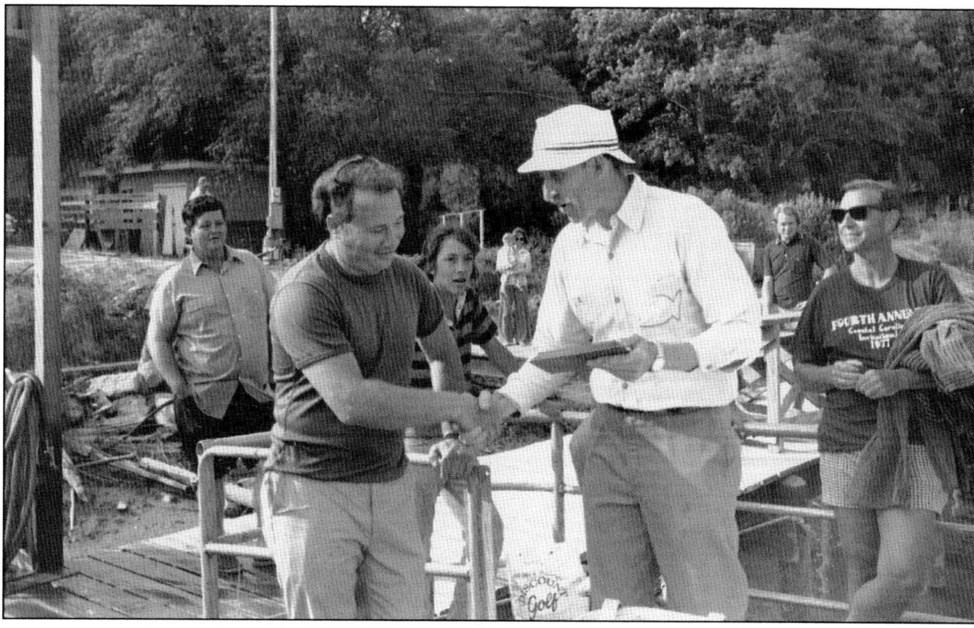

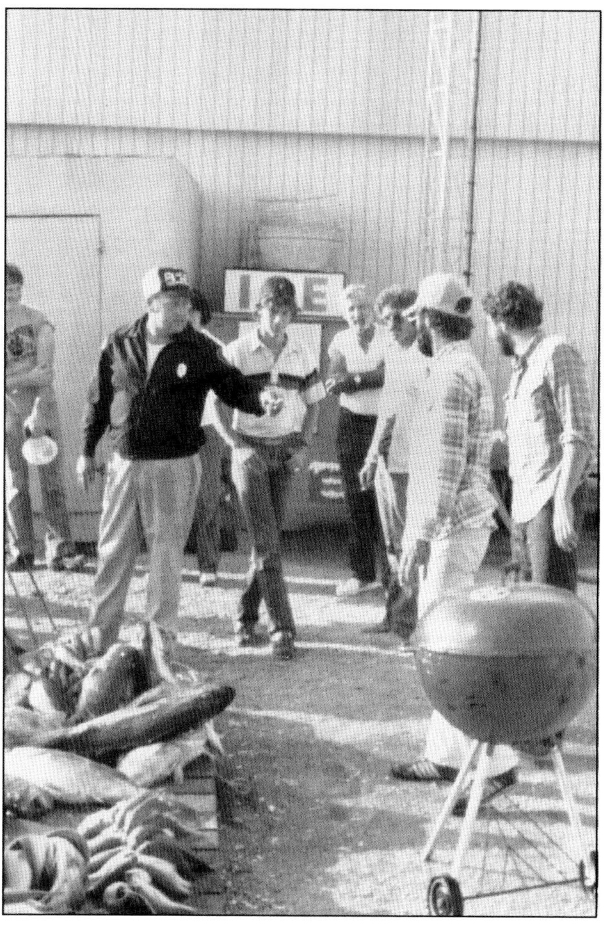

Capt. Don Lash is presented with an appreciation plaque by Prof. Don Milus from Coastal Carolina University after the Coastal Carolina Invitational Fishing Tournament in 1977. Professor Milus organized a collegiate fishing event every year and took students from different schools deep-sea fishing on the charter boats from Murrells Inlet. Timmy Altman is shown in the background to the left, Mike Goodwin is shown in the center background, and Linda is holding Dawn Lash in the right background. (Courtesy of Don and Linda Lash.)

Capts. Hoss Johnson and Everette Ayers would take the mates from the fishing boats on an overnight fishing trip at the end of the season every year on the *New Inlet Princess*. Hoss Johnson (second from left, in a black jacket and hat) is shown with several of the crew, and the load of fish caught is seen in the foreground. Chico Neyrey (second from right in hat) was one of the mates on this trip. (Courtesy of the Eason family.)

Nine

STORMS

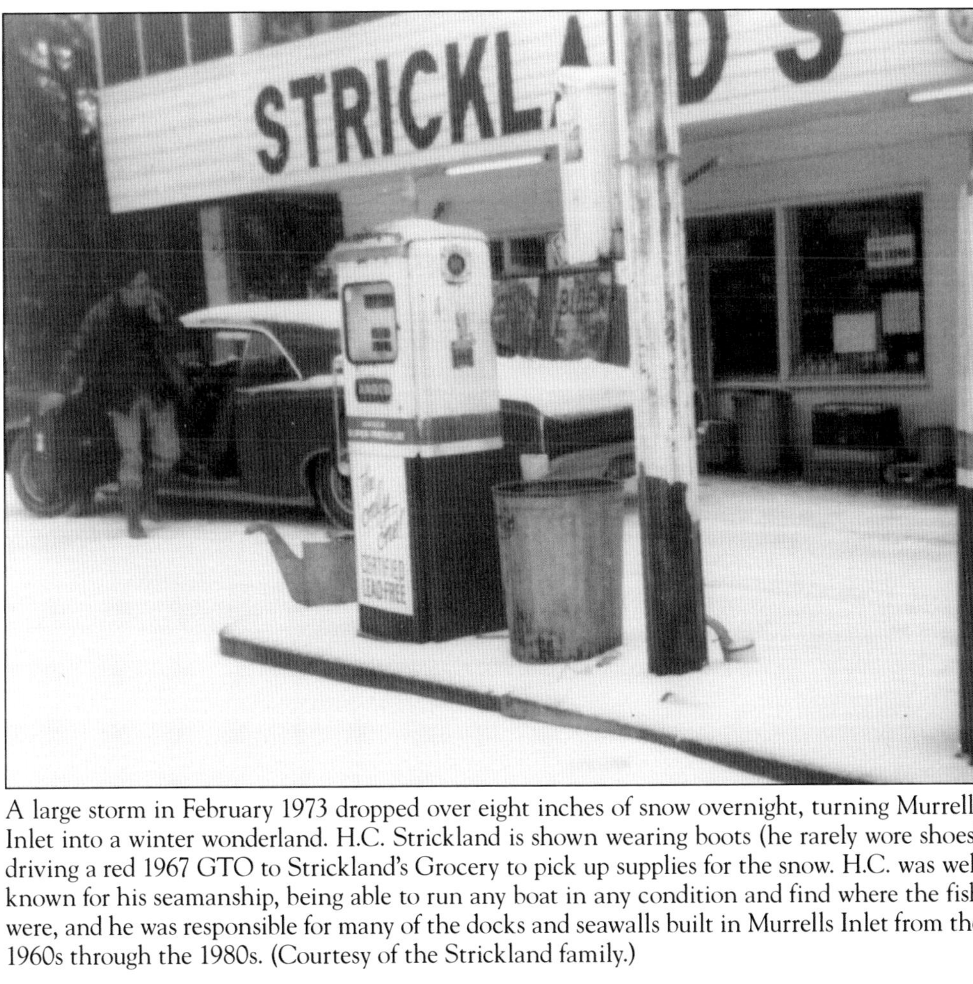

A large storm in February 1973 dropped over eight inches of snow overnight, turning Murrells Inlet into a winter wonderland. H.C. Strickland is shown wearing boots (he rarely wore shoes) driving a red 1967 GTO to Strickland's Grocery to pick up supplies for the snow. H.C. was well known for his seamanship, being able to run any boat in any condition and find where the fish were, and he was responsible for many of the docks and seawalls built in Murrells Inlet from the 1960s through the 1980s. (Courtesy of the Strickland family.)

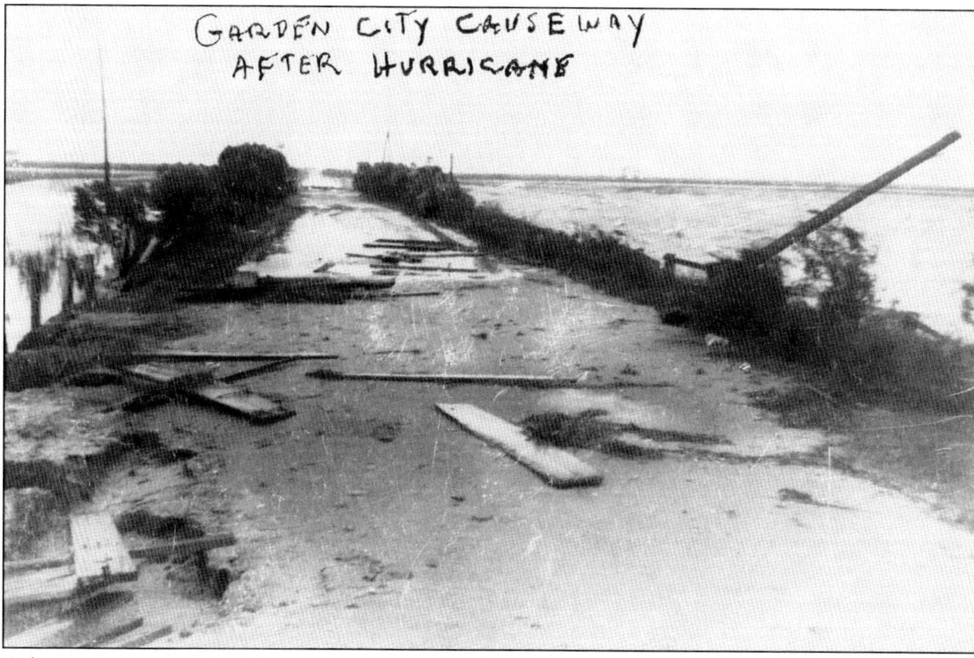

A hurricane passed by Murrells Inlet in 1944, leaving a trail of debris over the causeway out to Garden City Beach. The causeway at this time was an unpaved road that crossed over a small creek on the west side of the marsh. (Courtesy of Gwen Watson and Murrells Inlet 2020.)

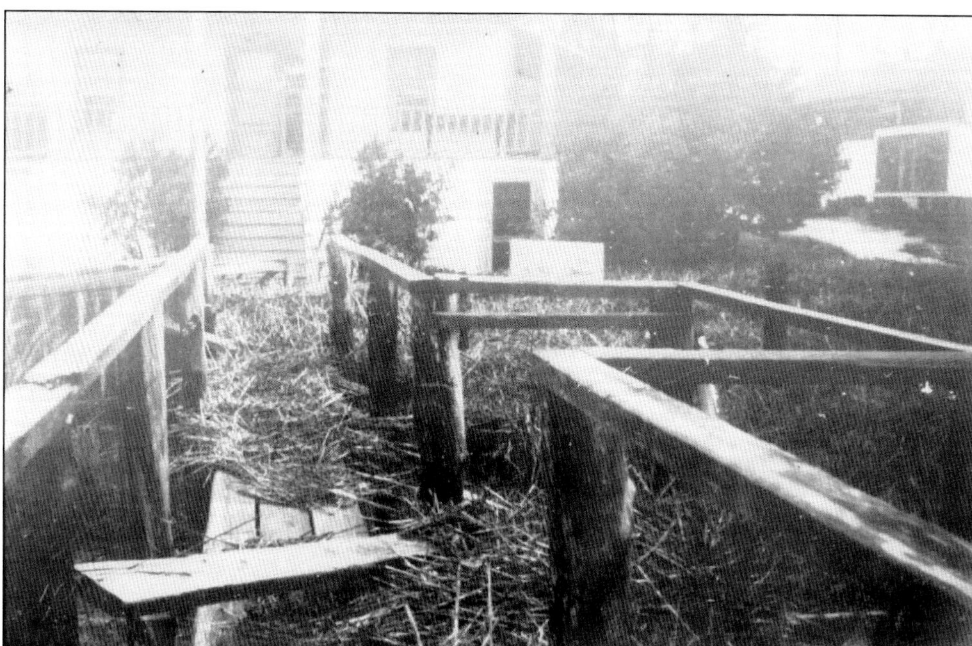

A view of the Army dock and the Army barracks depicts storm debris from a passing hurricane. The storm surge would push all of the debris and marsh grass from the creek into the properties on the creek front, leaving a mess to be cleaned up. (Courtesy of Gwen Watson and Murrells Inlet 2020.)

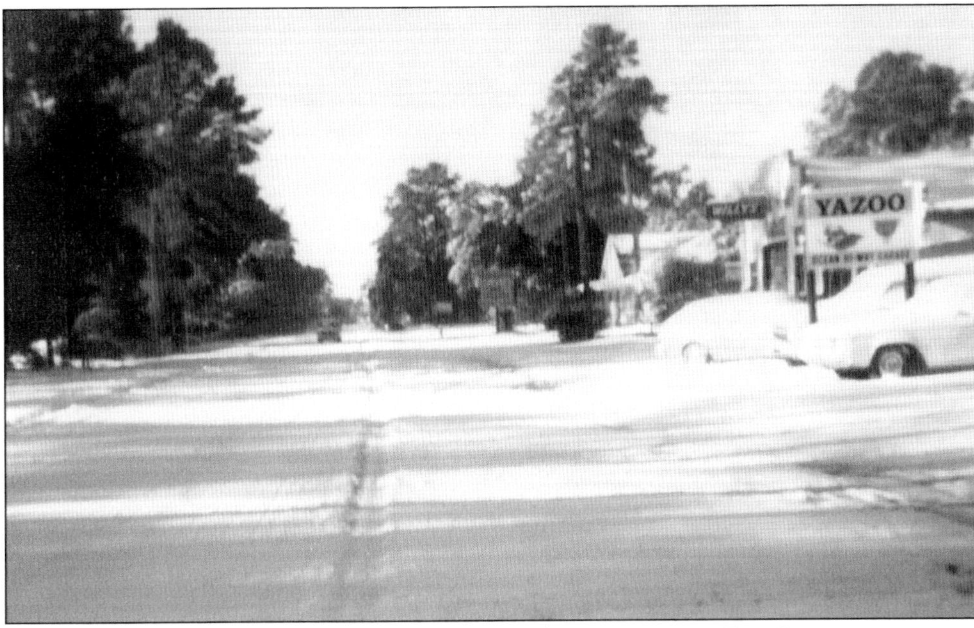

Here is a view of Ocean Highway Garage in 1973 after a snowstorm. Esau Lazarowitz operated the garage in the 1960s and 1970s after purchasing it from Sam Outlaw. Esau sold and repaired vehicles, lawn mowers, and various go-carts and three-wheelers and had an automotive junkyard in the rear. (Courtesy of the Strickland family.)

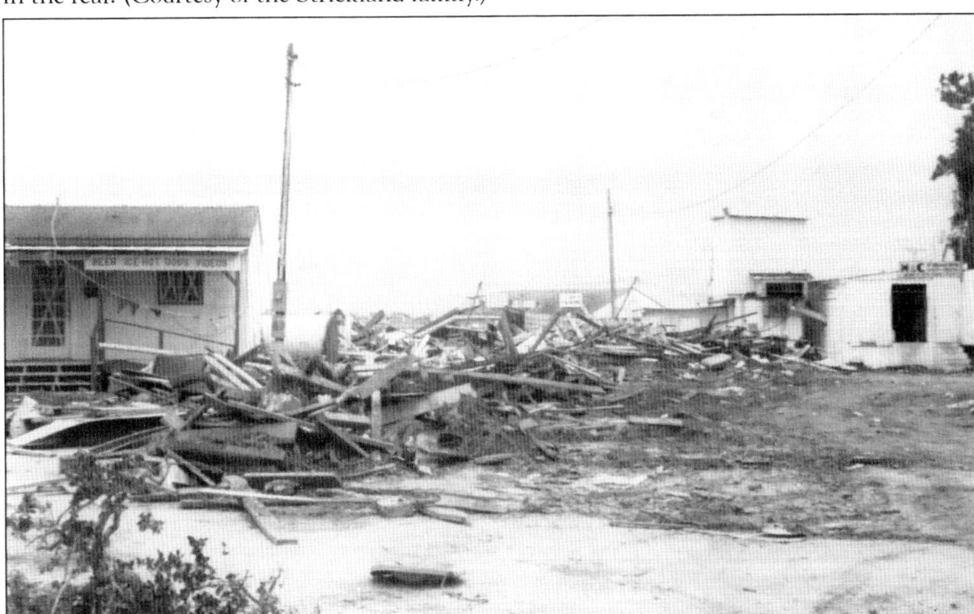

The storm surge from Hurricane Hugo washed all of the docks at H&C Fisheries up into the parking lot and caused significant damage to the buildings along the waterfront. The icehouse building (at right) was elevated and survived the storm, but the fish house at Capt Dick's (center) was not as fortunate. All of the Murrells Inlet commercial fleet survived the storm by moving into the river west of Murrells Inlet (White Creek) and tying the boats between the large cypress trees on either bank to secure them. (Courtesy of Dean Hair.)

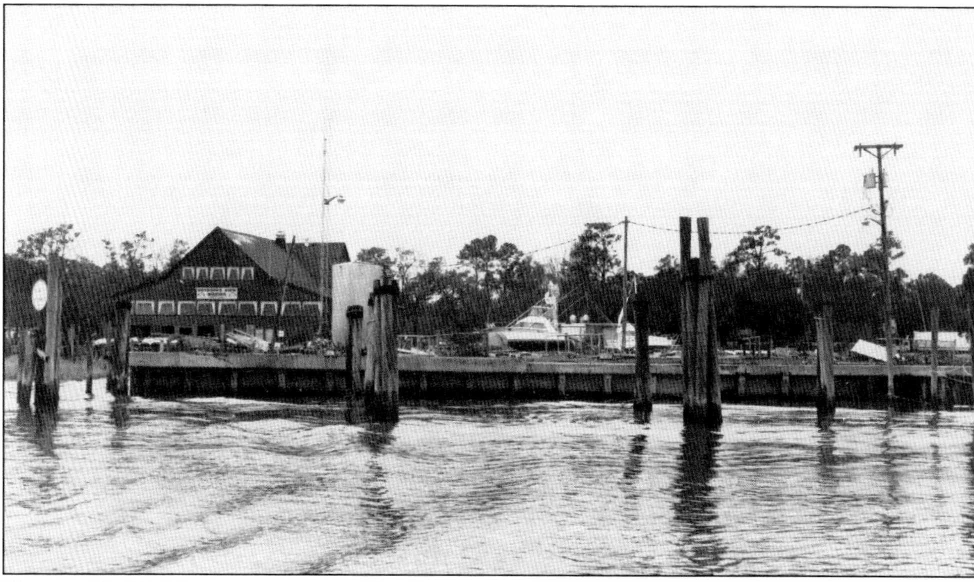

Captain Dick's Marina was ravaged by the storm surge from Hurricane Hugo on September 22, 1989, with the creek front stripped of boats, docks, and buildings. Several boats, including the *Silver Tongued Devil* (center), were picked up and floated into the parking lot beside Voyager's View Marina (left). The storm surge was six to eight feet at Captain Dick's Marina. (Courtesy of the Strickland family.)

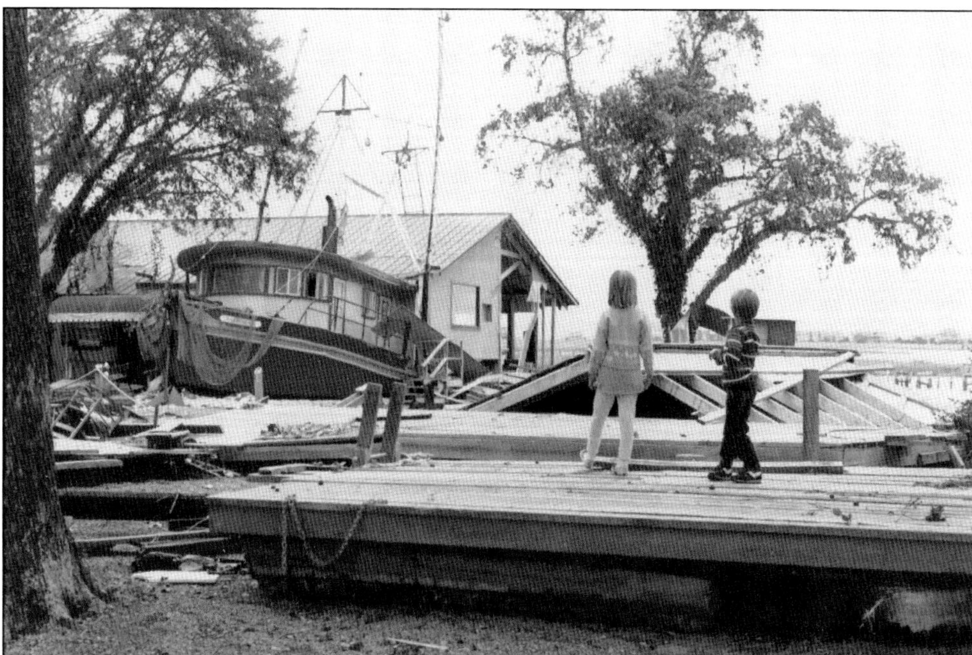

Amanda and J. Wesley Hughes are standing on some floating docks that were relocated by the storm surge of Hurricane Hugo. The Shrimp Boat restaurant was severely damaged by the hurricane. The shrimp boat was a working boat owned by Sam Vereen and Wesley Gordon that sank and was converted into a restaurant by excavating a slip into the high ground, towing the boat up into the hill, and sand bagging behind it around 1982. (Courtesy of Taryn Gordon Wilson.)

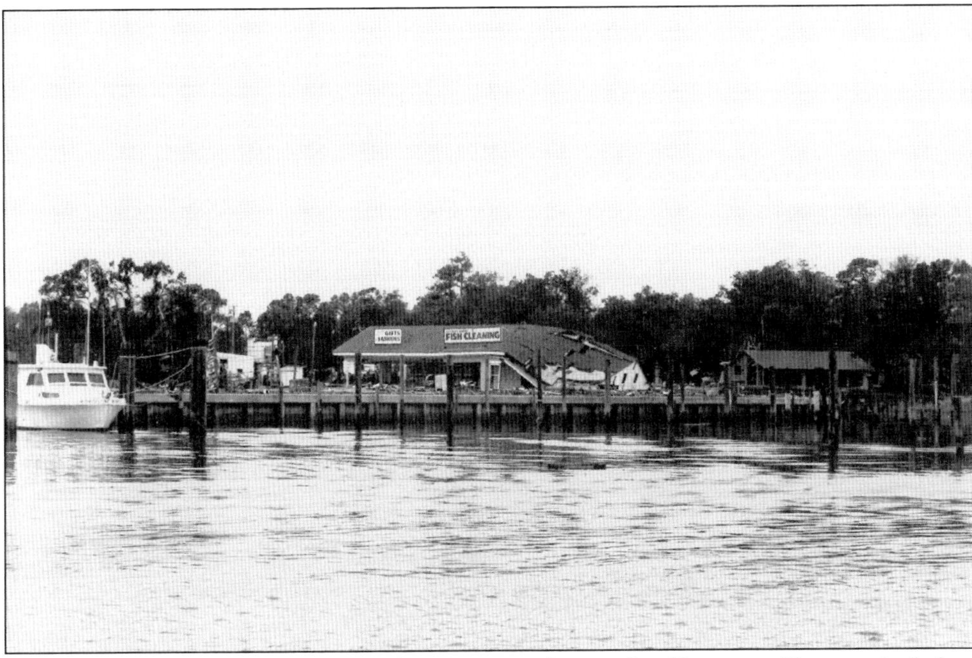

The northern portion of Captain Dick's Marina is shown after Hurricane Hugo; a single boat remains in the water after the storm surge, with Cook's Seafood and the fish-cleaning building having collapsed on the north side from the storm surge and debris. All of the floating docks were picked up and pushed into Highway 17 by the storm surge. (Courtesy of the Strickland family.)

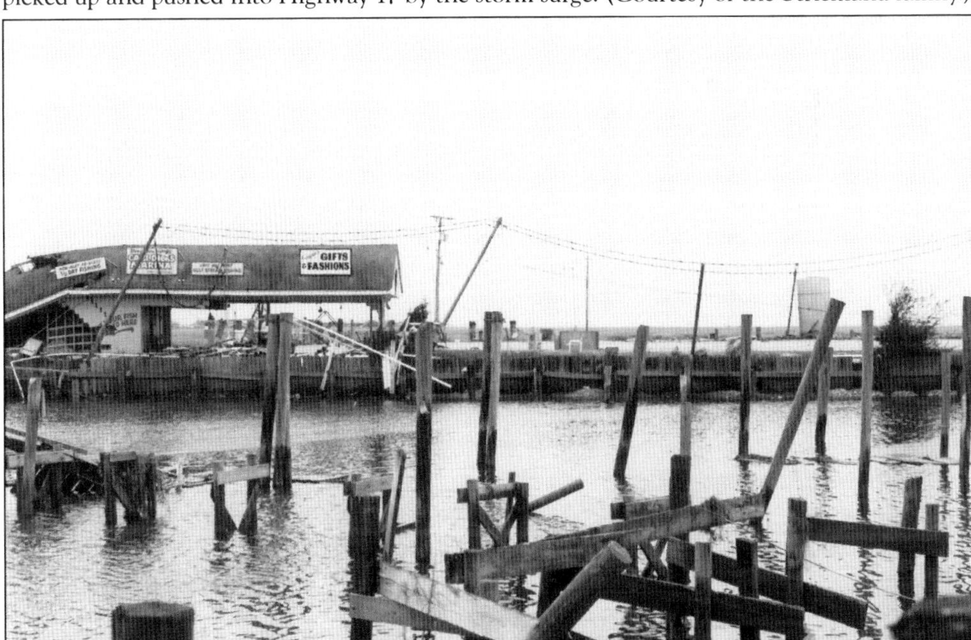

The docks at H&C Fisheries and Cook's Seafood at Captain Dick's Marina were destroyed by the storm surge during Hurricane Hugo in September 1989. The surge came up at least six to eight feet above the ground in this area, moving all of the floating docks into the parking lot and Highway 17 during the night. (Courtesy of Taryn Gordon Wilson.)

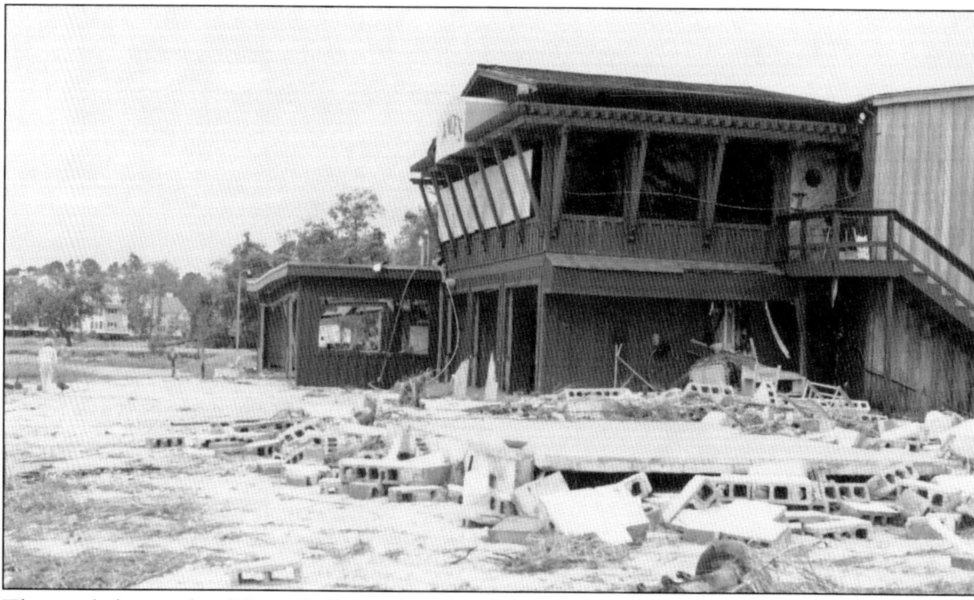

The creek-front side of Nance's Oyster Roast and the Crow's Nest lounge took a beating from the storm surge from Hurricane Hugo. The Crow's Nest portion of the building was moved from the creek location across Highway 17 to the site where Capt. George Morse and Mae Wesley Morse had lived and operated one of the first restaurants in Murrells Inlet. Russell Vereen had been a bartender at the Crow's Nest and in 1990 refurbished the building into Russell's Seafood Grill, which is still in operation today. (Courtesy of Taryn Gordon Wilson.)

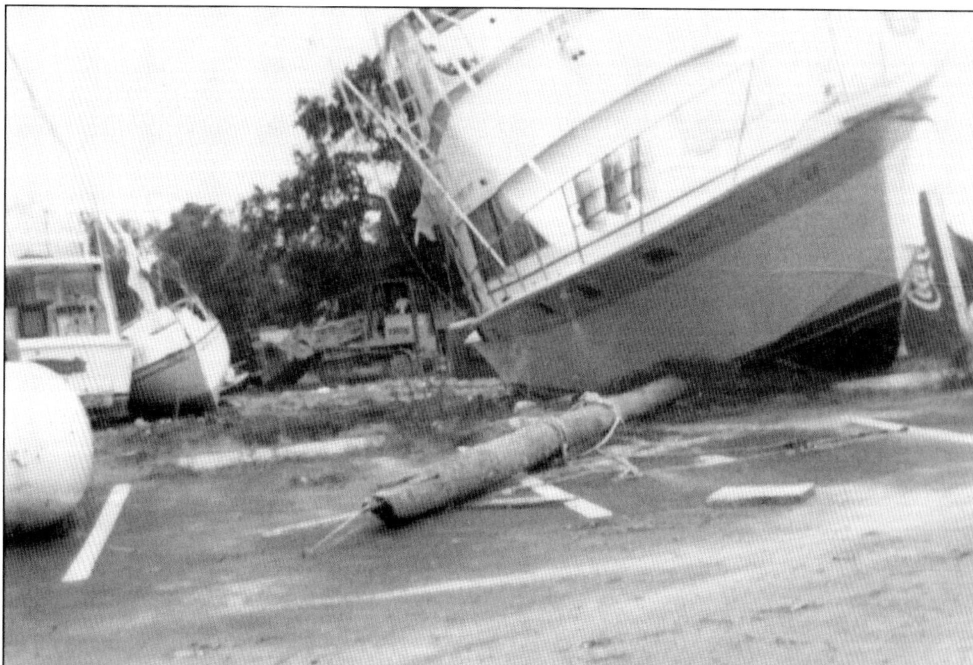

The *Silver Tongued Devil* was a Silverton sportfishing boat that was at the docks at Captain Dick's Marina during Hurricane Hugo. It was lifted up by the storm surge and set down in the parking lot about 100 yards west of its original location. (Courtesy of the Strickland family.)

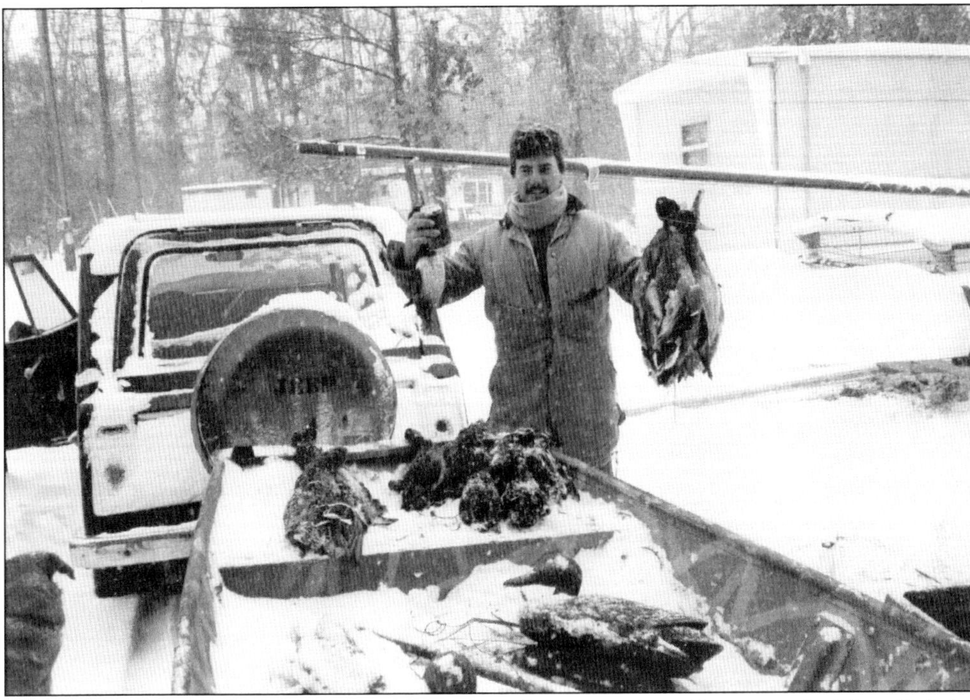

Christmas Day 1989 (after Hurricane Hugo) provided a rare white Christmas for Murrells Inlet, much to the joy of the local duck hunters who were fortunate enough to brave the snowy weather. Allen Curry (shown) and Bill Perry Jr. (taking picture) went to the Waccamaw River and were rewarded with a nice bag of mallards, teals, and wood ducks. (Courtesy of Allen Curry.)

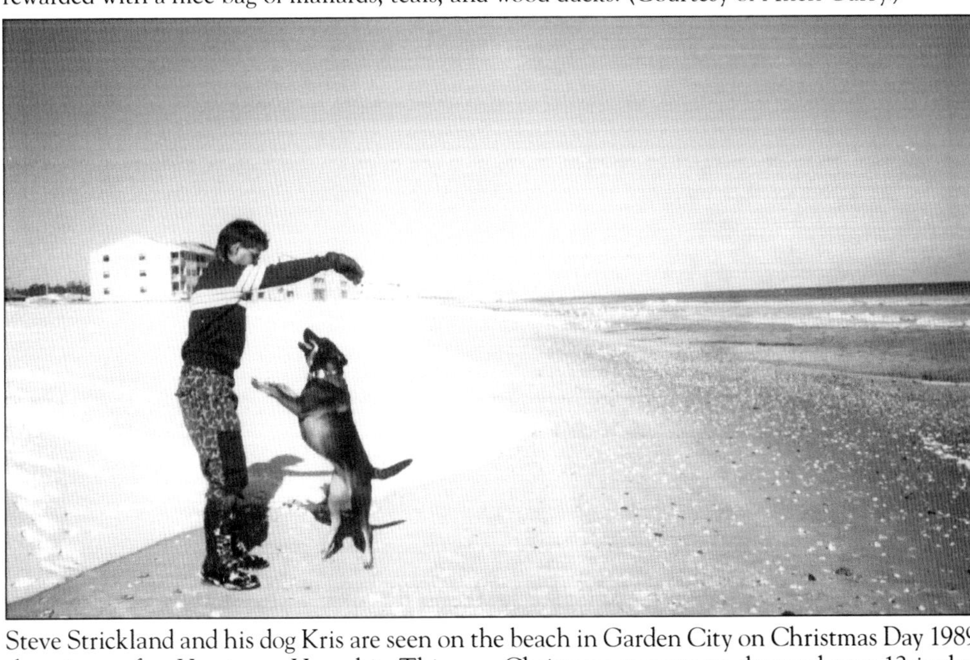

Steve Strickland and his dog Kris are seen on the beach in Garden City on Christmas Day 1989, the winter after Hurricane Hugo hit. This rare Christmas snowstorm dropped over 12 inches of snow in the Murrells Inlet area, while areas away from the coast up to 60 miles west received much lower amounts. (Courtesy of the Strickland family.)